Human Apolipoprotein Mutants
Impact on Atherosclerosis and Longevity

NATO ASI Series

Advanced Science Institutes Series

A series presenting the results of activities sponsored by the NATO Science Committee, which aims at the dissemination of advanced scientific and technological knowledge, with a view to strengthening links between scientific communities.

The series is published by an international board of publishers in conjunction with the NATO Scientific Affairs Division

A	Life Sciences	Plenum Publishing Corporation
B	Physics	New York and London
C	Mathematical and Physical Sciences	D. Reidel Publishing Company Dordrecht, Boston, and Lancaster
D	Behavioral and Social Sciences	Martinus Nijhoff Publishers
E	Engineering and Materials Sciences	The Hague, Boston, and Lancaster
F	Computer and Systems Sciences	Springer-Verlag
G	Ecological Sciences	Berlin, Heidelberg, New York, and Tokyo

Recent Volumes in this Series

Volume 105—The Physiology of Thirst and Sodium Appetite
edited by G. de Caro, A. N. Epstein, and M. Massi

Volume 106—The Molecular Biology of *Physarum polycephalum*
edited by William F. Dove, Jennifer Dee, Sadashi Hatano,
Finn B. Haugli, and Karl-Ernst Wohlfarth-Bottermann

Volume 107—NMR in the Life Sciences
edited by E. Morton Bradbury and Claudio Nicolini

Volume 108—Grazing Research at Northern Latitudes
edited by Olafur Gudmundsson

Volume 109—Central and Peripheral Mechanisms of Cardiovascular Regulation
edited by A. Magro, W. Osswald, D. Reiss, and P. Vanhoutte

Volume 110—Structure and Dynamics of RNA
edited by P. H. van Knippenberg and C. W. Hilbers

Volume 111—Basic and Applied Aspects of Noise-Induced Hearing Loss
edited by Richard J. Salvi, D. Henderson, R. P. Hamernik,
and V. Colletti

Volume 112—Human Apolipoprotein Mutants: Impact on Atherosclerosis
and Longevity
edited by C. R. Sirtori, A. V. Nichols, and G. Franceschini

Series A: Life Sciences

Human Apolipoprotein Mutants

Impact on Atherosclerosis and Longevity

Edited by

C. R. Sirtori

Institute of Pharmacological Sciences
University of Milan
Milan, Italy

A. V. Nichols

University of California
Berkeley, California

and

G. Franceschini

Institute of Pharmacological Sciences
University of Milan
Milan, Italy

Plenum Press
New York and London
Published in cooperation with NATO Scientific Affairs Division

Proceedings of a NATO Advanced Research Workshop on
Human Apolipoprotein Mutants: Impact on Atherosclerosis and Longevity,
held March 31–April 3, 1985,
at Limone sul Garda, Italy

QP
99
.3
.A65
N37
1985

Library of Congress Cataloging in Publication Data

NATO Advanced Research Workshop on Human Apolipoprotein Mutants: Impacts on Atherosclerosis and Longevity (1985: Limone sul Garda, Italy)
  Human apolipoprotein mutants.

  (NATO ASI series. Series A, Life sciences; v. 112)
  "Proceedings of a NATO Advanced Research Workshop on Human Apolipoprotein Mutants, Impacts on Atherosclerosis and Longevity, held March 31–April 3, 1985, at Limone sul Garda, Italy"—T.p. verso.
  "Published in cooperation with NATO Scientific Affairs Division."
  Includes bibliographies and index.
  1. Apolipoproteins—Congresses. 2. Human chromosome abnormalities—Congresses. 3. Atherosclerosis—Genetic aspects—Congresses. 4. Longevity—Genetic aspects—Congresses. I. Sirtori, Cesare R. II. Nichols, Alex V. III. Franceschini, G. IV. North Atlantic Treaty Organization. Scientific Affairs Division. V. Title. VI. Series. [DNLM: 1. Apolipoproteins—genetics—congresses. 2. Arteriosclerosis—etiology—congresses. 3. Longevity—congresses. 4. Mutation—congresses. QU 85 N279h 1985]
  QP99.3.A65N37   1985   616.1′36′071   86-15088
  ISBN 0-306-42370-7

© 1986 Plenum Press, New York
A Division of Plenum Publishing Corporation
233 Spring Street, New York, N.Y. 10013

Printed in the United States of America

Genealogic tree of the apo Al-Milano mutant

FOREWORD

From the best estimates we can obtain, we believe that an unusual event occurred in the sunny, pleasant community of Limone sul Garda in approximately 1780. This event was a mutation on chromosome 11 which took place in either the mother or father of an affected offspring. We have only recently discovered this biological occurrence in the far distant past and its implications. The mutant gene carries the genetic information in coding a variant of the normal apolipoprotein AI, which is the major apolipoprotein of HDL throughout nature, from higher to lower species. In fact, the evolutionary forces appear to have maintained within apo AI a structure unique for the apolipoproteins in that it contains repeating units of amphipathic helices, approximately 22 amino acids in length which function as specialized lipid binding regions. One of the parents of the offspring referred to above in 1780, had a genetic code for apo AI which had undergone a mutation. The protein produced by this offspring was thus not normal apo AI, but instead apolipoprotein AI-Milano ($\text{arg}_{173} \longrightarrow$ cysteine). Apo AI-Milano became only the first of a long series of mutants which have now been discovered, affecting human apolipoproteins. Since the discovery of apo AI-Milano by the Sirtori Group in Milano, the number of identified mutants has increased to over 30. It is interesting that in most cases, the results of these mutations are relatively benign and most appear to have trivial effects on either the general health and well being of the affected individual, or on apolipoprotein or lipoprotein metabolism. Some have speculated that the apo AI-Milano mutation may be associated with some biological benefit.

The unique volume we are now publishing contains the collected proceedings of a three day meeting held in Limone sul Garda. The purpose of the meeting was to review the current status of apolipoprotein mutations and to analyze their effects, not only on apolipoprotein, lipoprotein and lipid metabolism, but also on to consider any potential clinical implications. In a few years time, we may be discussing the apolipoproteinopathies as much as we are the hemoglobinopathies today.

The Mayor of Limone and his associates created a very friendly atmosphere in which to examine the exciting findings deriving from the discovery of this growing list of mutants. Professor Cesare Sirtori, in particular, and his organizing committee are to be highly congratulated. It was fitting that the meeting be opened by the Under Secretary of Health of the Republic of Italy to emphasize the importance of apolipoproteins in clinical medicine.

It soon became obvious that the current state-of-the-art of apolipoprotein mutants relies heavily on the methodology and advancements in molecular biology. However, the meeting in Limone sul Garda was not devoted entirely to molecular biology, but there was ample discussion of the importance of clinical judgement and of a sound genetic evaluation of affected kindreds. It became obvious to all of the participants that the basic researcher, the clinical geneticist and the physician, can take advantage of these mutant events in human biology to learn more of the role of apolipoproteins in lipid transport in atherosclerosis and in coronary heart disease. The field is evolving very rapidly and I would anticipate another such meeting in the near future to evaluate continued progress. As one of the participants, I speak for all of us in acknowledging our deep gratitude to Professor Sirtori for combining science, history and delightful scenery in such a unique way.

Antonio M. Gotto, Jr., M.D., D.Phil.
Chairman, Department of Internal Medicine
Baylor College of Medicine
The Methodist Hospital
Houston, Texas

CONTENTS

GENETICS AND EPIDEMIOLOGY

APOLIPOPROTEIN CII

APOLIPOPROTEIN E

THE FUNCTION OF HUMAN SERUM APOLIPOPROTEINS:
CLUES FROM INBORN ERRORS OF LIPOPROTEIN METABOLISM

Gerd Assmann

Institut für Klinische Chemie und Laborato-
riumsmedizin der Westf. Wilhelms-Universität
A. Schweitzer Str. 33, 4400 Münster, FRG

Lipoproteins are complexes composed of apolipoproteins and non-covalently bound lipids. Characterization of the various apolipoproteins, of cellular lipoprotein receptors and of enzymes cata- lyzing intravascular changes in the structure and composition of lipoproteins has permitted the iden- tification of the underlying molecular defect in a number of inborn errors of lipoprotein metabolism and ultimately may result in a reclassification of these disorders based upon molecular mechanisms (Table 1-3). Apolipoprotein disorders are diseases in which the aetiology and pathophysiology are directly related to a structural defect or a defect in the biosynthesis or secretion of apolipoproteins. Due to the numerous functions of serum apolipoproteins (Table 4), struc- tural defects of these proteins potentially cause complex metabolic consequences.
With the recent availability of screening techniques many apolipoprotein mutants have been detected.
In certain cases apolipoprotein variants have been described without pathological complications. How- ever, there is little doubt that subtle changes in metabolism may exist even in these, as it is very possible that more sophisticated methods may be required to precisely determine the effects involved here.

1

Table 1: Mutations of Apolipoproteins

Apolipo-protein	Defect
A-I	APO A-I Milano variant
	APO A-I Marburg, Giessen variants
	APO A-I Münster 1-4 variants
	HDL deficiency with planar xanthomas
	Familial deficiency of apolipoproteins A-I and C-III
	Apolipoprotein A-I absence
	Fish eye disease
	Hypoalphalipoproteinaemias
A-IV	APO A-IV Giessen variant
	APO A-IV Münster variants
B	Recessive abetalipoproteinaemia
	Homozygous hypobetalipoproteinaemia
	Normotriglyceridemic abetalipoproteinaemia
	Chylomicron retention disease
	Familial hypobetalipoproteinaemia with chylomicronaemia
C	Apolipoprotein C-II deficiency
	Apolipoprotein C-II Münster variants
	Apolipoprotein C-III-3 variant
E	Apolipoprotein E-2 homozygosity
	a) Dysbetalipoproteinaemia
	b) Familial type III hyperlipoproteinaemia
	Type V hyperlipoproteinaemia associated with the APO E-4 phenotype
	Apolipoprotein E deficiency
	Other apolipoprotein E variants

Table 2: Mutations of Lipolytic Enzymes

Enzyme	Defect
Lipoprotein lipase	Familial lipoprotein lipase deficiency (phenotypes: I, infrequently V)
Hepatic lipase	Familial hepatic lipase deficiency
LCAT	Familial LCAT deficiency

Table 3: Mutations of Lipoprotein Receptors/
Cellular Processing Defects

Receptor	Defect
APO B, E (LDL)	Familial hypercholesterolemia
HDL	Tangier disease
APO E	unknown
Scavenger	unknown

Table 4: Metabolic Roles of Plasma Apolipoproteins
in Lipid Transport

Function	Apolipoprotein
1. Lipoprotein biosynthesis/	B- 48 (intestine)
secretion	B-100 (liver)
2. Enzyme activity	
a) lipoprotein lipase	C-II
b) LCAT	A-I
	C-I
	A-IV
	E
3. Interaction of lipoproteins with cellular receptors	
a) LDL receptor recognition	B-100
	E
b) chylomicron remnant receptor recognition	E
c) inhibition of interaction with hepatic receptors	C-I
	C-II
	C-III

1) APO A-I

The gene coding for Apo A-I is located on
chromosome 11. Apolipoprotein A-I (apo A-I) is
synthesized as a 267 residue precursor protein
(preproapo A-I) in the liver and in the intestine.
Cotranslational cleavage of 18 amino acid residues
and posttranslational cleavage (plasma compartment)
of a hexapeptide from the amino terminus result in
the formation of the mature circulating apo A-I. In
vitro, apo A-I activates LCAT (lecithin: cholesterol
acyltransferase).

Structural Variants of Apolipoprotein A-I

Structural variants of apo A-I can be identified in native serum by isoelectric focusing.
In our own studies of 1000 patients investigated by
coronary angiography, four different familial
apolipoprotein A-I structural variants were discovered (apo A-I Münster 1-4). The mutant and
normal apo A-I in the probands were both reduced to
approximately 50 % of normal serum concentrations,
though there was no indication of hypoalphalipoproteinaemia. Apparently, despite the defective
structure of the apolipoproteins A-I Münster 1-4,
the physiocochemical properties (protein-protein
interaction, protein-lipid interaction with HDL)
are intact, such that functional deficiencies in
terms of altered HDL concentration are absent. This
is in contrast to findings in patients with the apo
A-I Milano variant, where hypoalphalipoproteinaemia
is a feature of the apolipoprotein defect.

Other Mutations of Apolipoprotein A-I

Several disorders characterized by the near or
complete absence of apo A-I have been recently
described. Since these disorders (HDL deficiency
with planar xanthomas; familial deficiency of
apolipoproteins A-I and C-III; apolipoprotein A-I
absence; fish eye disease) have only been described
in single probands or single kindreds, it is not
possible at present to relate the clinical findings
in each case to diminished plasma concentrations of
apo A-I.

Hypoalphalipoproteinaemias

The familial hypoalphalipoproteinaemias are a
biochemically heterogeneous group of disorders with
their origin in the reduced biosynthesis or accelerated catabolism of HDL. It is probable that the
defective metabolism of HDL is not due to an
apolipoprotein defect in every case, and thus the
classification chosen here may require modifica-

tion. The criteria for diagnosis of hypoalphalipoproteinaemia are as follows:

(1) HDL cholesterol < 25 mg/dl;
(2) exclusion of secondary causes (e.g. obesity,
hypertriglyceridaemia, diabetes mellitus);
(3) confirmation of hypoalphalipoproteinaemia in
family members;
(4) possibly determination of a structural
variant of apolipoprotein A-I.

In view of the fact that to date only a few
cases of primary hypoalphalipoproteinaemia (e.g.
heterozygous patients with Tangier disease) have
been observed, it is not yet possible to address
potential clinical complications or the risk of
arteriosclerosis.

Tangier Disease

Tangier Disease was first described by
Fredrickson in 1961 and is named for Tangier
Island, Virginia, where the patients first known to
have the disease lived. The most striking clinical
symptom in Tangier disease is substantial enlarge-
ment and yellow-orange discolouration of the
tonsils. In addition, splenomegaly and peripheral
neuropathy is seen in most patients. The disease is
characterized by the following laboratory findings:

(1) low plasma cholesterol concentrations
(< 100 mg/dl) and normal or elevated
plasma triglycerides;
(2) nearly total absence of high-density
lipoproteins (HDL) (= analphalipo-
proteinaemia) in plasma in conjunction
with altered chemical composition of
other plasma lipoproteins;
(3) increased concentration of cholesteryl
esters in numerous organs, primarily in
the macrophages of tonsils, lymph nodes,
thymus, bone marrow, liver, spleen and
rectal mucosa.The cellular concentration
of cholesteryl esters is also increased
in Schwann cells of peripheral nerves and
in intestinal smooth muscle cells.

Arterial smooth muscle cells or other
cells of the arterial wall are not
affected;
(4) in obligate Tangier heterozygotes,
both HDL cholesterol and apo A-I concentrations are reduced to 50 % of controls.
There is moderate increase in the
cellular concentration of cholesteryl
esters in macrophages in these patients.

Several hypotheses have been formulated to
explain the molecular defect in Tangier disease.
These include (i) accelerated catabolism of HDL
despite normal rates of apo A-I synthesis.
(ii) abnormal structure of apo A-I. (iii) impaired
interconversion of proapo A-I to mature apo A-I, and
(iv) a failure of proapo A-I to associate with HDL.
However, no unequivocal evidence of a
structural apolipoprotein defect causing HDL
deficiency has been established. In fact, recent
studies of the Tangier apo A-I gene have failed to
demonstrate a coding abnormality.

In an attempt to better understand the role
of HDL in macrophage cholesterol metabolism and to
relate the plasma deficiency of these lipoproteins
in Tangier disease to the observed accumulation of
cholesteryl esters in macrophages, we have under-
taken in vitro studies with mouse peritoneal
macrophages and human monocytes. It was demonstrated
that these cells express HDL receptors. Subsequent
to receptor-mediated binding, HDL are internalized
and intracellularly transported within endosomes.
The HDL containing endosomes do not fuse with the
lysosomal compartment, but interact with the margin
of lipid droplets and are ultimately resecreted from
the cells.

Treatment of Tangier monocytes with normal
HDL leads to cellular events quite different from
those observed in control monocytes. HDL binding
to Tangier monocytes was approx. 10-30 % higher
than in normals; however, in contrast to control
monocytes, only minor amounts of internalized HDL
were resecreted. Apparently, the majority of
internalized HDL was recognized by the lysosomal
compartment and degraded, thus not being available
for resecretion.

It appeared from our experiments that in Tangier monocytes receptor mediated recognition of HDL, internalization of the receptor-ligand complex, and recycling of the HDL receptor to the cellular surface are unimpaired. Therefore, it is unlikely that the molecular defect in Tangier disease resides in either abnormal HDL apolipo- proteins or abnormal HDL receptor recognition sites. Rather, some specific intracellular event directing the internalized HDL back to the extracellular compartment appears to be at fault. Thus, the biochemical alteration in Tangier disease might likely affect some mechanism important in the transcellular channeling of proteins. These can include the internalization site of the HDL receptor, some specific endosomal protein(s) normally preventing recognition by primary lysosomes, or Golgi membrane-associated proteins affecting resecretion.

If these in vitro observations can be extended to the in vivo metabolism of HDL and other monocyte-derived cells, such as tissue macrophages or Kupffer cells, they would have important pathophysiologic implications and could readily explain both the observed hypercatabolism of HDL and the dramatic tissue cholesteryl ester storage in Tangier disease. The hypercatabolism of HDL, reflecting an interrupted pathway for retroendo- cytosis, would result in low plasma concentrations of apo A-I and apo A-II; both cellular "trapping" of HDL and ineffective cellular cholesterol clearance may account for macrophage cholesteryl ester storage in Tangier disease.

The fact that serum HDL cholesterol-, apo A-I-, and apo A-II-concentrations in Tangier heterozygotes are reduced to 50 % of normals emphasizes the probable importance of cellular HDL retroendocytosis in the regulation of serum HDL concentrations. Due to the repeatedly demonstrated relationship of HDL deficiency to premature coronary artery disease, further unravelling of the detailed cellular events in HDL metabolism is not only of interest to Tangier disease but also to the pathogenesis of atherosclerosis.

2) APO A-II

The gene coding for apo A-II is located on chromosome 1. Apo A-II, the second major protein of HDL, is biosynthesized in the liver as a 100-residue precursor protein, prepro A-II. Co-translationally prepro apo A-II is cleaved to proapo A-II which contains a pentapeptide attached to mature apo A-II. Apo A-II contains 77 amino acid residues as monomer. As dimer it is linked by a disulfide bridge at position 6 in the sequence. No definitive function of apo A-II has been established; apo A-II mutants have not yet been described.

3) APO A-IV

The gene of apo A-IV is located on chromosome 11. Apo A-IV is a 393 residue protein with a MW of approx. 46.000 and can be found as a component of chylomicrons and the lipoprotein-free fraction of plasma. In approx. 10 % of all people an additional hereditary isoform of apo A-IV can be identified in serum using isoelectric focusing. Up to now, no function has been attributed to apo A-IV.

4) APO B

The gene coding for apo B is located on chromosome 2. Apo B is synthesized in the liver and in the small intestine. The structural integrity of apo B is a prerequisite for the regular formation and secretion of chylomicrons and VLDL. On SDS gels apo B migrates in two bands, apo B-100 and apo B-48. Apo B-100 has a molecular weight of approx. 365.000. It is considered to be important in the metabolism of cholesterol-rich lipoproteins and to bind to specific membrane receptors (apo-B,E receptor) in the liver and peripheral cells. A specific metabolic function of apo B-48 has not yet been elucidated.

8

Abetalipoproteinaemia

The disease first described by Bassen and
Kornzweig in 1950 is, analogous to Friedreich's
ataxia and fat malabsorption syndrome, characterized by retinitis pigmentosa, acanthocytosis and
neurological symptoms. The diagnosis is confirmed
by extremely low levels of cholesterol ($<$ 50 mg/dl)
and triglycerides ($<$ 30 mg/dl) and the total
absence of apolipoprotein B-containing lipoproteins
(chylomicrons, VLDL, LDL, Lp(a)).
On the basis of family studies, two forms of
abetalipoproteinaemia can be distinguished –
on the one hand, recessive abetalipoproteinaemia
(autosomal recessive inheritance) and on the other
hand, the homozygous form of hypobetalipoprotein-
aemia. In the case of recessive abetalipoproteinaemia the parents of the probands exhibit normal
concentrations of apolipoprotein B and LDL, while
in the other case both parents have low apolipoprotein B levels. The precise biochemical defect
responsible for the apolipoprotein B deficiency is
not yet known.

Normotriglyceridaemic Abetalipoproteinaemia

In this variant, in contrast to the classical
form of abetalipoproteinaemia, triglycerides are
regularly metabolized in the intestine and
chylomicrons are formed and secreted. Apo B-48 is
detectable in the serum compartment.
However, as a consequence of selective inhibition
of hepatic synthesis of B-100, neither VLDL nor LDL
are present in plasma. Normotriglyceridaemic
abetalipoproteinaemia is associated with modest
neurological changes.

Chylomicron Retention Disease

Recently several unrelated children have been
described with failure to thrive, malabsorption,
hypocholesterolaemia and hypotriglyceridaemia.
These patients do not show a rise in plasma

triglyceride following fat feeding, and chylomicrons can not be visualized in plasma by lipoprotein electrophoresis. Intestinal epithelial cells of these patients show large fat vacuoles and the immunochemical presence of apolipoprotein B. These patients appear to have a defect in chylomicron assembly or secretion.

5) APO C-II

The gene coding for apo C-II is located on chromosome 19. Apo C-II is synthesized in the liver as a 101-residue precursor, preapo C-II, which undergoes co-translational cleavage to mature 79-residue apo C-II.
Apo C-II is a cofactor for lipoprotein lipase, the major enzyme catalyzing the hydrolysis of plasma triglycerides. Patients with a deficiency of apo C-II are characterized clinically by high triglyceride concentrations in their plasma and type I hyperlipo-proteinaemia.

Apo C-II Deficiency

In the case of hyperchylomicronaemia it is imperative that a check is made to see whether the serum C-II concentration is normal. Clear semi-quantitative results are generally available by isoelectric focusing of lipoproteins d $<$ 1.006/ml in density; immunochemical tests (radioimmunoassay,immunoelectrophoresis) with monospecific antibodies confirm the diagnosis. To date, an apo C-II deficiency as the cause of reduced lipoprotein lipase activity with consecutive hyperchylomicronaemia has been described in only a very few cases. Similar to familial lipoprotein lipase deficiency, hyperchylo-micronaemia is seen as early as childhood and leads to similar clinical complications, particularly acute pancreatitis. In contrast to familial lipoprotein lipase deficiency, neither xanthoma-tosis nor hepatomegaly have been observed to date in patients with C-II deficiency. The few cases described up to now do not permit generalizations

with reference to clinical complications of this
disease.

6) APO C-III

    The gene for apo C-III is located on
chromosome 11. Apo C-III is synthesized in the
liver as a 99 residue protein, preapo C-III.
Cotranslationally it is cleaved to mature apo C-III
which is present in plasma as three isoforms
containing no carbohydrates (apo C-III$_0$) and a
carbohydrate chain with one (apo C-III$_1$) or two
neuraminic acid residues (apo C-III$_2$), respectively. Apo C-III presumably inhibits lipoprotein
uptake by the liver suggesting that it may modulate
the metabolism of triglyceride-rich lipoproteins.
Patients with apo A-I- apo C-III deficiency can not
synthesize these apolipoproteins due to a defect in
the A-I C-III gene cluster.
HDL in these patients are absent from plasma, LDL
concentrations are normal. Severe premature
atherosclerosis and xanthomatosis are prominent
clinical features of this disease.

7) APO E

    The gene for apo E is located on chromosome
19. Messenger RNA of apo E has been found in all
organs with major concentrations in the liver,
adrenal and spleen.
Apo E is synthesized as a 299-residue glycoprotein,
preapo E. After cotranslational cleavage of the 18
residue prepeptide, the mature apo E is secreted
into plasma as a sialylated apolipoprotein.
Apo E is located at a single gene locus with three
major alleles ϵ-2, ϵ-3, ϵ-4 resulting in six apo
E phenotypes (E 2/2, E 3/3, E 4/4, E 2/3, E 2/4 and
E 3/4) in the population. The common apo E isoforms
differ at two positions in the amino acid sequence
(112 and 158). Apo E-2 contains cysteine at
positions 112 and 158; apo E-3 contains cysteine at
position 112 and arginine at position 158, while
apo E-4 contains arginine at both positions.
Apo E is considered to be important in the
metabolism of triglyceride-rich lipoprotein
and to bind in vitro to specific membrane receptors
(apo-E receptors, apo-B,E receptors) in the liver.

Apo E and Cholesterol Metabolism

Apo E polymorphism has a pronounced effect on serum LDL cholesterol concentrations. Lowest serum cholesterol- and LDL-cholesterol concentrations are generally detected in apo E-2 homozygosity (see also next paragraph) and highest concentrations in apo E-4 homozygosity.
In a study with coronary angiography patients we have recently determined that differences in serum LDL cholesterol concentrations between E-3/E-4 heterozygosity and E-3/E-2 heterozygosity were 22 mg/dl. E-3/E-4 heterozygosity was related to the occurrence of myocardial infarction at age 48, five years earlier than E-2/E-3 heterozygous patients. The high LDL cholesterol concentrations in coronary angiography patients and myocardial infarction survivors presumably are of multifactorial origin (LDL receptor expression, apo B polymorphism etc.). Among these factors apo E polymorphism apparently has a significant effect on LDL cholesterol concentrations.

Apo E-2 Homozygosity

In the case of apo E-2 homozygosity (approx. 1 % of the population) there is resultant dysbetalipoproteinaemia as a consequence of disturbed catabolism of chylomicron remnants and IDL. In the lipoprotein electrophoresis, ß-VLDL are found in the $d < 1.006$ g/ml supernatant (i.e. dysbetalipoproteinaemia), VLDL cholesterol is elevated.
LDL cholesterol and total cholesterol are reduced. The abnormal ß-VLDL have the following properties:
(a) spherical particles 250 A in diameter on average (normal VLDL: approx. 400 A); .
(b) float in S_F-range 20-60 (normal VLDL: S 20-40);
(c) rich in cholesterol (normal VLDL: triglyceride-rich);
(d) high apolipoprotein E concentration;
(e) no normal apolipoprotein E (i.e. apo E-3 or apo E-4), only defective apolipoprotein E

It is assumed that the ß-VLDL are metabolic products of both chylomicrons (i.e. chylomicron remnants) and VLDL (i.e. VLDL remnants). Evidently, as a result of structural mutation of apolipoprotein E-3 yielding apolipoprotein E-2, the remnants of the triglyceride-rich molecules are not properly recognized by hepatic receptors and thus accumulate in the plasma. Apparently, more than one mutation accounts for the apolipoprotein E-2 phenotype. Arginine-cysteine interchanges may occur at different sites in the molecule not affecting the charge and the isoelectric focusing behaviour, but possibly affecting the function of this apolipo-protein.

It has not been possible to date to determine whether apo E-2 homozygosity causing dysbetalipoproteinaemia per se is associated with an increased coronary risk. In our own studies of a group of patients who underwent coronary angio-graphy, apo E-2 homozygosity occurred with similar frequency among unaffected patients or within the general population. At present, the low number of reported cases does not permit any conclusion as to whether apo E-2 may be considered a biochemical indicator of increased coronary risk. One or two per cent of the patients with apo E-2 homozygosity progress to a condition characterized by severe early coronary atherosclerosis, peripheral athero-sclerosis and xanthomatosis: type III hyperlipo-proteinaemia.

Familial Type III Hyperlipoproteinaemia

Familial type III hyperlipoproteinaemia was described initially in 1967 by Fredrickson et al. Employing a combination of ultracentrifugation and lipoprotein electrophoresis, these authors discovered abnormal VLDL in the plasma of affected patients which did not exhibit the usual pre-ß mobility, but rather ß mobility. These abnormal lipoproteins were designated 'ß-VLDL' or 'floating ß-lipoproteins', which yield a broad ß-band in the electrophoresis of native serum ('broad ß

(apo E-2) present.

disease'). Later studies by Havel and Kane showed a high concentration of apo E in the ß-VLDL. In 1975, Utermann et al. described the genetic defect of type III hyperlipoproteinaemia as an increase in apo E-2 with simultaneous absence of apo E-3 and apo E-4. In 1980 Weisgraber et al. identified a structural mutation of apolipoprotein E-3 as a biochemical defect of type III hyperlipoprotein-aemia.

Only 2 % of all patients with apo E-2 homozygosity develop clinical signs of type III hyperlipoproteinaemia. Type III hyperlipoprotein-aemia becomes ·manifest when, in addition to apo E-2 homozygosity, there is either a further inborn error of lipid metabolism present (e.g. familial hypercholesterolaemia, familial hypertriglycerid-aemia, familial combined hyperlipidaemia, polygenic hypercholesterolaemia) or there is a secondary hyperlipoproteinaemia (e.g. in hypothyroidism) present. Obviously, under these circumstances (apolipoprotein E-2 homozygosity combined with increased biosynthesis of VLDL or reduced catabolism of LDL) the condition in question is extreme dysbetalipoproteinaemia causally related to atherosclerosis and xanthomatosis.

The diagnosis of familial type III hyper-lipoproteinaemia (frequency approx. 1:5000) can be confirmed on the basis of the clinical findings (xanthomata of the hand lines, tuberous xanthomata, intermittent claudicatio, coronary heart disease) and the biochemical findings (apo E-2 homozygosity, ß-VLDL, hyperlipidaemia with elevated cholesterol and triglycerides). The early occurrence of coronary heart disease and/or peripheral vascular occlusion (often before age 40) are frequent complications of this disorder of lipid metabolism. The differentiation of apolipoprotein E-2 homozygosity from type III hyperlipoproteinaemia is at present possible only on the basis of clinical observations. Of particular clinical interest is the question of which patients, if any, with apolipoprotein E-2 homozygosity have an increased coronary risk. In any case, apolipoprotein E-2 homozygosity occurs in the population with a frequency of 1 % and is characterized by dysbetalipoproteinaemia which, at least in a number of patients, is accompanied by the early onset of coronary sclerosis. Between type III hyperlipo-proteinaemia with extreme elevation of ß-VLDL and apolipoprotein E-2 homozygosity with low serum cholesterol levels and slight elevation of ß-VLDL, there is an entire spectrum of metabolic anomalies whose relationship to coronary atherosclerosis is in need of explanation.

Type V Hyperlipoproteinaemia Associated with the

Apo E-4 Phenotype

A high frequency (74 %) of the homozygous and heterozygous E-4 phenotype has recently been discovered among type V hyperlipoproteinaemic patients. The apo E allele frequency was 53 % in contrast to 15 % in normals. Therefore, it was concluded that the ε-4 allele may predispose to a disturbance in the catabolism of triglyceride-rich lipoproteins. It is not unlikely that similar to type III hyperlipoproteinaemia - at least in certain kindreds with type V hyperlipoproteinaemia - a polygenic defect accounts for the extreme elevation of chylomicrons and VLDL.

Apo E Deficiency

A single kindred from Virginia was recently described in which four siblings exhibited the complete absence of apo E from plasma. Three of the four siblings had evidence of premature CAD and all had tuberoeruptive xanthomas. Upon lipoprotein electrophoresis, a broad beta band was the prominent feature corresponding to an increased concentration of intermediatedensity lipoproteins. The clinical picture in these patients resembles type III hyperlipoproteinaemia.

Other Apolipoprotein E Variants

Screening techniques to monitor for the isoelectric focusing behaviour of the apo isoforms permit the identification of structural apo E variants. Recently, a kindred in Bethesda area was observed in which the proband was a patient with type III hyperlipoproteinaemia associated with an abnormal isoform of apo E (apo E Bethesda). In our own screening analysis of coronary angiography patients for apo E isoforms among 2000 individuals, only a single case of abnormal apo E isoform pattern was observed (apo E Münster).

CONCLUSION

The detailed analysis of apolipoproteins, lipoprotein receptors and enzymes involved in the metabolism of serum lipoproteins has greatly improved our understanding of the pathophysiology of lipid disorders. Obligatory functions of apolipoproteins have been delineated from the study of rare mutants (Table 5).

Table 5: Lessons from Apolipoprotein Mutants: Obligatory Functions of Apolipoproteins

B-100/B-48	chylomicron, VLDL formation
C-II	lipoprotein lipase activation
E	chylomicron remnant removal
A-I	reverse cholesterol transport

With the recent availability of screening techniques permitting the structural analysis of apolipoproteins and their genes, it is expected that knowledge on apolipoprotein disorders will further increase. Undoubtedly, these techniques will be extended to lipoprotein receptors and lipolytic enzymes giving rise to a complex analysis of lipid disorders and a better understanding of their relationship to atherosclerosis.

DNA POLYMORPHISMS AND ANALYSIS OF HYPERLIPIDAEMIA

S.E. Humphries, P.J. Talmud and R. Williamson

Department of Biochemistry, St. Mary's Hospital
Medical School, Norfolk Place, London, W2 1PG.

Which genes are of interest in the study of inherited factors that predispose an individual to develop hyperlipidaemia? Table I shows a list of candidate genes that are known to be involved in the metabolism of cholesterol and triglycerides. Even though the list is not comprehensive, there is clearly a problem of how to decide which genes to study first. Some of the candidates, such as the LDL receptor, are already clearly implicated and warrant a detailed study, which would involve the isolation of the gene from patients for sequencing, and the identification of the defect at the DNA level.

The approach we are adopting is to use restriction fragment length polymorphism (RFPLs) to be able to follow the inheritance in a family of the genes, for example for an apoprotein. Thus in the model family in Figure 1 we can distinguish the two alleles of the apo CII gene in an individual with a particular type of hyperlipidaemia. When we look in his children we find that all the affected offspring have inherited the T2 allele and all the unaffected offspring the T1 allele. This is compatible with there being a defect in the apo CII gene on the T2 allele causing the hyperlipidaemia in this family, but requires similar results to be obtained in several families to confirm this result. The apo CII gene on the T2 allele in this family could then be isolated and sequenced to identify the defect at the DNA level.

TABLE 1

Candidate Genes Involved in the Development of Hyperlipidaemia

GENE	CLONE	CHROMOSOME	POLYMORPHISM	PIC VALUE	REF
APOPROTEINS					
A II	cDNA	1 p21-qt	Msp I	.33	14
AIV/AI/CIII	cDNA genomic	11 p11-q13	Sst I Pst I Xmn I	.14 .18 .5 .20	12 13
E/CI/CII	cDNA genomic	19 p13.2-q?	E PROTEIN CII Taq I CII Bgl I CI -	.4 .37 .37 .5 -	4 11 15 16
B	cDNA	2p	-	-	$
RECEPTORS					
LDL	cDNA genomic	19	Pvu II	.27	2
REMNANT	-	-	-	-	
LDL-MODIFIED	-	-	-	-	
HDL	-	-	-	-	
ENZYMES					
HMG CoA REDUCTASE	cDNA genomic	5q21	-	-	17
LCAT	cDNA genomic	16q21	-	-	18
LIPASE	-	-	-	-	
ACAT	-	-	-	-	

($ Dr. B. Brewer, Dr. J.Breslow personal communications)

Once the defect is identified, the other patients and families can be rapidly analysed for the same defect using oligonucleotides (1).

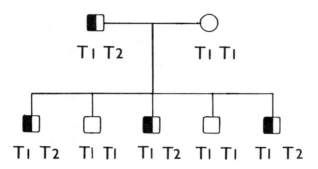

T₁ T₂ T₁ T₁

T₁ T₂ T₁ T₁ T₁ T₂ T₁ T₁ T₁ T₂

LINKAGE

Figure 1 Inheritance of alleles of a candidate gene in the family of an individual with Hyperlipidaemia. ■ individual with hyperlipidaemia; ○ □ normal individual.

We have already used this approach to identify defective genes of apo CII (2 and this conference) and the method can be used to study monogenic disorders such as Familial Hypercholesterolaemia (3) and LCAT deficiency, and more complex situations such as shown in Figure 2. Here we have a model family where hyper-lipidaemia is caused by the interaction of two sub-clinical alleles of the genes A and B. These defective alleles only raise cholesterol levels by say 25-30% and only individuals who have inherited both the A* and B* defective alleles develop hyperlipid-aemia. It should be noted that in order to understand this interaction, the inheritance of both genes has to be followed simultaneously in the same family. This may be the sort of approach that will help us to understand the genetic factors involved in the development of Familial Combined Hyperlipidaemia.

19

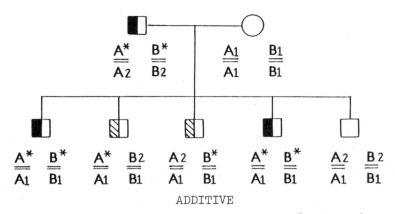

ADDITIVE

Figure 2 Interaction of two genes A* and B[4] in the development of Hyperlipidaemia. ■ individual with hyperlipidaemia; ▨ individual with slightly elevated levels of lipids; ○ □ normal individual.

Another form of interaction can be seen in families with type III hyperlipidaemia. Individuals who are homozygous for the variant apo E protein E2 are predisposed to develop Type III, but it requires another factor, probably genetic, to develop the hyperlipidaemia. About 50% of the first degree relatives of individuals with Type III hyperlipidaemia are themselves hyperlipidaemic (4), and this is compatable with the co-segregation in these families of a second "hyperlipidaemia gene".

Which of the candidate genes could this be? It will be interesting in these families to follow the inheritance of the genes for apo B or the remnant receptor, or even lipoprotein lipase, but as yet this has not been done. At the present time RFLPs have been reported for most but not all of the cloned genes of interest (Table 1). However, it has recently become clear that there are two clusters of the apoprotein genes on chromosome 11 (AIV; AI and CIII) and chromosome 19 (E, CII and CI). The genes for apo AI and apo CIII are only 2.6 kb apart (5) and apo E and apo CI about 6-8 kb apart (our unpublished results and

20

J. Breslow personal communication). The genes for apo CII (6) and apo AIV (7) have been linked to the others by genetic studies. Thus it is clear that in family studies a polymorphism in, for example the apo CII gene will allow the inheritance of the whole E/CII/CI cluster to be followed. It should be pointed out that although the gene for the LDL receptor is also on chromosome 19, the genetic distance between this gene and the apoprotein gene cluster is so great that the two segregate essentially independently in a family (i.e. as if they were in fact on different chromosomes (8)).

Usually several polymorphisms are required to be able to follow the inheritance of a gene unambiguously (9) and if many RFLPs are available they can be used in conjunction to construct a haplotype. This approach has been very useful in the study of the haemoglobinopathies to distinguish new variants (10) and this should also be applicable for the apoprotein genes.

It should be pointed out that the vast majority of the polymorphisms are neutral and are not in themselves causally involved in the defects under study. For example, the apo CII TaqI polymorphism is most probably caused by a single base change in the DNA about 2 kb from the 3' end of the coding region of the gene. The frequency of this RFLP is not significantly different in groups of patients with different hyperlipidaemias (11). There have been reports that the frequency of the SstI RFLP in the apo CIII gene is higher in patients with certain forms of hypertriglyceridaemia (12). However, the results of our study have not confirmed this (13) and neither does a blind study that we have conducted in collaboration with Professor Berg in Norway (in preparation). In general polymorphisms of these candidate genes will probably show no strong population associations with defects leading to the development of hyperlipidaemia, but will be useful as genetic markers for family studies. A possible exception to this has just been reported for a polymorphism of the apo AII gene. This may be in population assocation with an allele of the apo AI gene that overproduces apo AII protein (14).

The prospect for the next few years is very exciting. We will soon have the probes and the polymorphisms we need. We can then start to identify defective genes acting by themselves and in combination with others. We should be able to apply this to diagnosis of individuals at risk of developing hyperlipidaemia and premature atherosclerosis.

References

1. V.J. Kidd, R.B. Wallace and K. Itakura, α 1-antitrypsin deficiency detection by direct analysis of the mutation in the gene, Nature 304:230-234, (1983).
2. S.E. Humphries, L. Williams, O. Myklebost, A.F.H. Stalenhoef, P.N.M. Demacker, G. Baggio, G. Crepaldi, D.J. Galton and R. Williamson, Familial apolipoprotein CII deficiency: A preliminary analysis of the gene defect in two independent families. Hum. Genet. 67:151-155 (1984).
3. S.E. Humphries, A.M. Kessling, B. Horsthemke, J.A. Donald, M. Seed, N.I. Jowett, M. Holm, D.J. Galton, V. Wynn and R. Williamson, A common DNA polymorphism of the Low Density Lipoprotein (LDL) receptor gene and its use in diagnosis. Lancet, I:1003-1005 (1985).
4. G. Utermann, K.H. Vogelberg, A. Steinmetz, W. Shoenborn, N. Pruin, M. Jaeschke, M. Hees and H. Canzler, Polymorphisms of apolipoprotein E. II. Genetics of hyperlipoproteinemia type III. Clin. Genet. 15:37-62 (1979).
5. S.K. Karathanasis, J. McPherson, V.I. Zannis and J.L. Breslow, Linkage of human apolipoprotein AI and CIII genes. Nature 304:371-373.
6. O. Schamaun, B. Olaisen, B. Mevag, T. Gedde-Dahl, C. Ehnholm and P. Teisberg, The two apolipoprotein loci apo A-I and apo A-IV are closely linked in man, Hum. Genet. 68:181-184 (1984).
7. S.E. Humphries, K. Berg, L. Gill, A.M. Cumming, F.W. Robertson, A.F.H. Stalenhoef, R. Williamson and A-L. Borresen, The gene for apolipoprotein CII is closely linked to the gene for apolipoprotein E on chromosome 19, Clin. Genet. 26:389-396, (1984).

8.	J.A. Donald, S.C. Wallis, A. Kessling, P. Tippett, E.B. Robson, S. Ball, K.E. Davies, P. Scambler, K. Berg, A. Heiberg, R. Williamson and S.E. Humphries, Linkage relationships of the gene for apolipoprotein CII with loci on chromosome 19, Hum. Genet. 69:39-43. (1985).

9.	S.E. Humphries, N.I. Jowett, A. Kessling, J.A. Donald, S.C. Wallis and R. Williamson, The use of recombinant DNA technology to study polygenic hyperlipidaemia, Cologne Atherosclerosis Meeting II Lipids. Ed. M.J. Parnham, pp 35-40, (1984).

10.	S.E. Antonarakis, H.H. Hazazain and S.H. Orkin, DNA polymorphism and molecular pathology of the human globin gene clusters, Hum. Genet. 69:1-14 (1985).

11.	S.E. Humphries, N.I. Jowett, L. Williams, A. Rees, M. Vella, A. Kessling, O. Myklebost, A. Lydon, M. Seed, D.J. Galton and R. Williamson, A DNA polymorphism adjacent to the human apolipoprotein CII gene, Molecular Biology and Medicine 1:463-471 (1984).

12.	A. Rees, J. Stocks, C.C. Shoulders, D.J. Galton and F.E. Barralle, DNA polymorphism adjacent to human apoprotein AI gene: relation to hypertriglyceridaemia, Lancet I:444-446 (1983).

13.	A.M. Kessling, B. Horsthemke and S.E. Humphries, A study of DNA polymorphisms around the human Apolipoprotein, Clin. Genet., submitted, (1985).

14.	J. Scott, T.J. Knott, L.M. Priestley, M.E. Robertson, D.V. Mann, G. Kostner, G.J. Miller and N.E. Miller, High-density lipoprotein composition is altered by a common DNA polymorphism adjacent to apoprotein AII gene in man, Lancet, 6th April, 771-773.

15.	S.C. Wallis, J.A. Donald, L.A. Forrest, R. Williamson and S.E. Humphries, The isolation of a genomic clone containing the apolipoprotein CII gene and the detection of linkage disequilibrium between two common DNA polymorphisms around the gene, Hum. Genet., 68:286-289 (1984).

16.	F. Tata, I, Henry, A.F. Markham, S.C. Wallis, D. Weil, K.H. Grzeschik, C. Junien, R. Williamson and S.E. Humphries, Isolation and characterisation of a cDNA clone for human apolipoprotein CI and assignment of the gene to chromosome 19, Hum. Genet., 69:345-349.

17. M Azoulay, I. Henry, F. Tata, D. Weil, K.H. Grezchik. E. Chaves, N. McIntyre, R. Williamson, S.E. Humphries and C. Junien, The structural gene for lecithin:cholesterol acyl transferase (LCAT) maps to 16q22, Annals Hum. Genet. submited (1985).

18. S.E. Humphries, I. Henry, F. Tata, F. Banchard, M. Holm, R. Williamson and C. Junien, The gene for HMG-CoA reductase is on human chromosome 5, EMBO J. submitted, 1985.

MONOCLONAL ANTIBODIES AND GENETIC POLYMORPHISM OF APOLIPOPROTEINS

Ross W. Milne, P.K. Weech, and Y.L. Marcel

Laboratory of Lipoprotein Metabolism
Clinical Research Institute of Montreal
Montreal, Quebec H2W 1R7, Canada

Genetic polymorphism has been demonstrated for several of the human apolipoproteins. In most cases the polymorphism has been identified by demonstrating differences in the electrophoretic charge amongst isoforms and more recently the elucidation of amino acid and nucleotide sequences has provided insight into the molecular basis of the polymorphism. There are, in contrast, few examples of human apolipoprotein polymorphisms which have been identified immunologically. The Ag system of human LDL (1,2) has been defined by antibodies in the plasma of multitransfused patients and while it appears that the Ag determinants are associated with apo B, it remains to be shown definitively that the Ag system represents polymorphism of the apo B gene. Polymorphism in the lipoproteins of several animal species including swine (3), monkeys (4), mink (5) and rabbits (6) have also been identified by alloantibodies.

Monoclonal antibodies (MABS) have been demonstrated to be useful probes for studying apolipoprotein structure and heterogeneity. There have been several reports of MABS, notably against apo B, which show different immunoreactivities with lipoproteins of different individuals (8,9). However, as in the case of the polyclonal antibodies against Ag antigens, it isn't clear that these differences in immunoreactivities reflect polymorphism at the level of the apo B gene. One exception is the report of Schumaker and his colleagues (10). They have observed intersubject differences in the immunoreactivity of LDL with certain anti-apo B MABS which appeared to be independent of both the carbohydrate moiety of the apo B and LDL particle size. The described polymorphism appeared to be the product of 2 codominant alleles which are inherited in a Mendelian fashion and appear to

25

be different from the known Ag factors. The biological importance of this polymorphism remains to be demonstrated. The only other reported example of a MAB which is capable of discriminating amongst human apolipoprotein isoforms is the anti-apo E MAB 1D7 (11). Weisgraber et al (12) have shown that 1D7 blocks recognition of apo E by the LDL receptor and that its corresponding antigenic determinant is found within a region of apo E bounded by residues 139 and 169. When this MAB was tested against various apo E isoforms its reactivity was independent of a cysteine/arginine interchange at residue 158 of apo E but was markedly reduced by either a cysteine/arginine interchange at residue 145 or a lysine/glutamine interchange at residue 146. However as the differences in immunoreactivity were quantitative rather than absolute it is unlikely that 1D7 will prove useful as a screening reagent for apo E isoforms.

MABS may be potentially useful for both defining new polymorphisms and for discriminating amongst isoforms in already defined systems. As an example, MABS specific for the apo E isoforms would permit the phenotyping of subjects by direct analysis of the plasma and thus eliminating the steps of isolation ,delipidation and isoelectrofocusing of the lipoproteins. This would obviously facilitate studies involving the screening of large numbers of subjects. Moreover, a lack of concordance between results obtained with antibodies and those with isoelectrofocucusing could be indicative of a new unidentified variant.

One of the problems in most current protocols for producing MABS is that they rely on the immune system of the mouse for providing the specificity of the MABS. When the immune system is presented with an antigen from another species, antibodies directed against species-specific determinants predominate in the immune response and these, in general, will not detect the subtle differences which differentiate the isoforms. Not surprisingly, therefore, most human polymorphisms defined immunologically are based on the reactivities of human isoantibodies. These antibodies have classically come from multitransfused patients and multiparous women or, as in the case of the ABO blood group system, are so-called "natural" antibodies which have been produced in response to cross-reacting environmental antigens. Taking the above into consideration we will suggest several strategies which may prove more efficient than currently used protocols for the production of MABS capable of identifying genetic polymorphisms of human apolipoproteins.

When the molecular basis of the polymorphism is known, as in the case for apo E, it may be possible to use as immunogen synthetic peptides which mimic apolipoprotein sequences and which include the amino acid substitution responsible for the

polymorphism. To be useful, antibodies raised against such
synthetic peptides must satisfy two criteria; they must be capable
firstly, of reacting with the native apolipoprotein and secondly,
of discriminating amongst the isoforms. Based on the experience,
primarily of the group of Lerner at the Scripps Institute, a
number of rules have been formulated to optimize the chances of
obtaining antibodies against synthetic antigens which also
recognize the native protein (13). According to these rules it is
advisable to utilize hydrophilic peptides consisting of at least
six amino acids which, if possible, include a proline residue.
While in the case under consideration the choice is limited to the
sequence spanning the substitution site, these rules should
nevertheless help to predict the probability of success of the
immunization. Alexander et al. (14) have produced MABS against
short synthetic peptides which were capable of differentiating
between cell surface polymorphic proteins differing by a single
amino acid.

A second possible approach is through the induction of
immunological tolerance. When an animal is exposed to antigen
during foetal and neonatal life, instead of mounting an immune
response against the antigen the animal tends to develop a
specific immunological tolerance i.e. the animal becomes
unresponsive to the antigen. This state of unresponsiveness can
continue throughout the life of the animal and is probably related
to the fact that the ability to distinguish between self and
non-self is an acquired phenomenon. Thus, exposure to antigen
early in life would result in the antigen being recognized as
self. One might therefore envisage the injection of the neonate
with one isoform of an apolipoprotein and, then, once the animal
has matured and become immunologically competent, immunization
with a second isoform. One would hope that only those
determinants which differ between the isoforms will elicit
antibodies. The spleens of such animals could be used as the
source of lymphocytes for the production of hybridomas.

An alternative similar strategy may be to eliminate
immunocompetent cell precursors which are capable of binding
antigen by *in vitro* incubation of spleen cells with one
apolipoprotein isoform coupled to toxin. The surviving cells
could then be adoptively transferred to an irradiated recipient
which in turn could be challenged with a second isoform. Such a
protocol has been shown to be efficient at selectively eliminating
the immune response to one antigen while leaving the response to
other antigens intact (15,16).

A further approach could be the production of human
hybridomas. As described above, most human genetic polymorphisms
which are defined immunologically rely on human isoantibodies.
Thus, human monoclonal antibodies may prove to be better than

murine MABS for identifying apolipoprotein polymorphisms. The three major prerequisites for the production of human hybridomas are the availability of an immortal human cell partner, of immune human lymphocytes and of an efficient fusion system. There are now numerous appropriate human lymphoblastoid and myeloma cell lines which can serve as the immortal cell partner and a number of successful fusion protocols have been described and recently reviewed (17). The principal problem which plagues the production of human monoclonal antibodies remains the availability of immune lymphocytes.

The most accessible source of human lymphocytes is the peripheral blood, and peripheral blood lymphocytes as well as spleen, tonsil and lymph node lymphocytes have been used for production of human hybridomas (17). Immunization *in vivo* has been most efficient to date and is convenient for such antigens as tetanus toxoid or any of the vaccines. However, in the case of human antigens such as apolipoprotein one must consider the risk of eliciting autoantibodies. While immunization *in vitro* is widely used for production of murine hybridomas (18), the conditions for the generation of a primary *in vitro* immune response with human lymphocytes have not yet been satisfactorly defined. *In vitro* exposure of human lymphocytes to antigen, mitogen or Epstein-Barr virus can increase the frequency of antigen specific hybridomas if these lymphocytes had received a primary immunization *in vivo* (17). With the current interest in the production of human hybridomas, improvements in techniques of *in vitro* immunization should be forthcoming. In addition there are two of the classic sources of human isoantibodies; multitransfused patients and multiparous women. Human hybridomas secreting antibody against Rh antigens have been produced from peripheral blood lymphocytes isolated from women who have had Rh incompatible pregnancies (19). It remains to be seen if polymorphic determinants of apolipoproteins would be sufficiently immunogenic to elict an immune response under similar circumstances.

While MABS against apolipoproteins have been shown to be excellent probes for the study of lipoprotein structure and metabolism there are few examples of MABS capable of identifying genetic polymorphisms of apolipoproteins. Here we have suggested several strategies which may prove to be more efficient for the production of MABS which will be more discriminating than those currently available for detecting apolipoprotein polymorphisms.

ACKNOWLEDGEMENTS

We acknowledge the superb secretarial assistance of Mrs Louise Lalonde. We wish to thank the mayor and people of Limone sul Garda for their kindness and hospitality during the NATO Advanced Workshop.

REFERENCES

1. G. M. Kostner, Lp(a) Lipoproteins and the genetic polymorphisms of lipoprotein B, in: "Low density lipoproteins", C.E. Day and R.S. Leung, eds., Plenum Press, New York (1976).
2. R. Butler, E. Butler-Brunner, R. Scherz, and R. Pflugshaupt, The Ag-system of low density lipoproteins - an updating, in: "Protides of the Biological Fluids", H. Peeters, ed., Pergamon Press, New York (1977).
3. J. Rapacz, R. H. Grummer, J. Hasler, and R. M. Shachelford, Allotype polymorphism of low density beta lipoproteins in pig serum, Nature 225:941 (1970).
4. J. Hasler-Rapacz, and J. Rapacz, Lipoprotein immunogenetics in primates. I. Two serum B-lipoprotein allotypes (Lmb 1 and Lmb 11) in Rhesus monkeys and the LP-B immunological relationship with other primates, J. Med. Primatol. 11:352 (1982).
5. O. K. Baranov, and M. A. Savina, Immunogenetic study on the polymorphism of serum alpha 2- lipoproteins in mink IV Duallelism of the Ld locus of low-density lipoproteins, Biochem. Genet. 19:997 (1981).
6. J. J. Albers, and S. Dray., Identification and genetic control of two new low density lipoproteins allotypes, Biochem. Genet. 2:25 (1968).
7. R. W. Milne, and Y. L. Marcel, The use of monoclonal antibodies to probe human apo B structure and function, Can. J. Biochem. (in press).
8. M. J. Tikkanen, T. G. Cole, and G. Schonfeld, Differential reactivity of human low density lipoproteins with monoclonal antibodies, J. Lipid Res. 24: 1494 (1983).
9. J. G. Patton, J.-J. Badimon, and S. J. T. Mao, Monoclonal antibodies to human plasma low density lipoproteins. II. Evaluation for use in radioimmunoassay for apolipoprotein B in patients with coronary artery disease, Clin. Chem. 29:1889 *1983).
10. V. N. Shumaker, M. T. Robinson, L. K. Curtiss, R. Butler, and R. S. Sparkes, Anti-apoprotein B monoclonal antibodies detect human low density lipoprotein polymorphism, J. Biol. Chem. 259:6423 (1984).
11. R. W. Milne, Ph. Douste-Blazy, L. Retegui, and Y. L. Marcel, Characterization of monoclonal antibodies against human apolipoprotein E, J. Clin. Invest. 68:111 (1981).
12. K. H. Weisgraber, T. L. Innerarity, K. H. Harder, R. W. Mahley, R. W. Milne, Y. L. Marcel, and J. T. Sparrow, The receptor binding domain of human apolipoprotein E: monoclonal antibody inhibition of binding, J. Biol. Chem. 258: 11348 (1982).

13. J. G. Sutcliffe, T. M. Shinnick, N. Green, and R. A. Lerner, Antibodies that raect with predetermined sites on proteins, Science 219:660 (1983).

14. H. Alexander, D. A. Johnson, J. Rosen, L. Jeraliek, N. Green, I. L. Weissman, and R. A. Lerner, Mimicking the alloantigenicity of proteins with chemically synthesized peptides differing in single amino acids, Nature 306:697 (1983).

15. D. J. Volkman, A. Ahmad, A. S. Fauci, and D. M. Neville, Selective abrogation of antigen-specific human B cell responses by antigen-ricin conjugates, J. Exp. Med. 156:634 (1982).

16. E. S. Vitetta, K. A. Krolick, M. Miyama-Inala, W. Cushley, and J. W. Uhr, Immunotoxins: a new approach to cancer therapy, Science 219: 644 (1983).

17. D. Kozbor, and J. C. Roder, The production of monoclonal antibodies from human lymphocytes, Immunol. Today 9:72 (1983).

18. C. L. Reading, Theory and methods for immunization in culture and monoclonal antibody production, J. Immunol. Meth. 53:261 (1982).

19. P. Bron, M. B. Feinberg, N. N. H. Teng, and H. S. Kaplan, Production of human monoclonal IgG antibodies against Rhesus (D) antigen, Proc. Natl. Acad. Sci. 81:3214 (1984).

NORMAL GENETIC LIPOPROTEIN VARIATIONS AND ATHEROSCLEROSIS

Kåre Berg

Chairman, Institute of Medical Genetics
University of Oslo, Oslo, Norway

INTRODUCTION

Disorders that exhibit great frequency variations over relatively short time periods must necessarily have important environmental,nutritional or life style factors in their etiology. The demonstration of a direct connection between such factors and parameters that are known to be strongly associated with the disorder in question would add credence to the hypothesis that these factors are etiologically important. Genetic studies may nevertheless uncover evidence of an effect of genes on the same parameters, or show that the disorder aggregates in families in a way suggestive of either simple inheritance or genetic pre-disposition. We are then confronted with the complex problem of interaction between environmental, nutritional or life style factors on the one hand and the individual's genotype on the other. Atherosclerotic disease, especially coronary heart disease (CHD) poses such a problem.

It has been well known since documentation published in the 1930ies that the triad of xanthomas, a high level of serum cholesterol and heart disease behaves as an autosomal dominant trait in many kindreds (Müller 1939). It was, however, believed that CHD as observed in this syndrome represented an exceptional case of genetic factors contributing to the etiology of premature CHD. Because of the impressive evidence that nutritional or life style factors are of importance, atherosclerosis has often been thought of as exclusively caused by such factors. For example, the highly significant difference in mean cholesterol level between the high-morbidity area of East Finland and the low-morbidity area of South Japan has been described as purely cultural in origin.

However, the differences between the populations of Finland and
Japan are not exclusively of a cultural nature. Thus, there are
great differences in frequencies of genes at many loci between
populations as widely separated as the Finns and the Japanese,
and some of these genes appear to influence lipid levels.

There are well established relationships between lipid or
lipoprotein levels in the blood, accumulation of lipid or lipoproteins in the artery wall, and coronary heart disease (for
review, see Berg 1979, 1982, 1983, 1985). Direct evidence that
serum lipoproteins are involved in the atherosclerotic process has
emerged from studies in man with labelled antibodies in which
presence of serum lipoproteins in atherosclerotic lesions has been
established. Also, a wealth of clinical and epidemiological data
implicates lipoproteins in the etiology of atherosclerosis. Lipids
or lipoproteins are therefore of central importance in research
concerning the etiology of atherosclerosis and in the discussion of
the prospects for preventing atherosclerotic disease.

Normal, genetic lipoprotein variation could be quantitative
(i.e. genes contributing to the population distribution of lipids
or lipoprotein levels) or qualitative (distinct, non-overlapping
phenotypes).

MONOGENIC HYPERLIPIDEMIAS

The monogenic hyperlipidemias, represent the extreme in terms
of quantitative lipid variation. Among these disorders, familial
hypercholesterolemia (FHC) (Müller 1939, Fredrickson et al. 1967,
Goldstein et al. 1972, Heiberg & Berg 1976, Motulsky 1976,
Goldstein & Brown 1983, 1984) is by far the best studied and
understood condition. It is an autosomal dominant trait that
occurs in Western populations with a frequency of approximately
1/500, caused by an error in the low density lipoprotein (LDL)
receptor pathway. Goldstein and Brown who in a long series of
elegant studies uncovered the molecular basis of this serious
disorder have, with coworkers cloned and sequenced the LDL
receptor gene and determined the amino acid sequence of the
receptor protein (Yamamoto et al. 1984, Lehrman et al. 1985,
Südhof et al. 1985). The present level of understanding of
autosomal dominant hypercholesterolemia gives reason for cautious
optimism concerning the possibility to develop more effective
treatment of this disease.

The LDL receptor activity is to a great extent determined by
genes, also in the healthy population (Magnus et al. 1981a).
Studies on LDL receptor activity in our laboratory suggested that
there could be multiple normal alleles at the receptor locus
(Maartmann-Moe et al. 1981) but this problem was difficult to
completely solve by receptor activity studies. It is therefore of

32

considerable interest that the new DNA technology has led to a definite identification of normal genetic polymorphism at the LDL receptor locus. It will doubtless be examined in the very near future if these normal alleles relate to level of receptor activity and in turn to cholesterol level. According to classical genetic theory polymorphism implies some selective advantage to the bearers of one specific gene or combination of genes. Thus, if the LDL receptor locus should turn out to be highly polymorphic the question of which forces underlie the polymorphisms will become of interest. Presumably, variant genes at loci involved in the control of lipoprotein structure or metabolism could have carried a selective advantage under the widely different nutritional or life style conditions that prevailed hundreds or thousands of years ago.

GENETIC INFLUENCE ON LIPID AND APOPROTEIN LEVELS IN THE GENERAL POPULATION

The question if genes contribute to the distribution of lipid and lipoprotein levels in the general population is of great interest because of the importance of quantitative lipid or lipoprotein variation for susceptibility or resistance to athero-sclerotic disease. Animal as well as human data indicate significant influences of genes.

Animal Data

Roberts and Thompson (1976) found that different strains of inbred mice react to a high-fat, high-cholesterol diet in different ways, and that the mother and father exert an equal influence on the development of fatty deposits in the aortic sinus wall and on serum total cholesterol level. Breeding experiments indicated a polygenic system of inheritance of susceptibility to develop fatty deposits in the wall of the aortic sinus and this was strongly correlated to serum cholesterol levels. Adams et al. (1972) observed breed differences in the response of rabbits to an atherogenic diet with regard to both hypercholesterolemia and atheroma, presumably reflecting genetic differences between breeds.

Stufflebean and Lasley (1969) examined cholesterol levels in beef cattle and found that the blood level of cholesterol of young bulls is a heritable trait, apparently influenced by additive gene action. From an evolutionary point of view, it is of interest that there was a positive correlation between post weaning growth rate and serum cholesterol level, since a high post weaning growth rate (known to be controlled by additive gene action) may well carry a selective advantage. Thus, selection for polygenes determining a relatively high cholesterol level seems possible in that species. In squirrel monkeys, Clarkson et al. (1971) found a heritability for serum cholesterol level as high as 0.92.

Shore and Shore (1976) compared New Zealand White (hyper-responder) and Dutch Belt (hyporesponder) rabbits and found significant differences between the strains with respect to lipoprotein patterns following cholesterol feeding.

The above and other studies (for review, see Berg 1979, 1983) indicate significant genetic influences on lipid and lipoprotein levels in animals.

Human Data

Mayo et al. (1969) studying serum cholesterol in Greek families found significant parent-offspring and sib-sib correlations but no significant correlation between spouses. Rao et al. (1982) reported heritability estimates for total cholesterol of 0.62 and 0.49, from the Cincinnati Lipid Research Clinic Study and the Honolulu Heart Study, respectively. The estimates for LDL cholesterol were 0.62 and 0.39, for high density lipoprotein (HDL) cholesterol 0.47 and 0.28 and for very low density lipoprotein (VLDL) cholesterol 0.34 and 0.17. Namboodiri et al. (1984) studying more than 900 families found that genetic factors played a more substantial role than cultural factors in the determination of total and LDL cholesterol. Again, there was no significant correlation between spouses. In an Israeli study (Friedlander et al. 1982) a heritability estimate of 0.46 was obtained for total cholesterol. They also obtained significant heritability estimates for HDL cholesterol, as did Laskarzefsky et al. (1984). Glueck et al. (1984) suggested that the higher HDL cholesterol levels in blacks than in whites are due to genetic differences and proposed a mechanism that could give people with high HDL a selective advantage.

The above studies and others indicate significant contributions of genes to the population distribution of total-, LDL-, and HDL-cholesterol levels whereas the situation concerning triglyderides and VLDL remains unclear.

Since blood lipids are distributed on different lipoprotein classes, determination of specific populations of lipoprotein particles would appear to be more informative than lipid determination. This can to some extent be achieved by analysing the apoproteins that are characteristic of the various lipoprotein classes. Using this approach we find that apoB, the apoprotein that is characteristic of LDL, exhibits a higher degree of heritability than does total cholesterol, despite the fact that LDL is the main transporter of cholesterol in the blood (Berg 1981). Table 1 shows our best estimates of heritability of serum lipid and apoprotein levels from the study of 98 monozygotic and 100 dizygotic Norwegian twin pairs.

Table 1

Estimates of heritability (h^2) of serum
lipid and apoprotein levels from studies
of 98 monozygotic and 100 dizygotic pairs
(Data extracted from Berg 1983)

Parameter	h^2
Cholesterol level	0.34
Triglycerides (fasting)	0.40
ApoB level	0.66
ApoA-I level	0.53
ApoA-II level	0.69

Table 2

Interaction between environmental and
genetic factors: the most significant
results of a study of possible marker
gene effects on the variability in
serum lipoprotein parameters that
environmental/nutritional factors can
cause
(Data extracted from Berg 1985)

Marker system	Lipoprotein parameter	p-value
MNSs[1]	Cholesterol	0.001
ADA[2]	Fasting triglycerides	0.003
Kidd[1]	Cholesterol	0.005
Rh[1]	Fasting triglycerides	0.02

[1] Blood group system
[2] Polymorphism in the enzyme adenosine
deaminase

It appears from the heritability estimates that gene effects may explain a significant part of the quantitative variation in apoproteins present in atherogenic LDL as well as in "anti-atherogenic" HDL. When male and female twin pairs were analysed separately the heritability estimate for triglycerides was zero for male pairs, strengthening the previous impression that heritability of triglyceride level may be very low.

It is clear from Table 1 that there is ample space for strong effects also of nutritional or life style factors on the parameters examined. It is an interesting question how combinations of genes that act in a "favourable" or "unfavourable" way on the serum lipoprotein profile would influence the risk for CHD, and how nutritional or life style factors may interact with such gene combinations. This makes attempts to identify individual genes that influence lipoprotein parameters an important task for research in medical genetics.

ASSOCIATION BETWEEN LIPID LEVEL AND GENETIC MARKERS

Evidence for genetic influence on lipid levels in man has also emerged from association analyses between normal genetic markers and lipid levels. Association with cholesterol level has been found for genetic factors belonging to the AB0 and Secretor blood group system, and the Gm and Hp serum type systems. The combination of types in these four systems gives an additive effect when any two systems are combined whereas no additional effect is obtained by combining three or four systems (Sing and Orr 1976). Comparisons between such "two systems combined" genotypes show differences between the "highest" and "lowest" combined genotypes of 8-9 mg/dl for total serum cholesterol. Thus, a not ignorable part of the variation in total serum cholesterol may be determined by combinations of genes belonging to these four blood group and serum type systems.

Three genetic systems belonging to the lipoproteins themselves: the Ag system, the Lp system and the ApoE system also exhibit associations with lipid level and the Lp and ApoE systems show direct associations with CHD (associations between genetic markers and lipid levels are extensively reviewed in Berg 1983).

The new possibilities to study normal genetic polymorphisms in DNA itself is likely to uncover more examples of association between genetic markers and lipid or lipoprotein levels, and indeed such associations have already been reported (see below).

INTERACTION BETWEEN GENOTYPE AND ENVIRONMENTAL FACTORS

Marker genes may not only exhibit association with lipid levels but could also contribute to a genetically determined framework

which would limit the variation that nutritional or life style
factors could cause. We have developed an approach to study such
interactions between environmental factors and the genotype (Magnus
et al. 1981 b, Berg 1983). Since monozygotic twins have identical
genotypes, any difference between two members of a pair must be
caused by nutritional or life style factors. Therefore, a
"permissive" or "restrictive" effect of a given gene on variation
in a parameter such as serum cholesterol would be detectable by
comparing the within-pair difference in cholesterol level between
pairs that possess and pairs that lack the gene in question. When
we conducted this comparison between 75 monozygotic twin pairs
possessing and 22 monozygotic pairs lacking the M gene in the MNSs
blood group system, we found that the within-pair difference in
serum cholesterol level was almost twice as large in the latter as
in the former group. At face value this would seem to suggest a
restrictive effect of the M gene on variability in cholesterol
level caused by nutritional or life style factors. Alternatively,
such an effect could be exerted by genes at a locus that is closely
linked to the MNSs locus.

Since a number of loci and parameters were examined, the
apparently significant result could have arisen by chance alone.
With the experimental design used, 85 variance analyses were
conducted on 17 loci and 5 quantitative lipoprotein parameters.
With the number of analyses conducted one would expect chance
alone to cause 4 significant results at the 5% level and 1 at the
1% level. The actually observed numbers were 7 results that were
significant at the 1-5% level and 3 that were significant at the
1% level or lower. Thus, it seems likely that some of the observed
significant results were not due to chance alone. Table 2 shows
the most significant results and hence the results that are most
likely to reflect a true biological effect.

At this stage we cautiously conclude that it is likely that
at least one of the effects listed in Table 2 reflects a true
biological relationship, and the strongest candidate would seem
to be the apparent effect of the MNSs system on cholesterol
variability.

More important than the finding is the potential usefulness
of this new method to detect restrictive or permissive effects
of a great number of genes, on a wide spectrum of quantitative
biological or clinical parameters.

The clinical implications if any of the apparent effects of
marker genes on the amount of variation in cholesterol level that
nutritional or life style factors can cause, is unknown.

Lp(a) LIPOPROTEIN AND CORONARY HEART DISEASE

The genetically determined Lp(a) lipoprotein has been shown in several studies to be associated with CHD, and apparently intact Lp(a) lipoprotein has been demonstrated in atherosclerotic lesions (for review see Berg 1983). A major collaborative, blind study of Japanese living in Hawaii has recently been completed. The study adds to both our genetic knowledge and to the knowledge concerning Lp(a) lipoprotein as a risk factor for CHD. In the genetic study, 227 families with a total of 557 children were analysed. The results strongly indicate a major locus, a dominant major gene and a residual heritable component that may reflect one or more alleles of weaker effect. There was no evidence against Mendelian transmission (Morton et al. 1985).

The study design was such that problems of uncertain comparability of cases and controls, of unblinded, non-simultaneous laboratory determinations, of damage to serum caused by storage or of inappropriate immunological reagents were completely avoided. The agreement in quantitative Lp(a) determination between the two laboratories involved was close with a correlation of 0.90. CHD cases had higher Lp(a) lipoprotein levels than controls and the difference was highly significant ($p < 0.005$) and most pronounced in the younger patients. The association with myocardial infarction was not explained by differences in total cholesterol, HDL cholesterol, subscapular skin fold, systolic blood pressure, history of smoking, alcohol consumption or age. The increased risk was largely confined to persons in the upper quartile or the Lp(a) lipoprotein distribution. The authors concluded that Lp(a) lipoprotein is quantitatively the most important defined genetic risk factor for myocardial infarction and should be considered when CHD risk is assessed in younger individuals (Rhoads et al. 1985).

Thus, the study of Japanese living in Hawaii have yielded results that strongly support the major locus concept and that confirm the association between Lp(a) lipoprotein and CHD.

Since the first report in 1974 (Berg et al. 1974) of association between immunologically determined Lp(a) lipoprotein and CHD, a number of studies have confirmed the association and shown that it is particularly pronounced in the younger age groups. The new confirmation from a totally different ethnic group strongly suggests that the association between Lp(a) lipoprotein and CHD is a ubiquitous phenomenon and that Lp(a) lipoprotein testing should be included in attempts to establish CHD risk profiles. Earlier studies on the Lp(a) lipoprotein have been summarized elsewhere (Berg 1979, 1983).

THE ApoE POLYMORPHISM AND CORONARY HEART DISEASE

It is now well established that the apoE isoforms apoE-2, apoE-3 and apoE-4 are determined by three alleles at one single locus and that the apoE polymorphism is closely related to type III hyperlipiproteinemia (Zannis and Breslow 1981, Børresen and Berg 1981, Berg 1983, Utermann et al. 1979 a, b).

Utermann et al. (1979 b) were the first to report an association between genetic types within the apoE polymorphism and lipid levels in the general population. The data indicated **that** people possessing the isoform apoE-3 had a higher cholesterol level that those lacking it. Utermann et al. (1984 a) recently reported that the isoform apoE-2 is significantly more frequent in patients with hypertriglyceridemia than in controls, that isoform apoE-4 is significantly more frequent in patients with hyper-cholesterolemia than in controls and that both isoforms are frequent in patients with mixed hyperlipidemia.

We have examined the apoE isoforms in a group of 40-50 years old males with moderate hypercholesterolemia who were otherwise healthy (Leren et al. 1985). They all had cholesterol levels between 7.5 and 10 mmol/l. The apoE-4 isoform was present in 42% of persons with hypercholesterolemia and only in 19% of the controls. The difference is statistically significant ($0.01 < p < 0.02$). If confirmed, this result suggests that persons possessing the apoE-4 isoform have a relative risk of 3 over those lacking it to have a moderate hypercholesterolemia by middle-age.

The apparent effect of the apoE polymorphism on serum lipid levels raises the possibility of an association also between apoE and CHD. In a recent paper by Utermann et al. (1984 b) there were fewer persons possessing the apoE-4 isoform among the patients than among the controls whereas in the recent paper by Cumming and Robertson (1984) there were more people with the apoE-4 isoform among the patients than among controls. The reason for the apparent discrepancy between the two studies is not clear. The difference between patients and controls is in one of the studies (Utermann et al. 1984 b) not statistically significant if presence or absence of the apoE-4 isoform is compared in a simple two-by-two table. When the same analysis is conducted on data from the other study (Cumming and Robertson 1984) the difference between patients and controls is highly significant ($p < 0.01$). There is a need to collect more information on the apoE polymorphism in CHD. An association between CHD and the apoE-4 isoform would be plausible because of the association between that isoform and hypercholesterolemia.

It is an important research task to study the atherogenic

effect of apoE genotypes in the presence of other genes that affect susceptibility or resistance to atherosclerotic disease and in the presence of various environmental or nutritional factors.

DNA STUDIES

By the combined use of restriction enzymes and specific DNA probes, it is possible to study pathological as well as normal DNA variation that was previously not possible to analyse, and a new type of genetic polymorphisms has been identified: restriction fragment length polymorphisms (RFLPs). Presence or absence of a recognition site for a restriction enzyme forms the basis for this type of DNA variation which can be analysed by simple laboratory techniques.

It may be predicted that DNA variation reflecting atherosclerosis risk will be identified and that the DNA technology will add a new dimension to predictive testing. Prime targets in research to arrive at a better predictive testing will be genetic variation at the apolipoprotein loci. Eight apolipoprotein genes have been cloned over a 3-year period and the cloning of the apolipoprotein B gene in four different laboratories was reported recently (Knott et al. 1985, Lusis et al. 1985, Deeb et al. 1985, Huang et al. 1985).

Karathanasis et al. (1983) studying a family with premature coronary atherosclerosis, very low HDL levels and deficiencies of apoA-I and apoC-III found that both probands were homozygous for a DNA defect in the apoA-I gene (Breslow et al. 1982). First degree relatives who were heterozygotes for the defect had intermediate HDL levels. It may be quite rare that a defect such as this causes low HDL. However, reduced level of HDL and apoA-I was also found in heterozygotes for the deficiency condition (variant II) described by Schäfer et al. (1985).

Rees et al. (1983) studied a DNA polymorphism adjacent to the human apoA-I gene and found association between one of the DNA types studied and hypertriglyceridemia. However, Kessling et al. (1985) could not detect such an association. There is a need for more study in order to finally assess the possibility that DNA variations (other than those underlying apoA-I deficiencies) in this gene complex affect lipid level and atherosclerosis risk. It is now clear that also the apoA-IV locus belongs to this cluster of apolipoprotein genes (Schamaun et al. 1984) and future studies will have to address haplotypes that reflect variation in all three apolipoprotein loci.

Work with a probe for human apoA-II (Knott et al. 1984 a, b) uncovered DNA polymorphism at the apoA-II locus. Scott et al. (1985) found association between this polymorphism and apoA-II concentration, and proposed that homozygosity for the gene that caused higher apoA-II concentration may have a protective effect against atherosclerosis. If confirmed this and similar associations may indeed become very useful for predictive testing and preventive counselling.

Scott and his coworkers have uncovered several DNA polymorphisms at the apoB locus (Priestley et al. 1985). Although the biological and clinical implications are still unknown, the high degree of genetic variability in the apoprotein of atherogenic low density lipoprotein poses several interesting questions. It will be important tasks to find out if any of the DNA polymorphisms at the apoB locus correlates with overt atherosclerotic disease, cholesterol level or apoB level. Interestingly, a rich genetic variability in LDL detectable by rare immunological reagents is known but the study of such variability has been hampered by extreme shortage of high quality antisera (see Berg 1979). It is fortunate that the DNA technology now offers new possibilities to study genetic poly-morphisms in apoB. Interestingly, the Ag variation of immunologically detectable allotypes exhibits association with serum lipid levels, at least in middle-aged people (Berg et al. 1976).

ApoC-II is closely linked to apoE (Humphries et al. 1984) and since genetic variation in the latter apolipoprotein affects lipid levels, the possibility of interaction between apoE and apoC-II genes must be entertained.

Clearly, genetic variation in any one of the apolipoprotein loci could contribute to the risk for atherosclerosis. In addition, genes in polymorphisms that exhibit association with lipid level could contribute to atherosclerosis risk. In Table 3, such genes are referred to as "level genes" as opposed to "variability genes" which are those that appear to have a restrictive or permissive effect with respect to the amount of variation that nutritional or life style factors can cause, in lipid levels (see above). It appears that there are many genes distributed over the human genome that could contribute to predisposition or resistance to atherosclerotic disease, but more research is needed in most instances. The impression that chromosomes 11 and 19 are particularly rich in genes that could be relevant to athero-sclerosis persists. In addition to the loci listed in Table 3 comes the quantitatively very important Lp(a) variation whose locus has not yet been asigned to a specific human chromosome.

ECOGENETICS OF HUMAN ATHEROSCLEROSIS

Ecogenetics is the study of heritable variations in response to environmental agents including nutritional or life style factors. It may be a useful concept in relation to human atherosclerosis and

Table 3

Genes in the human genome that could contribute to atherosclerosis
risk (see text)

Chromo-some	Apolipoprotein gene	"Level gene"	"Varia-bility gene"	Other relevant gene
1	apoA-II		Rh	
2	apoB	Ag	Jk	
4			MNSs	
9		ABO		
11	apoA-I) very apoA-IV) close apoC-III)			Insulin
14		Gm		
16		Hp		
19	apoC-I) very apoC-II) close apoE)	Se (apoE)		LDL receptor
20			ADA	

Table 4

Theoretical coronary heart disease risk,
resulting from different combinations of genes
affecting risk factor level and variability,
respectively

"Level genes"	"Variability genes"	
	Permissive	Restrictive
More than average	High, but reducible	Very high
Average	Average, but changeable	Average
Less than average	Low, but changeable	Very low

it may help to avoid considering exogenous factors to the exclusion of genetic determinants or vice-versa. It is self-evident that people vary in their response to environmental agents and there are many examples of genes causing or contributing to such variability, for example in reaction to chemical compounds.

The existing evidence that environmental as well as genetic factors contribute to atherosclerotic development (at least to premature CHD) must mean that environmental, nutritional or life style factors preferentially cause atherosclerotic disease in those who have a genetic predisposition. The genetic factors may be of such a strength that disease is virtually unavoidable such as in homozygotes for familial hypercholesterolemia, but many heterozygotes for this condition enjoy a long life and they may even have cholesterol levels in the normal or near-normal area, presumably because other genetic or environmental factors have favourable effects (Nora et al. 1985).

Most people with atherosclerosis or other common disorders do not have a disease that to an overwhelming degree is caused by a single mutant gene. Rather, several genes and several life style factors interact to produce an overall atherosclerosis risk profile. Each single gene may not have a strong effect but shifts the risk profile slightly in an unfavourable or favourable direction if not counteracted by other genes or environmental factors. Those who contract premature atherosclerosis may have an unfortunate combination of several atherogenic genes and life style factors. We know from the very significant drop in CHD frequency in occupied European countries during World War II that even those with a quite strong genetic predisposition to atherosclerosis may avoid CHD, at least for several years, if life style factors are changed in an "anti-atherogenic" direction. This knowledge gives reason for cautious optimism and argues against the defeatist attitude that "if it is genetic, there is nothing one can do".

Atherosclerotic diseases are frequent and the effect of pre-disposing genes appears to be strong. It is therefore not surprising that the genes that render the individual susceptibility to atherosclerosis are frequent, such as genes belonging to normal polymorphisms are. The best prediction would in fact be that genetic predisposition to CHD would be associated with normal polymorphisms. The approach of searching for associations between atherosclerotic disease and polymorphisms at gene loci believed to be relevant to the atherosclerotic process is therefore sound and such studies should be encouraged. They are likely, in the long run, to result in meaningful predictive testing and it is even possible that the most effective preventive measures will differ between various genetic risk categories.

Much remains to be understood in the area of association between genetic markers and disease. The association between CHD and (high levels of) Lp(a) lipoprotein can probably best be explained by trapping of Lp(a) lipoprotein particles in arterial walls, since apparently intact Lp(a) lipoprotein has been detected in atherosclerotic lesions, Lp(a) lipoprotein particles readily form aggregates in the presence of glycosaminoglycans, and since Lp phenotypes have only a moderate effect on lipid levels.

Associations between genetic markers and risk factor level (such as lipid level) may be more difficult to explain. In principle, the relationship between quantitative risk factors and genetic marker genes could be of two different types. Those marker genes that exhibit a direct association with risk factor level, may exert their effect by helping to maintain a risk factor such as cholesterol at a given level. One may think of such genes as "level genes". On the other hand we have developed a method to uncover (by examining monozygotic twins) any "permissive" or "restrictive" effect of a marker gene on the degree of variability that environmental factors may cause (see above), and we do have evidence for such effects of marker genes on cholesterol variability. We may refer to such genes as "variability genes". One may predict that additional "level genes" as well as "variability genes" will be detected by DNA technology.

Although it is premature at this stage to speculate on the possible clinical consequences of "variability genes", the data presented above would, if confirmed, suggest complicated inter-actions between the two types of genetic effects. Such inter-actions are summarized in Table 4 where the column "level genes" refers to more than average, average or less than average effect (number) of such genes. In Table 4, it is speculated how permissive or restrictive "variability genes" could interact with "level genes". According to the hypothesis presented in Table 4 those at highest risk for atherosclerotic disease would be indi-viduals who have both genes that determine a high risk factor level and genes that restrict the amount of variability that environmental, nutritional or life style factors can cause. Persons with genes determining a high risk factor level who have permissive "variability genes" should have a better chance of risk factor reduction. Presumably, those who benefit most from "total population" approaches to the prevention of CHD are persons who have genes that determine average or low risk factor levels and at the same time have permissive "variability genes". The best protected group would be those who both have genes determining low risk factor levels and restrictive "variability genes". If this concept were to be proven correct, genetic tests may in the future become a useful tool in a "high risk" strategy that should probably be added on to "total population" strategies for preventing CHD adn other atherosclerotic diseases.

CONCLUDING REMARKS

Normal genetic variations at lipoprotein and other loci should be included in an extended risk profile concept together with familial clustering of premature CHD. Exact evaluation of the risk connected with each factor and combinations of factors should be given priority in atherosclerosis research.

Knowledge of genetic risk factors can already be utilized in attempts to control CHD by including genetic analyses in screening programs aimed at instituting active preventive action in those who have the highest risk to contract early CHD. It appears likely, that in the future, predictive tests to determine CHD risk will be widely used and this will hopefully lead to more effective disease prevention. Problems that need to be handled include transmitting risk information and conducting counselling in an efficient way without creating excessive anxiety, as well as appropriate protection, of data concerning predisposition to disease. The latter problem is potentially very important because it could limit use of predictive tests if people had reason to fear that the results of such tests could be used to their disadvantage, for example by employers or insurance companies. If in the future a wide variety of predictive tests become available the best way to secure an optimal use would be to make laws that would make such information the exclusive property of the individual.

ACKNOWLEDGMENTS

The work in the author's laboratory was supported by grants from the Norwegian Research Council for Science and the Humanities, The Norwegian Council on Cardiovascular Disease, and Anders Jahre's Foundation for the Promotion of Science.

REFERENCES

Adams, W.C., Gaman, E.M., Feigenbaum, A.S., 1972, Breed differences of rabbits to atherogenic diets. Atherosclerosis, 16: 405.
Berg, K., Dahlén, G., and Frick, M.H., 1974, Lp(a) lipoprotein and pre-β_1-lipoprotein in patients with coronary heart disease. Clin. Genet., 6: 230.
Berg, K., Hames, C., Dahlén, G., Frick, M.H., and Krishan, I., 1976, Genetic variation in serum low-density lipoproteins and lipid levels in man. Proc. Natl. Acad. Sci. USA, 73: 937.
Berg, K., 1979, Inherited lipoprotein variation and atherosclerotic disease, in: "The Biochemistry of Atherosclerosis", A.M. Scanu, R.W. Wissler, and G.S. Getz, eds., Marcel Dekker Inc., New York, pp. 419.

Berg, K., 1981, Twin research in coronary heart disease, in:
    "Twin Research 3: Epidemiological and Clinical Studies",
    pp. 117.
Berg, K., 1982, The genetics of the hyperlipidemias and coronary
    artery disease, in: "Human Genetics, Part B: Medical Aspects",
    Alan R. Liss Inc., New York, pp. 111.
Berg, K., 1983, Genetics of coronary heart disease, in: "Progress
    in Medical Genetics Volume 5", A.G. Steinberg, A.G. Bearn,
    A.G. Motulsky, and B. Childs, eds., Saunders Company,
    Philadelphia, pp. 35.
Berg, K., 1985, Genetics of coronary heart disease and its risk
    factors, in: "Medical Aspects: Past, Present, Future",
    Alan R. Liss Inc., New York, pp. 351.
Børresen, A.-L. and Berg, K., 1981, The apoE polymorphism studied
    by two-dimensional, high-resolution gel electrophoresis of
    serum. Clin. Genet., 20: 438.
Breslow, J.L., Ross, D., McPherson, J., Williams, H.W., Kurnit,
    D., Nussbaum, A.L., Karathanasis, S.K., and Zannis, V.I.,
    1982, Isolation and characterization of cDNA clones for human
    apolipoprotein AI. Proc. Natl. Acad. Sci. USA, 79: 6861.
Clarkson, T.B., Lofland, H.B.Jr., Bullock, B.C., and Goodman, H.O.,
    1971, Genetic control of plasma cholesterol. Studies on
    squirrel monkeys. Arch. Pathol., 92: 37.
Cumming, A.M. and Robertson, F.W., 1984, Polymorphism at the apo-
    protein-E locus in relation to risk of coronary disease.
    Clin. Genet., 25: 310.
Deeb, S.S., Motulsky, A.G., and Albers, J.J., 1985, A partial cDNA
    clone for apolipoprotein B. Proc. Natl. Acad. Sci. USA, 82:
    4983.
Fredrickson, D.S., Levy, R.I., and Lees, R.S., 1967, Fat transport
    in lipoproteins. New Engl. J. Med., 276: 32.
Friedlander, Y., Cohen, T., Stenhouse, N., Davis, A.M., and Stein,
    Y., 1982, Familial aggregation of total cholesterol,
    triglyceride and high-density lipoprotein-cholesterol in an
    Israeli population sample. Israel J. Med. Sci., 18: 1137.
Glueck, C.J., Gartside, P., Laskarzewski, P.M., Khoury, P., and
    Tyroler, H.A., 1984, High-density lipoprotein cholesterol in
    blacks and whites: potential ramifications for coronary
    heart disease. Amer. Heart J., 108: 815.
Goldstein, J.L., Hazzard, W.R., Schrott, H.G., Bierman, E.L., and
    Motulsky, A.G., 1972, Genetics of hyperlipidemia in coronary
    heart disease. Trans. Assoc. Amer. Physns., 85: 120.
Goldstein, J.L. and Brown, M.S., 1983, Familial hyper-
    cholesterolemia, in: "The Metabolic Basis of Inherited
    Disease", 5th ed., J.B. Stanbury, J.B. Wyngaarden, D.S.
    Fredrickson, J.L. Goldstein, and M.S. Brown, eds, McGraw-
    Hill, New York, pp. 672.
Goldstein, J.L. and Brown, M.S., 1984, Progress in understanding
    the LDL receptor and HMG-CoA reductase, two membrane proteins
    that regulate the plasma cholesterol. J. Lipid Res., 25: 203.

Heiberg, A. and Berg, K., 1976, The inheritance of hyper-
    lipoproteinaemia with xanthomatosis. A study in 132 kindreds.
    Clin. Genet., 9: 203.
Huang, L.S., Bock, S.C., Feinstein, S.I., and Breslow, J.L., 1985,
    Human apolipoprotein B cDNA clone isolation and demonstration
    that liver apolipoprotein B mRNA is 22 kilobasis in length.
    Proc. Natl. Acad. Sci. USA, 82: 6825.
Humphries, S.E., Berg, K., Gill, L., Cumming, A.M., Robertson, F.W.,
    sStalenhoef, A.F.H., Williamson, J.R., and Børresen, A.-L.,
    1984, The gene for apolipoprotein C-II is closely linked to the
    gene for apolipoprotein E on chromosome 19. Clin. Genet., 26:
    389.
Karathanasis, S.K., Norum. R.A., Zannis, V.I., and Breslow, J.L.,
    1983, An inherited polymorphism in the human apolipoprotein
    A-I gene locus related to the development of atherosclerosis.
    Nature, 301: 718.
Kessling, A.M., Horsthemke, B., and Humphries, S.E., 1985, A study
    of DNA polymorphisms around the human apolipcprotein AI gene
    in hyperlipidaemic and normal individuals. Clin. Genet., in
    press.
Knott, T.J., Priestley, L.M., Urdea, M., and Scott, J., 1984a,
    Isolation and characterization of a cDNA encoding the
    precursor for human apolipoprotein AII. Biochem. Biophys.
    Res. Comm., 120: 734.
Knott, T.J., Eddy, R.L., Robertson, M.E., Priestley, L.M., Scott,
    J., and Shows, T.B., 1984b, Chromosomal localization of the
    human apoprotein CI gene and of a polymorphic apoprotein AII
    gene. Biochem. Biophys. Res. Comm., 125: 299.
Knott, T.J., Rall, S.C. Jr., Innerarity, T.L., Jacobson, S.F.,
    Urdea, M.S., Levy-Wilson, B., Powell, L,M., Pease, R.J.,
    Eddy, R., Nakai, H., Byers, M., Priestley, L.M.,
    Robertson, E., Rall, L.B., Betscholtz, C., Shows, T.B.,
    Mahley, R.W., and Scott, J., 1985, Human apolipoprotein B:
    structure of carboxyl-terminal domains, sites of gene
    expression and chromosomal localization. Science, 230: 37.
Laskarzewski, P.M., Glueck, C.J., and Rao, D.C., 1984, Family
    resemblance for plasma lipids and lipoprotein concentrations
    in blacks. Cincinnati Lipid Research Clinic Study.
    Arteriosclerosis, 4: 65.
Lehrman, M.A., Schneider, W.J., Südhof, T.C., Brown, M.S.,
    Goldstein, J.L., and Russell, D.W., 1985, Mutation in LDL
    receptor: alu-alu recombination deletes exons encoding
    transmembrane and cytoplasmic domains. Science, 227: 140.
Leren, T.P., Børresen, A.-L., Berg, K., Hjermann, I., and
    Leren, P., 1985, Increased frequency of the apolipoprotein
    E-4 isoform in male subjects with multifactorial hyper-
    cholesterolemia. Clin. Genet., 27: 458.
Lusis, A.J., West, R., Mehrabian, M., Reuben, M.A., LeBoeuf, R.C.,
    Kaptein, J.S., Johnson, D.F., Schumaker, V.N., Yuhasz, M.P.,

Schotz, M.C., and Elovson, J., 1985, Cloning and expression of apolipoprotein B, the major protein of low and very low density lipoproteins. Proc. Natl. Acad. Sci. USA, 82: 4597.

Maartmann-Moe, K., Magnus, P., Golden, W., and Berg, K., 1981 a, Genetics of the low density lipoprotein receptor: II. Genetic control of variation in cell membrane low density lipoprotein receptor activity in cultured fibroblasts. Clin. Genet., 20: 104.

Magnus, P., Berg, K., Børresen, A.-L., and Nance, W.E., 1981 b, Apparent influence of marker genotypes on variation in serum cholesterol in monozygotic twins. Clin. Genet., 19: 67.

Mayo, O., Fraser, G.R., and Stamatoyannopoulos, G., 1969, Genetic influences on serum cholesterol in two Greek villages. Hum. Hered., 19: 86.

Morton, N.E., Berg, K., Dahlén, G., Ferrell, R.E., and Rhoads, G.G., 1985, Genetics of the Lp lipoprotein in Japanese-Americans. Genet. Epidemiol., 2: 113.

Motulsky, A.G., 1976, Current concepts in genetics. The genetic hyperlipidemias. New Engl. J. Med., 294: 823.

Müller, C., 1939, Angina pectoris in hereditary xanthomatosis. Arch. Intern. Med., 64: 675.

Namboodiri, K.K., Green, P.P., Kaplan, E.B., Morrison, J.A., Chase, G.A., Elston, R.C., Owen, A.R.G., Rifkin, B.M., Glueck, C.J., and Tyroler, H.A., 1984, The Collaborative Lipid Research Clinics Program Family Study. IV. Familial association of plasma lipids and lipoproteins. Amer. J. Epidemiol., 119: 975.

Nora, J.J., Lortscher, R.M., Spangler, R.D., and Bilheimer, D.W., 1985, I. Familial hypercholesterolemia with "normal cholesterol in obligate heterozygotes. Amer. J. Med. Genet., 22: 585.

Rao, D.C., Laskarzewski, P.M., Morrison, J.A., Khoury, P., Kelly, K., Wette, R., Russell, J., and Glueck, C.J., 1982, The Cincinnati Lipid Research Clinic Family Study: Cultural and biological determinants of lipids and lipoprotein concentrations. Amer. J. Hum. Genet., 34: 888.

Rees, A., Stocks, J., Shoulders, C.C., Galton, D.J., and Baralle, F.E., 1983, DNA polymorphism adjacent to human apoprotein A-I gene: relation to hypertriglyceridemia. The Lancet, i: 444.

Rhoads, G.G., Dahlén, G., Berg, K., Morton, N.E., and Dannenberg, A.L., 1985, Lp(a) lipoprotein as a risk factor for myocardial infarction. Submitted for publication.

Roberts, A. and Thompson, J.S., 1976, Inbred mice and their hybrids as an animal model for atherosclerosis research, in: "Atherosclerosis Drug Discovery", C.E. Day, ed, Plenum Press, New York, pp. 313.

Schaefer, E.J., Ordovas, J.M., Law, S.W., Ghiselli, G., Kashyap, M.L., Srivastava, L.S., Heaton, W.H., Albers, J.J., Connor, W.E., Lindgren, F.T., Lemeshev, Y., Segrest, J.P., and Brewer, H.B. Jr., 1985, Familial apolipoprotein A-I and C-III deficiency, variant II. J. Lipid Res., 26: 1089.

Schamaun, O., Olaisen, B., Mevåg, B., Gedde-Dahl, T. Jr., Ehnholm, C., and Teisbe-g, P., 1984, The two apolipoprotein loci, apoA-I and apoA-IV are closely linked in man. Hum. Genet., 68: 380.

Scott, J., Priestley, L.M., Knott, T.J., Robertson, M.E., Mann, D.V., Kostner, G., Miller, G.J., and Miller, N.E., 1985, High-density lipoprotein composition is altered by a common DNA polymorphism adjacent to apoprotein AII gene in man. The Lancet, i: 771.

Shore, B. and Shore, V., 1976, Rabbits as a model for the study of hyperlipoproteinemia and atherosclerosis, in:"Atherosclerosis Drug Discovery", E. Day, ed, Plenum Press, New York, pp. 123.

Sing, C.F. and Orr, J.D., 1976, Analysis of genetic and environmental sources of variation in serum cholesterol in Tecumseh, Michigan. III: Identification of genetic effects using 12 polymorphic genetic marker systems. Amer. J. Hum. Genet., 28: 453.

Stufflebean, C.E. and Lasley, J.F., 1969, Hereditary basis of serum cholesterol level in beef cattle. J. Hered., 60: 15.

Südhof, T.C., Goldstein, J.L., Brown, M.S., and Russell, D.W., 1985, The LDL receptor gene: A mosaic of exons shared with different proteins. Science, 228: 815.

Utermann, G., Vogelberg, K.H., Steinmetz, A., Schoenborn, W., Pruin, N., Jaeschke, M., Hees, M., and Canzler, H., 1979 a, Polymorphism of apolipoprotein E. II. Genetics of hyper-lipoproteinemia type III. Clin. Genet., 15: 37.

Utermann, G., Pruin, N., and Steinmetz, A., 1979 b, Polymorphism of apolipoprotein E. III. Effect of a single polymorphic gene locus on plasma lipid levels in man. Clin. Genet., 15: 63.

Utermann, G., Kindermann, I., Kaffarnik, H., and Steinmetz, A., 1984 a, Apolipoprotein E phenotypes and hyperlipidemia. Hum. Genet., 65: 232.

Utermann, G., Hardewig, A., and Zimmer, F., 1984 b, Apolipoprotein E phenotypes in patients with myocardial infarction. Hum. Genet., 65: 237.

Yamamoto, T., Davis, C.G., Brown, M.S., Schneider, W.J., Casey, M.L., Goldstein, J.L., and Russell, D.W., 1984, The human LDL receptor: a cysteine-rich protein with multiple Alu sequences in its mRNA. Cell, 39: 27.

Zannis, V.I., Breslow, J.E., 1981, Human very low density lipoprotein apolipoprotein E isoprotein polymorphism is explained by genetic variation and posttranslational modification. Biochemistry, 20: 1033.

EPIDEMIOLOGY OF LIPIDS AND LIPOPROTEINS AS A GUIDE TO THE DETECTION OF MUTANTS

Alessandro Menotti

Laboratory of Epidemiology and Biostatistics
Istituto Superiore di Sanità
Viale Regina Elena 299, Rome Italy 00161

Along the last 40 years epidemiology has largely contributed to the advance of knowledge in the etiology of atherosclerosis and its complications. The main single achievement can be considered the identification of the so called risk factors and the evaluation of their predictive and, at least partially, causal role.[1] Among them the most investigated have been plasma lipids, lipoproteins and their fractions.

Field epidemiologists, working on population samples or groups from the observational point of view, usually look for risk factors, their distribution and secular trends and mainly for their ability to predict fatal and non fatal events of coronary, cerebrovascular and peripherial type. Due to the mass approach of the problem and the consequent probabilistic statistics employeed in the analysis of data, rare genetic conditions of the plasma lipid profile are usually buried into the mass of data and their influence on mass phenomena and on the risk-disease relationships might be neglegible. From this point of view it is well known, p.e., that in the general population only 1 out of 1000 individuals can be classified as carrier of an eterozygote type II, and only one out of 300.000 or more as homozygote type II. This means that epidemiology is not necessarily the best tool for the discovery of rare conditions also because it has proved more suitable for the study of the relationship of environment vs disease than that of genetics vs disease unless the genetic condition is very common. However epidemiology can help and give some contribution, at least indirectly, to the detection of rare

51

conditions and to their study.

There are two different approaches. In the first case a rare genetic condition is identified, almost by chance, in a single individual. The study of the individual moves then to the family and only later into the community if it is reasonable to expect that it contains many other cases. At this stage the structure of the study becomes a typical epidemiological survey with all its methodological implications. This type of approach corresponds to that followed in the Limone study where a mutant of the apo-A1 lipoprotein, called Milano A1, has been suspected, detected and throughly investigated in the original proband, in its family and finally in the whole community.[2]

In the second case it may happen that the analysis and the results of an epidemiological study on population groups or samples conducted for other reasons suggest the existence of relatively rare and abnormal conditions. The suspect may rise from the shape of a frequency distribution which might be bimodal, either in the certer of the curve or in one of the tails; it may also rise from the location of the distribution curve and the value of its mean as compared with the location and the mean of a neighbour population which is expected to be similar while it is not; or it may rise from the abnormal relationship between factor and disease as compared with the expected patterns. The latter type of approach does correspond to a personal yet unpublished experience[3] which started from the inspection of the frequency distribution curve of cholesterol in the adult population sample of Campodimele, a village located 150 km south of Rome, where a small peak was found in the class of less than 100 mg/dl. In fact 8 subjects (4 males and 4 females) aged 30-76 showed a total serum cholesterol ranging 44 to, 89 mg/dl. Subsequent investigations showed in those subjects a complete lack of VLDL lipoproteins, whereas LDL and HDL made up 50% each, with an excess of HDL2 as compared to HDL3. The analysis of the proteic component of HDL by high performance iso-electric focusing has shown an abnormality of Apo-AI whose intensity is reduced and an abnormal band is located in A-I3. Other abnoramlities from the electro-microscopy observation of HDL have been found as well as an uncommon fatty acid distribution in plasma and red blood cells. The suspect of a familiar genetic situation is well funded.

In any case one of the main problems, related to rare genetic conditions is the interpretation of their role which might be either promoting or protecting from the occurrence of a

disease. Statistical theory and clinical experience suggest that
an extremely rare condition carrying a very high risk for subsequent morbid events can be easily identified for such extra risk.
On the other hand it is extremely complex to identify the
protective role of a rare condition even in the case that its
characteristics have a location in the distribution curve which
would normally correspond to a high risk perspective. The scheme
reported in Table 1 represents a model comparing a "usual
relationship", say, between total cholesterol and coronary heart
disease (CHD) and a "deformed relationship" bound to the
existence in the high risk class of a relatively high proportion
(one fourth) of individuals unexpectedly protected for some other
reason, and whose risk is actually the same as that in the lowest
risk class.
The net result, in terms of incidence cases observed in 10 years,
is a difference of 3 individuals which may occur by chance in
about one out of 1.6 trials simply considering the outcome in the
highest risk class of cholesterol.

Table 1. Model on the usual relationship between total serum
cholesterol and coronary heart disease (CHD) incidence in
a 1000 subjects population and on the distorted relationship due to the presence of 50 subjects located in the
upper cholesterol class but carrying the risk of the lowest one.

USUAL RELATIONSHIP

	low risk	middle risk	high risk
rate % in 10 years	2	4	8
CHD cases in 10 years	4	24	16
subjects exposed to risk	200	600	200
cholesterol class (mg/dl)	< 200	200-239	240+

DISTORTED RELATIONSHIP

	low risk	middle risk	high risk
rate % in 10 years	2	4	2 and 8
CHD cases in 10 years	4	24	1 + 12
subjects exposed to risk	200	600	50 + 150
cholesterol class (mg/dl)	< 200	200-239	240 +

Such difficulties in the interpretation of data should be kept in mind when trying to label, as prone or protected, a given lipoprotein profile. In fact the follow-up for the detection of a morbid event must be extremely long and the small numbers involved may hide anyhow the true relationship. In front of rare conditions whose role is still uncertain, other approaches should likely be considered i.e. the possibility of non-invasive exploration of the arterial wall and, in perspective, new statistical types of evaluation.

References

1. Report of Intersociety Commission for Heart Disease Resources: Optimal Resources for Primary Prevention of Atherosclerotic Diseases. Circulation 70: 155A. (1984)
2. G., Franceschini, C.R., Sirtori, G. Gianfranceschi, A., Menotti, A., Cerrone, G.B., Orsini and V. Gualandri: AI Milano Apoprotein. Identification of the complete kindred and evidence of a dominant genetic transmission. In press. Am. J. Hum. Genetics. (1985)
3. A., Menotti and V. Cinosi: unpublished data. (1985)

DETECTION AND GENETIC HANDLING OF MUTANTS

Valter Gualandri

Inst. of Human Genetics
University of Milan
Corso Venezia 55 - 20121 Milano, Italy

Our present knowledge about the normal and pathological lipid metabolism and about its clinical manifestations, leads us to the recognition of two different situations:

A) An interaction between idiotype and environment, both represented by numerous not easily definable factors, is present. The normal and the diseased conditions are, therefore, not recognized as defined conditions, but as quasi-continuous traits.

In this particular case, the research methodology will be prevalently epidemiological and statistical. Statistical method are available[1], which are adequately specific and sensitive to recognize the familial correlations of lipid parameters and their individual associations[2,3,4]. The environmental conditions, as pertaining to the studied cases, should be fully characterized, in order to quantitate, as much as possible, the influence of the idiotype in the definition of the various phenotypes[5].

B) The idiotype is the sufficient etiological factor and the fondamental pathogenetic moment. This is the condition where pathological states, consequent to point mutations, take place[6].

EXAMPLES OF STUDY PROTOCOLS

In the situation expressed as A, a complete population research should be carried out. We have completed one such study, of which the major features are the following[7,8].

The LIMONE SUL GARDA Study

- study of social conditions (age, sex-ratio, etc.)
- definition of consanguineity
- biochemical research
- statistical evaluations

Major Results

- plasma total Cholesterol
  no correlation between spouses
  CORRELATION between parent-offspring
  CORRELATION between siblings

- plasma triglycerides
  no correlation between spouses
  no correlation between parent-offspring
  no correlation between siblings

- plasma HDL-Cholesterol
  no correlation between spouses
  no correlation between parent-offspring
  no correlation between siblings

CORRELATION INDEXES BETWEEN DIFFERENT LIPID-LIPOPROTEIN PARAMETERS

Comparison	n	r	t	P
Cholesterol/Triglycerides	310	0.327	6.092	<0.001
Cholesterol/HDL-Cholesterol	310	0.248	4.511	<0.001
Triglycerides/HDL-Cholesterol	310	-0.250	4.546	<0.001

In the condition expressed as $\underline{B}$, the opposite route should be followed:

a) in the individual

- knowledge of the clinical phenotype
- knowledge of the biochemical phenotype, i.e. deficiency or excess
  of some metabolic parameter

- knowledge of the primary phenotype, i.e. of the genic product (transport protein or enzyme): possible population screening
- euphenics

b) in the family

- heterozigote detection
- familial segregation
- Mendelian law of heredity
- eugenics

c) in the population
- epidemiology
- Hardy-Weinberg balance

An example is the detection of the mutants for glucose-6-phosphate dehydrogenase deficiency[9]. In this case, the primary phenotype may be defined from the evaluation of enzyme activity (Motulsky test[10]). The biochemical phenotype is defined by the stability of the reduced glutathione in red cells. Finally, the clinical phenotype is characterized by the presence of hemolytic anemia (fava-bean sensitivity, etc.).

EFFECT OF NATURAL SELECTION ON A MUTATION

A significant problem today is that of identifying the possible interference of natural selection against some mutations. A case in point may be offered by the apo AI-Milano mutant. Some preliminary considerations should be stated:

- the natural selection takes place for or against the phenotype, therefore the genotype is only indirectly involved;

- if, by chance, a new mutation alters a specific gene, for example codifiying a carrier protein or an enzyme, we may considered a priori unlikely that the individual may receive a selective advantage.

This tentative conclusion stems from a statistical consideration: it is rather difficult to believe that a chance event may cause an improvement in the balance within the actual environment, a balance as achieved through the evolution of the species. A pratical consideration also forces us to negatively judge the impact of mutations: our experience on mutations derives from the observation of phenotypes, which are almost always pathological. I do not believe it is correct to judge the selective effect of the mutation, being aware that it corresponds to a pathological phenotype. On the other hand, it is true that we cannot perceive any mutation, if not starting from its phenotype.

From these considerations I can visualize the uniqueness of the AI-Milano mutation: there is no pathological phenotype, corresponding to it and it may, indeed, represent an individual advantage[8]. However, there is one question which may be asked: for the AI-Milano mutation the date of occurrence in the studied population is known, or at least likely. From that date to the present day, three centuries and eight generations have gone by. At present, in the population under study, the mutation has a prevalence of 33 cases out of 1,000.

We may ask: if this mutation were really a selective advantage, for example if the carriers had a greater fitness, should we not observe a higher prevalence today? We may pose the following answer: the environment in which this population has lived in the past and up to the present day may not have challenged the AI-Milano mutation, which interferes with the lipid-lipoprotein metabolism. I believe we can exclude that in the past, significant environmental factors may have been present, leading to atherogenesis, in particular as relates to the type of diet, physical activity and other potential atherogenic traits. It is unlikely that the apo AI-Milano may have conferred to the carriers an advantage, compared to others, in an environment almost free of atherogenic risks. This same may not be necessarily true for the future and, therefore, I believe that in the future we may be able to see the selective effect of the mutation.

REFERENCES

1. A.E.H. Emery, "Methodology in Medical Genetics. An Introduction to Statistical Methods" Churchill Livingstone, Edinburgh, 1976.
2. A. Donner, The use of correlation and regression in the analysis of family resemblance. Am. J. Epidemiol. 110: 335, 1979.
3. G.W. Snedecor and G.W. Cochran, "Statistical Methods" (ed. 6), The Iowa State University Press, Ames, 1976.
4. B. Rosner, A. Donner and C.H. Hennekens, Significance testing of interclass correlation from familial data, Biometrics 35: 461, 1979.
5. D.C. Rao, N.E. Morton, and C.L. Gulbrandsen, Cultural and biological determinants of lipoprotein concentrations. Am. J. Hum. Genet. 42: 467, 1979.
6. H. Galjiaard, "Genetic Metabolic Diseases", Elsevier Biomedical Press, New York, 1980.

7. V. Gualandri, G.B. Orsini, A. Cerrone, G. Franceschini, and C.R. Sirtori, Familial associations of lipids and lipoproteins in a highly consanguineous population: The Limone sul Garda Study, Metabolism 34-212, 1985.
8. V. Gualandri, G. Franceschini, C.R. Sirtori, G. Gianfranceschi, G.B. Orsini, A. Cerrone, and A. Menotti, AI-Milano apoprotein. Identification of the complete kindred and evidence of a dominant genetic transmission, Am. J. Hum. Genet. in press.
9. V. Gualandri, G.B. Orsini, and E. Porta, Le déficit de glucose-6-phosphate deshydrogenase dans la population scolaire de Milan, J. Génét. Hum. 31-201, 1983.
10. E. Beutler, "Red Cell Metabolism. A Manual of Biochemical Methods" 2-ed., Grune & Stratton Inc., New York, 1975.

AI MILANO – HISTORY AND CLINICAL PROFILE

Cesare R. Sirtori*, Guido Franceschini*, Valter Gualandri**, Antonio Cerrone*** and Demetrio Fedrici§§

*Chair of Chemotherapy and Center E. Grossi Paoletti
Istitute of Pharmacology and Pharmacognosy, **Dept. of
Genetics, University of Milano, Italy, ***Medical
Officer, Limone sul Garda, §§ Mayor, Limone sul Garda
Italy

Plasma apolipoproteins have been long considered as stable
and invariable structures, characterized by the presence of long
linear stretches and, particularly, by amphipathic helical
segments[1]. Although some apoprotein polymorphism was earlier
suggested, based on the detection of apo E variations in type III
hyperlipoproteinemia[2], the possibility that significant changes
in the apolipoprotein structure might be associated with
phenotypic abnormalities, seemed remote.

AI-Milano history – Pt. D.V. born in 1938, was first
examined in 1970 at the Niguarda Hospital in Milano, because of
gastric discomfort. He was gastrectomised at age 43, when no
other significant clinical abnormalities could be detected. An
unstable hypertriglyceridemia (300–600 mg/dl) had been followed
for a number of years by his personal physician. Apparently, pt.
D.V. showed an inappropriate response to clofibrate, characterised by a marked increase of triglyceridemia during drug therapy.
The initial biochemical investigations at our Center in
1975, immediately detected a very marked reduction of the high
density lipoprotein (HDL) cholesterol levels (range 10–15 mg/dl
by selective precipitation). This reduction was confirmed by
visual inspection of the agarose electrophoretograms. In view of
the known significant negative correlation between HDL–cholesterolemia and plasma triglycerides[3], these findings did not
particularly impress some of our co-workers. On the other hand,

the very good cardiovascular conditions, reportedly present in the proband's family, as well as the detection of a similarly altered lipid-lipoprotein patterns in two of the proband's children, suggested that some further studies be carried out on this unusual syndrome (Table 1).

International contacts with colleagues with expertise in the field of HDL metabolism, also suggested some "therapeutic" attempts. These involved other drugs, different from "fibrates", e.g. metformin[4] and essential phospholipids (EPL)[5]. From Fig. 1, it appears that there was little advantage from any of these treatments, including a fat enriched diet, also in an effort to raise HDL-cholesterolemia[6]. What seems remarkable was, however, the stability of HDL cholesterolemia in this subject, the only apparent fluctuations being observed in the HDL levels determined by a selective precipitation procedure. By preparative ultracentrifugation, HDL cholesterol always ranged between 7 and 9 mg/dl[6].

Table 1. Plasma and Lipoprotein Lipids in the D. family

	D.V. father 49 y	D.M. son 19 y	D.A. daughter 12 y	D.E. daughter 13 y
PLASMA		mg/dl, May 1979		
Cholesterol	231.4	190.3	183.9	216.2
Triglycerides	318.8	272.6	180.6	116.6
Apo AI	35.2	50.2	73.6	126.5
Apo B	127.0	97.7	94.2	96.3
VLDL				
Cholesterol	40.8	26.6	11.5	15.6
Triglycerides	206.0	189.0	102.0	73.8
LDL				
Cholesterol	183.9	156.3	154.8	156.3
Triglycerides	105.0	75.0	67.0	25.0
HDL				
Cholesterol	6.7	7.4	17.6	44.3
Triglycerides	7.3	7.6	10.6	17.0
AI$_{MILANO}$	+	+	+	−

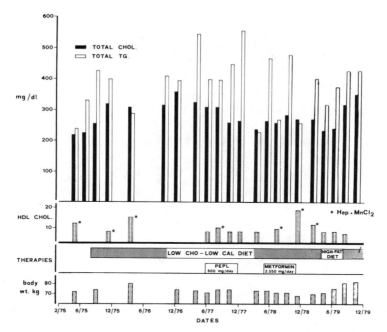

Fig. 1. Clinical and biochemical findings from the proband D.V. Data with an * indicate that HDL-cholesterol was determined by precipitation. The subject was on a low carbohydrate-low calorie diet, except for the final part of the study.

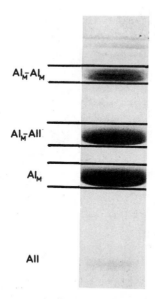

Fig. 2. Multiple apolipoprotein bands in the HDL of a subject with the AI-Milano apolipoprotein variant. The AI-Milano monomer (AI_M-AI_M) and complex (AI_M-AII) are evident.

In the meanwhile, examination of the proband's parents, both well beyond 70 years of age, disclosed that only the father, then aged around 78 y (now 84) had a remarkable reduction of HDL cholesterol (10-12 mg/dl), not so the mother (HDL cholesterol 42 mg/dl), suffering from a cerebral stroke and eventually succumbing to it. Also one of the three brothers of the proband had a marked HDL cholesterol reduction, with significant hypercholesterolemia and hypertriglyceridemia.

Discovery of the "mutant" – The conclusion that there was indeed an altered composition of apoprotein AI in the examined subjects was simultaneously reached at the end of 1979 in our Laboratory and at the Gladstone Foundation Research Laboratory in San Francisco. By carrying out, in fact, SDS polyacrylamide electrophoretic profiles of HDL isolated from these subjects, both in non-reduced and in mercaptoethanol reduced conditions, two different patterns were observed. In the non-reduced samples, multiple apoprotein bands were detected, whereas the normal apo AI-apo AII pattern was observed after reduction (Fig. 2). By the use of appropriate molecular weight standards, it could be tentatively concluded (and this was confirmed by aminoacid analysis), that one or more cysteine substitutions were present in the apo AI itself and of complexes with apo AII[7]. The name of: apoprotein AI-Milano (AI_M) was proposed for the variant molecule, thus indicating, respectively, as AI_M-AI_M and AI_M-AII, the dimers and complexes.

More recently, detailed analyses of the sequence of the AI_M variant could disclose that the molecular error occurs at just one residue. This residue was identified at aminoacid 173, with a substitution of arginine with cysteine (Arg → Cys). This last study[8] also indicated that the examined subjects are heterozygous for the mutant apoprotein, all carrying a varying amount of normal AI (from 15 to 50% of total AI).

Genetic transmission of the mutant and clinical studies – The very interesting observation on the genetic origin of the apo AI_M, prompted a large scale attempt to discover new cases, sharing the same family background of the known carriers. At the end of 1981, the City Hall of Limone sul Garda was contacted. It was known that the D. family originated from this small community. Limone sul Garda, now approximately 1,000 citizens, is a small village on lake Garda, which was separated from

64

neighbouring communities up to 1954, due to the lack of incoming roads. For this reason, Limone has one of the highest rates of consanguineity in Northern Italy (the F coefficient of consanguineity is 2.36×10^{-3} in Limone vs 0.159×10^{-3} for, e.g. Milano), and just about eleven family names cover the entire community. In spite of the negative consequences, generally attributed to a high rate of consanguineous weddings, Limone has developed into a healthy and prosperous community, mostly engaged in touristic activities.

The plan for the in-depth search for AI_M carriers was laid out at the end of 1981, with the full help of the Mayor and of the entire community. In the early months of 1982, during the weekends, 94% of those invited (all citizens beyond the age of 10 y) came for a brief check up, measurement of blood pressure and blood sampling for the evaluation of the presence of the mutant apoprotein. Aside from this specific search, the Limone sul Garda Study allowed the collection of important data on the familiarity and inheritance of traits related to plasma lipoprotein metabolism[9] and to blood pressure[10].

The identification of the AI_M carriers was achieved, after selective precipitation of HDL from serum[11], by an isoelectric focusing (IEF) procedure. An example is given in Fig. 3. By this methodology, a total of 28 carriers (in addition to the original 5 of the D. family), could be detected. It was also possible to reconstruct a complete genealogic tree, spanning back to the XVIII century.

Analysis of the mortality data of Limone sul Garda provided evidence for a slightly lower incidence of cardiovascular mortality in the village (years 1971-1981), compared of the rest of Italy. Limone is characterised by a high percentage of citizens beyond 80 years of age (2.6% as of now, vs 2.0% in the rest of the country). It is, of course, difficult to attribute this relative longevity of the Limone population to any specific trait. The gene for the AI_M mutant (from now on called the Limone gene), phenotypically present in only a few individuals, involves however a large number of families in the Limone community, i.e. about one fifth of the population. Among the on-going investigations is an attempt to find any accompanying gene, possibly indicative of a wider involvement of the population in some other specific trait.

A detailed clinical analysis was carried out in the carriers, directly originating from the Limone community, and in age and sex matched individuals from the same families, non

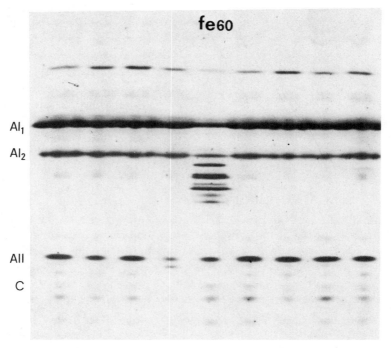

Fig. 3. Isoelectric focusing pattern of HDL isolated from 9 citizens of Limone sul Garda. In one (fe 60), the polymorphic bands of the AI-Milano are evident.

carriers of the mutant. This study has taken into consideration both the clinical, particularly cardiovascular findings, as well as a complete analysis of the plasma lipid-lipoprotein and apoprotein profiles. The clinical evaluation of the carriers and of the reference group has clearly shown that the former have a marked reduction of HDL cholesterol levels, approximately to one third of the controls (17.8 ± 8.1 vs 54.2 ± 11.7 mg/dl; p <0.001). Another interesting finding in the AI_M carriers is the higher mean triglyceridemia (184.5 ± 78.5 vs 126.5 ± 70.1 mg/dl; p <0.005), with a definite tendency for this biochemical parameter to rise with age[12]. Interestingly, in one early study on the lipoprotein findings in the original carriers, we could note that triglyceridemia was inversely related to both total HDL cholesterol and to apo AI levels[13].

Clinical findings in both AI-M carriers and controls were, on the whole, unremarkable. Among the 29 carriers, only one suffers from a disease clearly attributable to atherosclerosis. He underwent, in fact, an aortobifemoral bypass for an aortic aneurysm at age 67. No other carrier, including the oldest ones, has any evidence of atherosclerotic disease. More numerous atherosclerosis-linked abnormalities could he found among non-carriers, although there was no evidence for a statistically significant difference. Table 2 reports the general clinical findings in the two groups. Finally, also the analysis of the electrocardiograms according to the Minnesota code did not indicate any marked difference between the two groups, with a possibly higher prevalence of ST-abnormalities in the reference population.

DISCUSSION AND CONCLUSIONS

It was our intention to prepare an outline of the major findings in this unusual group of individuals, carriers of the AI_M trait. Way back from the earlier observations, we were struck by the apparent unusually low prevalence of vascular disorders in these subjects, in spite of the extremely low HDL cholesterol, the absence of HDL_2, and the concomitant hypertriglyceridemia or even hypercholesterolemia in some. Except for one subject who has, on the other hand, a relatively high HDL cholesterol for this group (25 mg/dl), no degenerative vascular disease has been detected in these individuals, who generally show large and patent arteries. Moreover, none of them shows any significant retention of lipids in major parenchymal tissues. Although it may seem inappropriate to indicate the Limone gene as protective since, as discussed in other parts of this book, very little challenge has been placed on the carriers, in terms of other cardiovascular risk factors (smoking, diet), still many facets of this unusual gene are worth underlining.

First, in spite of the growing number of observations indicating a consistent increase of metabolic disorders of genetic origin, e. g. diabetes, in the past several years[14], this syndrome puts together one apparent major atherosclerosis risk factor, i.e. low HDL cholesterol, with a complete wellbeing. In second place, from on-going studies on the biochemical properties of the mutant apoprotein, it appears that AI_M may have a faster rate of association and dissociation from lipids, as compared to normal AI, thus explaining a potential "anti-atherogenic" role, superior to that of normal AI. Third, the somewhat ambiguous correlation between the HDL mutant and hypertriglyceridemia has provided us and many other investigators with considerable food for thought in the understanding of the complex movements of triglycerides between lipoprotein[15].

Table 2. Major clinical observations in the AI$_{Milano}$ carriers (n=33) and in their close relatives (n=43)

	AI$_{Milano}$ carriers	Close relatives
Appendectomy	5	10
Arterial bypass procedure	1	
Arthrosis	1	3
Atherosclerotic peripheral arterial disease	1	1
Cardiac arrythmias	1	
Discal hernia	1	1
Gallstone disease		2
Gastroduodenitis - Peptic ulcer	2	1
Eye ground vascular abnormalities	1	5
Heart murmurs	2	1
Hemiparesis		1
Hepatomegaly	4	4
Hyperbilirubinemia	3	
Hypertension	1	5
Inguinal hernia	1	4
Peripheral arterial bruits	3	1
Pleuritis	3	1
Poliomyelitis	1	1
Silicosis	1	
Thyroid dysfunction		1
Tonsillectomy	12	10
Tonsillitis		2
Venous disease	7	5
Xanthelasma	1	1

68

Finally, by analyzing the present long list of ascertained apo AI mutants (with the exception of Tangier disease, for which a protein mutation has not been identified as yet), it is remarkable that only in the case of the AI$_M$ carriers, there is a significant reduction of HDL cholesterol levels.

The sudden and never to be explained appearance, two centuries ago, of an unusual, apparently friendly mutant in a small and healthy community on lake Garda marks a unique event in mankind, opening perhaps a tiny hole into the mystery of arterial disease and senescence. We express our gratitude to those who, with their non pretensive, loyal and abiding help made this contribution to the progress of science possible.

Supported by Grant N. 1 RO1 HL28961-01 awarded by the National Heart Lung and Blood Institute, and by the Consiglio Nazionale delle Ricerche of Italy (PF Ingegneria Genetica e Basi Molecolari delle Malattie Ereditarie).

REFERENCES

1. R.L. Jackson, J.D. Morrisset and A.M. Gotto, Lipoprotein structure and metabolism, Physiol. Rev., 56: 259 (1976).

2. G. Utermann, M. Jaeschke and J. Menzel, Familial hyperlipo-proteinemia type III: deficiency of a specific apolipo-protein (apo E III) in the very low density lipoproteins, FEBS Lett., 56: 352 (1975).

3. G.J. Miller and N.E. Miller, Plasma high density lipoprotein concentration and development of ischaemic heart disease, Lancet, i: 16 (1975).

4. C.R. Sirtori, G. Franceschini, G. Gianfranceschi, M. Sirtori, G. Montanari, E. Bosisio, E. Mantero and A. Bondioli, Metformin improves peripheral vascular flow in nonhyperlipidemic patients with arterial disease, J. Cardiovasc. Pharmacol., 6: 914 (1984).

5. V. Blaton, F. Soeteway, D. Vandanne, B. Declercq and H. Peeters, Effect of polyunsaturated phosphatidylcholine on human types II and IV hyperlipoproteinemias, Artery, 2: 309 (1976).

6. G. Franceschini, C.R. Sirtori, A Capurso, K.H. Weisgraber and R.W. Mahley, AI-Milano apoprotein. Decreased high density lipoprotein cholesterol levels with significant lipoprotein modification and without clinical atherosclerosis in an Italian family, J. Clin. Invest., 66: 892 (1980).

7. K.H. Weisgraber, T.P. Bersot, R.W. Mahley, G. Franceschini and C.R. Sirtori, AI-Milano apoprotein. Isolation and characterization of a cysteine-containing variant of the AI apoprotein from human high density lipoproteins, J. Clin. Invest., 66: 901 (1980).

8. K.H. Weisgraber, S.C. Rall jr., T.P. Bersot, R.W. Mahley, G. Franceschini and C.R. Sirtori, Apolipoprotein AI-Milano. Detection of normal AI in affected subjects and evidence for a cysteine for arginine substitution in the variant AI, J. Biol. Chem., 257: 9926 (1983).

9. V. Gualandri, G.B. Orsini, L. Stangoni and E. Porta, Familiarità della pressione arteriosa. Studio in una popolazione chiusa, Min. Cardioangiol., 31: 1 (1983).

10. G.R. Warnick, J. Benderson and J.J. Albers, Dextran sulfate precipitation procedure for quantitation of high density lipoprotein, Clin. Chem., 28: 1379 (1982).

11. V. Gualandri, G. Franceschini, C.R. Sirtori, G. Gianfranceschi, G.B. Orsini, A. Cerrone and A. Menotti, AI-Milano apoprotein. Identification of the complete kindred and evidence of a dominant genetic transmission, Am. J. Human Gen., (1985), in press.

12. G. Franceschini, M. Sirtori, G. Gianfranceschi and C.R. Sirtori, Relation between the HDL apoproteins and AI isoprotein in subjects with the AI-Milano abnormality, Metabolism, 30: 502 (1982).

APOLIPOPROTEIN AI-MILANO: A STRUCTURAL MODIFICATION IN AN

APOLIPOPROTEIN VARIANT LEADING TO UNUSUAL LIPID BINDING PROPERTIES

Guido Franceschini, Laura Calabresi, Paola Apebe,
Marina Sirtori, Giuseppe Vecchio* and Cesare R. Sirtori

Center E. Grossi Paoletti, Institute of Pharmacology
and Pharmacognosy, University of Milano – *Institute of
Chemistry of Hormones, C.N.R., Milano, Italy

INTRODUCTION

Several molecular variants[1] of human apolipoproteins, particularly of apo AI and apo E[1], have been described since 1980, when the apolipoprotein AI-Milano (AI_M) mutant was identified in an Italian family[2,3]. The apo E mutants are often associated with severe hyperlipidemia, primarily dysbetalipoproteinemia, and premature atherosclerosis[1]. By contrast, with the exception of the apo AI_M, there is no convincing evidence associating any of the described apo AI variants with pathological conditions or with significant alterations of lipid and lipoprotein metabolism.

In the case of apo E, the severe hyperlipidemia in the carriers of variants results from a defective interaction between the mutated apolipoprotein and apo E receptors in the liver[4], leading to accumulation of atherogenic lipoproteins in plasma[4]. The aminoacid substitutions in these mutants occur in a region of apo E devoted to receptor interaction and often involve basic residues, early shown to be determinant for a correct binding[5]. The definition of the molecular error in the mutants and the quantitation of their receptor binding allowed the identification of the apo E fragment, ie segment 140–160, responsible for receptor recognition[6].

In the same way, studies on apo AI mutants will help in the understanding the structure-activity relationships in the apo AI molecule. The function of apo AI is, however, apparently more

71

complex, compared to apo E. Apo AI is, in fact, the major activator[7] of the lecithin–cholesterol acyl transferase (LCAT) enzyme[8], participates in the interaction of HDL with specific receptors[8] and is involved in the cholesterol removal from peripheral tissues[9]. Furthermore, it shows the highest lipid–binding potential among apolipoproteins[10]. None of these activities has been related to any specific sequence or conformation in apo AI, although the repeated units, able to assume amphipathic helical conformation[11], which constitute the terminal part of the molecule[10], may represent the structural basis for the activity of the apo AI in binding lipids and activating LCAT[12]. The molecular errors in two human apo AI variants, ie AI–Giessen (Pro$_{143} \longrightarrow$ Arg) and AI–Marburg (Lys$_{107} \longrightarrow$ 0)[13,14], both unable to activate LCAT <u>in vitro</u>, perturb the structure of the amphiphilic region near the substituted residue. Furthermore, the Ala$_{158} \longrightarrow$ Glu variant, in which the 143–162 fragment is more hydrophilic and has a lower helical moment, compared to the same region of normal AI, shows altered lipid binding properties[15].

The apo AI$_M$, differently from other apo AI mutants, is associated with significant alterations of lipid and lipoprotein metabolism[1,16]. These abnormalities may be the consequence of an altered function of the mutant and/or of the presence of non functional AI$_M$ dimers and complexes. Preliminary studies demonstrated that AI$_M$/AI$_M$ and AI$_M$/AII dimers are inactive in stimulating LCAT <u>in vitro</u>, whereas the monomeric AI$_M$ behaves as normal AI[1]. The present study focuses on the lipid binding properties of monomeric AI$_M$ and reports how the Arg$_{173} \longrightarrow$ Cys substitution in the variant modifies the interaction with lipids, altering the secondary structure of the apo AI molecule.

Characterization of the apo AI–Milano/phospholipid complexes

Purified apo AI and apo AI$_M$ were mixed with synthetic phosphatidylcholines (PCs), ie dimyristoylphosphatidylcholine (DMPC) and dipalmitoylphosphatidylcholine (DPPC), at 100/1 PC/AI molar ratio, and incubated for 20 hrs. The incubation temperatures were chosen near the transition T° of the phospholipid, in order to obtain the maximun yield of PC–apoprotein complexes[17]. After detergent removal, the mixtures were filtered through a calibrated agarose column. With both PCs, apolipoprotein and phospholipid coeluted from the column in the form of well defined lipid–protein complexes. About 70% of the incubated DPPC was detected in the complexes, compared to a nearly total incorporation of DMPC. A lower percentage of DPPC was found in DPPC-AI_M complexes, compared to particles containing normal AI (Table). DMPC-AI and DMPC-AI_M particles are similar for dimensions and stoichiometries[18]. By contrast, different complexes are formed upon interaction with DPPC (Table), since particles containing the AI_M mutant are larger, compared to DPPC-AI complexes (Fig. 1). The DPPC-AI_M particles also show a slightly lower DPPC/apolipoprotein ratio (Table).

The anomalous interaction of apo AI_M with DPPC may be explained on the basis of an altered structure of the mutant apolipoprotein. Experiments carried out by Wetterau and Jonas[19] showed that dansylated apo AI forms larger complexes with DPPC, compared to those produced by unlabeled apo AI, whereas both apolipoproteins display an identical reactivity with DMPC. These results, comparable with those obtained by us with apo AI_M, suggest that minor modifications of the apolipoprotein structure may alter the lipid binding capacity, particularly under restrictive reaction conditions.

The stability of the purified DMPC-AI and DMPC-AI_M particles was investigated by exposure to increasing concentrations of Guanidinium-HCl (Gdn-HCl). The addition of the denaturant to the complexes induced a progressive shift of the fluorescence wavelength maxima to higher values, with a concomitantly decreased fluorescence intensity[18]. The denaturation pattern is similar for both DMPC-AI and DMPC-AI_M, however the midpoint of the denaturation curve for DMPC-AI_M is shifted toward lower Gdn-HCl concentrations (3.4 M vs 4.0 M). The easier desorption of apo AI_M from the surface of the apolipoprotein-DMPC particles is indicative of a more labile structure for complexes with apo AI_M than with apo AI, due to a less tight binding of the mutant apolipoprotein to lipids.

Kinetics of DMPC interaction with apo AI and apo AI-Milano

The association kinetics of DMPC with apo AI and apo AI_M were monitored by measuring the decrease of liposomal turbidity with time, at the transition temperature of the phospholipid[18]. A 70% increase in the rate of association with DMPC ($K_{1/2}$=0.17 vs 0.10 min^{-1}), was detected for apo AI_M compared to apo AI (Fig. 2), suggesting a higher affinity of apo AI_M for lipids.

The kinetic behavior of the PC-apolipoprotein interaction is dependent upon different factors[17]: incubation conditions, molecular weight and secondary structure of the apolipoprotein.

Table I. Characteristics of the phosphatidylcholine (PC) complexes with Apo AI and Apo AI$_{Milano}$

	DMPC-AI	DMPC-AI$_{Milano}$	DPPC-AI	DPPC-AI$_{Milano}$
Elution volume (ml)	125.9 ± 2.1	124.0 ± 3.2	141.0 ± 0.6	138.9 ± 1.0*
PC/AI (molar)	95.4 ± 4.7	94.3 ± 4.3	128.9 ± 10.9	125.3 ± 19.1
% PC in complex	93.4 ± 3.1	90.6 ± 4.2	76.7 ± 1.9	70.2 ± 1.1*

* $p < 0.001$ vs DPPC-AI

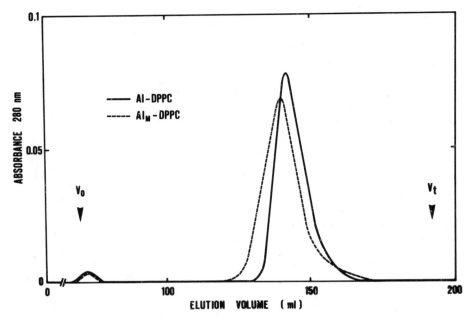

Fig. 1 Elution profiles from a 6% agarose column of apo AI-DPPC and apo AI_M-DPPC mixtures.

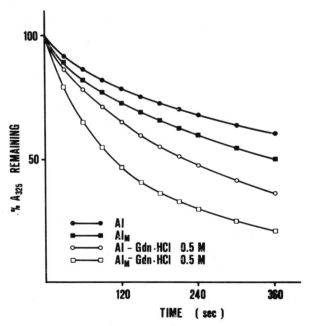

Fig. 2 Association kinetics of DMPC with apo AI and apo AI_M, both in native conditions and in the presence of 0.5 M Gdn-HCL.

75

The accelerated kinetics of the apo AI_M interaction with DMPC is not due to the phospholipid matrix, as identical reaction conditions were employed in all the experiments.

The molecular weight effect was carefully investigated as the apo AI_M can form high molecular weight dimers[3]. Purified apo AI_M has been incubated alone at different temperatures, under the experimental conditions used in the recombination experiments, and the formation of AI_M dimers was monitored by SDS–PAGE in non reducing conditions (Fig. 3). After 24 hrs of incubation at 4°C, 25°C and 37°C, 1.6%, 17.8% and 47.9% of the monomeric apolipoprotein was converted to high molecular weight complexes. Furthermore, unreduced SDS–PAGE of delipidated DMPC–AI_M complexes clearly showed that the mutant remains nearly completely monomeric during the recombination studies. Finally, as apo AI is known to self-associate, giving high molecular weight aggregates, the kinetic experiments were repeated in the presence of 0.5 M Gdn–HCl, which prevents protein self-association[20]. Again, the interaction of apo AI_M with DMPC is faster than for normal AI (Fig. 2), the calculated $K_{1/2}$ being 0.56 min^{-1} and 0.28 min^{-1}, respectively[18].

Physico–chemical properties of apo AI–Milano

In order to evaluate which difference between apo AI_M and apo AI is responsible for the anomalous interaction of the variant with lipids, investigations on the secondary structure of the two apolipoproteins were carried out by experimental and theoretical methods.

The fluorescence emission spectra of apo AI and apo AI_M, excited at 280 nm were recorded on a Jasco FP–550 spectrofluorometer between 250 and 500 nm, using a protein concentration of 0.05 mg/ml. A 2 nm red shift in the wavelength maximum of the emission spectrum of apo AI_M (337.4 ± 0.7 vs 335.2 ± 0.7 nm) was recorded with different preparations of the two apolipoproteins[18] suggesting an increased exposure to the solvent of the hydrophobic residues in the variant.

The higher hydrophobicity of apo AI_M is confirmed by theoretical methods, predicting protein conformational features from aminoacid sequence. We examined the apo AI fragment 167–184 by the Hopp and Woods method[21], which assignes a hydrophilicity value to each aminoacid and averages these values along the protein sequence (Fig. 4). The central portion of this region turns from a hydrophilic to a hydrophobic character following the

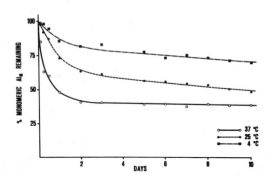

Fig. 3 In vitro formation of AI_M-AI_M dimers following incubation of monomeric apo AI_M in buffer of different temperatures.

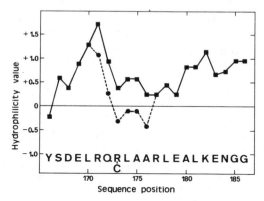

Fig. 4 Hydrophilicity analysis of the 167–184 fragment of apo AI (——) and apo AI_M (– – –). The **y** axis represents the range of hydrophilicity values assigned according to (21).

$Arg_{173} \longrightarrow$ Cys substitution: the mean hydrophilicity of the fragment decreases from 0.89 to 0.67. Using a different prediction method, Rosseneu et al[15] calculated a hydrophobicity of −.31 and −.12 for the 167–181 segments of apo AI and apo AI_M, respectively. Since the hydrophobicity of the amphiphile is one of the controlling factors in the association of the apolipoproteins with lipids[17], the higher hydrophobicity of AI_M may explain the increased affinity for lipids of the variant, compared to normal AI.

The secondary structure of apo AI_M has been also studied in terms of far-ultraviolet circular dichroism. Spectra were recorded with a Jasco J500A spectropolarimeter and the analyses of the secondary structural information were carried out using 16 reference proteins of known secondary structure[18]. A lower α-helical content was calculated for apo AI_M (39%) compared to normal AI (54%). This experimental finding, obtained with different preparations of the two apolipoproteins[22], cannot be confirmed by the prediction method of Chou and Fasman[22]. However, an explanation for the reduced helical structure in the variant apolipoprotein derives from the altered distribution of charged residues induced by the aminoacid substitution. The apo AI fragment 167–184 has the typical amphipathic structure, described by Segrest et al[11], the hydrophobic face being occupied by four Leu residues, and the opposite polar side by Asp_{168}, Glu_{169}, Glu_{179} and Glu_{183} (Fig. 5). Four positively charged residues (Arg_{171}, Arg_{173}, Arg_{177} and Lys_{182}) are located at the interface between the polar and apolar sides of the amphipathic helix. Two ion pairs[11] are present in close proximity in this fragment of apo AI: Asp_{168}-Arg_{171} and Glu_{169}-Arg_{173}. One of these is lost in the apo AI_M, where the positively charged Arg_{173} is substituted with a neutral cysteine. As "salt bridges" between oppositely charged residues are known to stabilize an α-helix[23], the disappearance of the Glu_{169} – Arg_{173} ion pair in the apo AI_M results in the loss of some amphipathic structure. The number of helical regions, involved in lipid binding, will be lower in the apo AI_M compared to normal AI, the former being more easily removed from lipid-protein complexes and giving different particles with the less reactive DPPC.

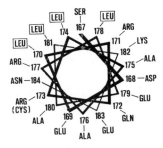

Fig. 5 Helical wheel presentation of the presumed α-helical segment 167–184 of apo AI. In the apo AI_M the Arg_{173} is substituted with cysteine.

Conclusions

In the present report, we demonstrated how the single $Arg_{173} \longrightarrow Cys$ substitution in the apo AI_M mutant leads to a remodeling of the secondary structure of the apo AI molecule, with a reduced amphipathic helical content and an increased hydrophobicity. Because of these modifications, the variant interacts more promptly with lipids, is more readily displaced from stable lipid–apolipoprotein particles, and forms large complexes upon reaction with DPPC. A relationship between structural alterations in normal AI and formation of larger lipid–apolipoprotein particles has been recently reported[24]; the chemical modification of amino groups in apo AI resulted in a red shift of the fluorescence wavelength maximum, in a 10% decrease of α-helix content and in an increase of the overall size of lipid–apolipoprotein complexes, compared to unmodified apo AI.

The reported studies, as well as others carried out on different apo AI mutants[13–15], will help in the definition of the functions of apo AI in lipid metabolism and in the characterization of the structural requirements. In the case of the apo AI_M variant, the high flexibility in the interaction with lipids may contribute to its accelerated catabolism[25], and, _via_ an increased uptake of tissue lipids, may be responsible of the anti-atherogenic potential of the mutant apolipoprotein[26].

Acknowledgements. Supported by Grant N. 1 RO1 HL 28961 awarded by the National Heart Lung and Blood Institutes, and by the Consiglio Nazionale delle Ricerche of Italy (PF Ingegneria Genetica e Basi Molecolari delle Malattie Ereditarie).

REFERENCES

1. R.W. Mahley, T.L. Innerarity, S.C. Rall jr, and K.H. Weisgraber, Plasma lipoproteins: apolipoprotein structure and function, J. Lipid Res. 25: 1277 (1984).

2. G. Franceschini, C.R. Sirtori, A. Capurso, K.H. Weisgraber, and R.W. Mahley, AI$_{Milano}$ apolipoprotein. Decreased high density lipoprotein cholesterol levels with significant lipoprotein modifications and without clinical atherosclerosis in an Italian family, J. Clin. Invest. 66: 892 (1980).

3. K.H. Weisgraber, T.P. Bersot, R.W. Mahley, G. Franceschini, and C.R. Sirtori, AI$_{Milano}$ apolipoprotein. Isolation and characterization of a cysteine-containing variant of the AI apoprotein from human high density lipoproteins, J. Clin. Invest. 66: 901 (1980).

4. R.W. Mahley, Apolipoprotein E and cholesterol metabolism, Klin. Wochenschr. 61: 225 (1983).

5. R.W. Mahley, T.L. Innerarity, R.E. Pitas, K.H. Weisgraber, J.H. Brown, and E. Gross, Inhibition of lipoprotein binding to cell surface receptors of fibroblasts following selective modification of arginyl residues in arginine-rich and B apoproteins, J. Biol. Chem. 252: 7279 (1977).

6. T.L. Innerarity, E.J. Friedlander, S.C. Rall jr., K.H. Weisgraber, and R.W. Mahley, The receptor-binding domain of human apolipoprotein E, J. Biol Chem. 258: 12341 (1983).

7. C.J. Fielding, V.G. Shore, and P.E. Fielding, A protein cofactor of lecithin: cholesterol acyltransferase, Biochem. Biophys. Res. Comm. 46: 1493 (1972).

8. V.A. Rifici, and M.A. Eder, A hepatocyte receptor in high density lipoproteins specific for apolipoprotein AI, J. Biol. Chem. 259: 13814 (1984).

9. N.E. Miller, A. La Ville, and D. Crook, Direct evidence that reverse cholesterol transport is mediated by high density lipoprotein in rabbit, Nature 314: 109 (1985).

10. H.N. Baker, A.M. Gotto jr., and R.L. Jackson, The primary structure of human plasma high density apolipoprotein glutamine I (Apo AI), J. Biol. Chem. 250: 2725 (1975).

11. J.P. Segrest, R.L. Jackson, J.D. Morrisett, and A.M. Gotto jr., A molecular theory of lipid-protein interactions in the plasma lipoproteins, FEBS Lett. 38: 247 (1974).

12. J.T. Sparrow, and A.M. Gotto jr., Apolipoprotein/lipid interactions: studies with synthetic polypeptides, CRC Crit Rev. Biochem. 13: 87 (1982).

13. G. Utermann, J. Haas, A. Steinmetz, R. Paetzold, S.C. Rall jr., K.H. Weisgraber, and R.W. Mahley, Apolipoprotein AI-Giessen: apo AI (Pro$_{143}$ $\longrightarrow$ Arg). A mutant that is defective in activating lecithin: cholesterol acyltransferase, Eur. J. Biochem. 144: 325 (1984).

14. S.C. Rall jr., K.H. Weisgraber, R.W. Mahley, Y. Ogawa, C.J. Fielding, G. Utermann, J. Haas, A. Steinmetz, H.J. Menzel, and G. Assmann, Abnormal lecithin: cholesterol acyltransferase activation by a human apolipoprotein AI variant in which a single lysine residue is delated, J. Biol. Chem 259: 10063 (1984).

15. M. Rosseneu, H. DeLoof, G. Assmann, U. Jads, and M. Phillips, Lipid binding properties of human apo AI mutants, in: NATO ARW: Human Apolipoprotein Mutants-Impact on Atherosclerosis and Longevity, Plenum Press, N.Y., in the press.

16. G. Franceschini, C.R. Sirtori, E. Bosisio, V. Gualandri, G.B. Orsini, A.M. Mogavero, and A. Capurso, Relationship of the phenotypic expression of AI$_{Milano}$ apoprotein with plasma lipid and lipoprotein patterns, Atherosclerosis (1985), in the press.

17. H.J. Pownall, A. Pao, D. Hickson, J.T. Sparrow, S.K. Kusserow, and J.B. Massey, Kinetics and mechanism of association of human plasma apolipoproteins with dimyristoylphosphatidylcholine: effect of   protein structure and lipid clusters on reaction rates, Biochemistry 20: 6630 (1981).

18. G. Franceschini, G. Vecchio, G. Gianfranceschi, D. Magani, and C.R. Sirtori, Apolipoprotein AI$_{.Milano}$: accelerated binding and dissociation from lipids of a human apolipoprotein variant, J. Biol. Chem. (1985), in the press.

19. J.R. Wetterau, and A. Jonas, Factors affecting the size of complexes of dipalmitoylphosphatidylcholine with human apolipoprotein AI, J. Biol. Chem. 258: 2637 (1983).

20. J.B. Massey, A.M. Gotto jr., and H.J. Pownall, Human plasma high density apolipoprotein AI: effect of protein interaction on the spontaneous formation of a lipid–protein recombinant, Biochem. Biophys. Res. Comm. 99: 466 (1981).

21. T.P. Hopp, and K.R. Woods, Prediction of protein antigenic determinants from amino acid sequences, Proc. Natl. Acad. Sci. USA 78: 3824 (1981).

22. P.Y. Chou, and G.D. Fasman, Prediction of the secondary structure of proteins from their amino acid sequence, Adv. Enzymol. Relat. Areas Mol. Biol. 47: 45 (1978).

23. A. Bierzynski, P.S. Kim, and R.L. Baldwin, A salt bridge stabilizes the helix formed by isolated C–peptide of RNase A, Proc. Natl. Acad. Sci USA 79: 2470 (1982).

24. A. Jonas, K.E. Covinsky, and S.A. Sweeny, Effect of amino group modification in discoidal apolipoprotein AI–egg phosphatidylcholine–cholesterol complexes on their reaction with lecithin cholesterol acyltransferase, Biochemistry 24: 3508 (1985).

25. G.C. Ghiselli, J.A. Summerfield, E.J. Schaefer, E.A. Jones, and H.B. Brewer jr., Abnormal catabolism of AI_{Milano}, Clin. Res. 30: 291A (1982).

26. V. Gualandri, G. Franceschini, C.R. Sirtori, G. Gianfranceschi, G.B. Orsini, A. Cerrone, and A. Menotti, AI_{Milano} apoprotein: identification of the complete kindred and evidence of a dominant genetic transmission, Am. J. Human Genet. (1985), in the press.

THE AI-MILANO HDL PARTICLES

Alex V. Nichols,* Guido Franceschini,†
Cesare R. Sirtori,† and Elaine L. Gong*

* Donner Laboratory
  University of California
  Berkeley, California 94720

† Center Enrica Grossi Paoletti
  University of Milan
  20129 Milan, Italy

Interest in the structure and function of human high density lipoproteins (HDL) derives in major part from epidemiologic observations of their inverse correlation with the risk of arterial disease (1,2). Based on such observations, an increased incidence of premature disease would be expected in individuals with very low levels of HDL. Surprisingly, several rare familial disorders characterized by decreased levels of HDL do not show the presence of premature vascular lesions (3,4). One such disorder appears to be the apolipoprotein variant designated AI_{Milano} or AI_M, which is generally associated with reduced plasma levels of HDL and elevated levels of triglyceride (5). The mutant apolipoprotein AI is characterized by a single cysteine-for-arginine replacement at position 173 (6). The apolipoprotein is capable of forming intermolecular disulfide bonds that can produce dimers and mixed disulfide complexes. Since AI is the major apolipoprotein component of normal HDL and thereby plays a crucial role in determining both the

lipid-binding capacity and the ultimate particle size properties of
HDL, considerable change in HDL particle properties and distribution
might be expected from participation of AI_M dimers and mixed
disulfide complexes in HDL structure.

Franceschini et al. (7) have shown that HDL from affected
carriers (designated AI_M^+) are characterized by a predominance of
HDL_3 (d 1.125-1.200 g/ml) which are enriched in triglyceride and low
in cholesterol content. By means of chemical crosslinking, at least
three apparent HDL_3 subspecies with differential apolipoprotein
composition of the protein moiety were identified by these
investigators.

Table I

Identification and Characterization of AI_M Carriers (AI_M^+)

and Nonaffected Kindred (AI_M^-)

Case #	Age (yr)	Sex	TG	HDL-C	$F_{1.20}^o$ 0-9 (Total HDL)	$F_{1.20}^o$ 0-3.5 (HDL_3)	$F_{1.20}^o$ 3.5-9 (HDL_2)
AI_M^+							
445	48	M	476	9	25	25	0
456	22	M	96	10	na	na	na
447	56	M	126	10	na	na	na
449	41	M	250	11	47	47	0
487	12	M	60	15	na	na	na
454	35	M	65	21	138	119	19
444	33	F	316	8	18	18	0
455	14	F	96	18	88	75	13
458	16	F	93	20	na	na	na
473	66	F	170	35	238	183	55
AI_M^-							
17	75	M	115	42	201	197	4
18	56	M	78	51	na	na	na
21	56	M	105	70	288	164	124
22	36	F	110	50	na	na	na
19	60	F	220	61	309	214	95
20	38	F	64	76	305	172	133

Abbreviations: TG, triglyceride; HDL-C, HDL cholesterol; $F_{1.20}^o$ 0-9, 0-3.5,
and 3.5-9: flotation rate intervals measured by analytic ultracentrifugation.
All values in mg/dl. na, not analyzed by analytic ultracentrifugation.

In the present investigation, the particle polydispersity of HDL in plasma of ten AI_M^+ and six AI_M^- (nonaffected kindred) was evaluated (Table I). For determination of HDL particle size distribution, gradient gel electrophoresis (protein stain) was performed on the ultracentrifugal d $\leq$ 1.20 g/ml fraction isolated from plasma of all of the above subjects (8). For determination of the flotation rate distribution of HDL, the same ultracentrifugal fraction isolated from a smaller subgroup (six AI_M^+ and four AI_M^-, see Table I) of the above subjects was analyzed by analytic ultracentrifugation (9). Total HDL and HDL subclass levels determined by analytic ultracentrifugation are listed in Table I.

Analytic ultracentrifugal patterns of HDL of the six AI_M^+, whose plasma levels of HDL-cholesterol (HDL-C) ranged from 8 to 35 mg/dl, are shown in Fig. 1. Total plasma HDL of this group of AI_M^+ ranged from 18 to 238 mg/dl and showed a predominance of HDL_3 as gauged by the pattern area within the flotation interval of $F_{1.20}^{\circ}$ 0-3.5. HDL material in the flotation interval of $F_{1.20}^{\circ}$ 3.5-9.0, corresponding to the HDL_2 subclass, was observed in AI_M^+ with higher plasma HDL-C levels. Plasma concentrations of HDL_2 in these subjects ranged from 0 to 55 mg/dl. At the higher levels of HDL-C, the flotation rate of the major HDL schlieren peak was also shifted to higher values, consistent with the presence of the additional faster floating HDL_2 species. Analytic ultracentrifugal patterns (not shown) of HDL from the four AI_M^-, with HDL-C and total plasma HDL levels ranging from 42 to 76 mg/dl and 201 to 309 mg/dl, respectively, generally showed higher HDL_3 levels than those in AI_M^+; the range of HDL_2 levels in AI_M^- was 4-133 mg/dl. The analytic ultracentrifugal results were consistent with the rate zonal ultracentrifugal data reported by Franceschini et al. (7).

As indicated above, the particle size distributions of HDL of AI_M^+ and AI_M^- were determined directly by gradient gel electrophoresis.

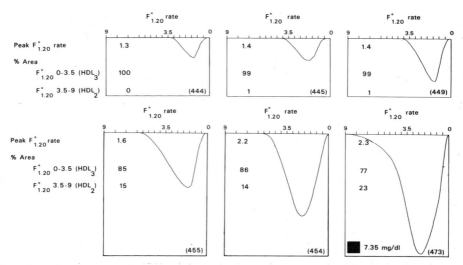

Fig. 1. Analytic ultracentrifugal patterns of AI_M^+ HDL ($F_{1.20}^o$ 0-9.0).
Total HDL and HDL subfraction concentrations from above
patterns (identified by number at lower right of each
pattern) are given in Table I. Patterns are organized in
sequence of increasing plasma HDL-C levels starting from
upper left to right to lower left to right. Small square in
lower right pattern denotes calibration of analytic ultracentrifugal area.

By means of this technique, we had previously described the occurrence in normal human plasma of at least five major subpopulations:
three within the HDL_3 subclass ($(HDL_{3a})_{gge}$, $(HDL_{3b})_{gge}$, and
$(HDL_{3c})_{gge}$) and two within the HDL_2 subclass ($(HDL_{2b})_{gge}$ and
$(HDL_{2a})_{gge}$) (10). Peak maxima of the above subpopulations fall
within specific particle size intervals which define the subpopulations: 12.9-9.7 nm, $(HDL_{2b})_{gge}$; 9.7-8.8 nm, $(HDL_{2a})_{gge}$; 8.8-8.2 nm,
$(HDL_{3a})_{gge}$; 8.2-7.8 nm, $(HDL_{3b})_{gge}$; and 7.8-7.2 nm, $(HDL_{3c})_{gge}$.

Gradient gel electrophoresis patterns of AI_M^+ HDL were
characterized by two major peaks with maxima located primarily
within the particle size intervals of the $(HDL_{3a})_{gge}$ and $(HDL_{3b})_{gge}$
subpopulations (Fig. 2). Compared to AI_M^- HDL (Fig. 3), the AI_M^+ HDL
were unique in consistently exhibiting a distinct peak within the

86

PATTERN

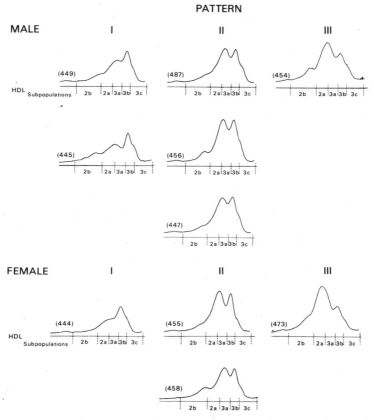

Fig. 2. Gradient gel electrophoresis patterns of male and female AI_M^+. Patterns are obtained by densitometry of protein-stained gradient gels (4-30% polyacrylamide) (8). Intervals corresponding to particle size ranges of HDL subpopulations in normal human plasma are indicated below patterns. See text for numerical values of particle size intervals corresponding to the HDL subpopulations. Numbers appearing at lower left of each pattern designate AI_M^+ described in Table I.

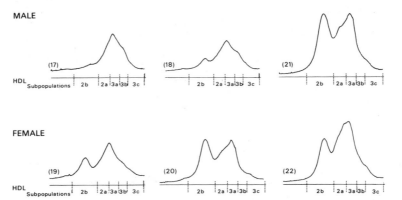

Fig. 3.   Gradient gel electrophoresis patterns of male and female AI_M^- (see legend of Fig. 2 and Table I).

$(HDL_{3b})_{gge}$ interval. Peaks with maxima in the $(HDL_{2b})_{gge}$ interval, which in normal subjects contains the larger species of the HDL_2 subclass, were either minor or nondetectable. Patterns of AI_M^- HDL were similar to patterns previously reported for normal subjects (8). They were characterized by a major peak with maximum in the $(HDL_{3a})_{gge}$ interval and by peaks of varying amplitude in the $(HDL_{2b})_{gge}$ interval. The latter peaks, when present, were correlated with the presence of material in the HDL_2 flotation interval $F^\circ_{1.20}$ 3.5-9.0 in corresponding analytic ultracentrifugal patterns. In some patterns of control subjects, a shoulder on the major $(HDL_{3a})_{gge}$ peak was noted, indicating the occurrence of material within the $(HDL_{3b})_{gge}$ interval.

In HDL patterns of all AI_M^+, the mean particle sizes of the major components, with peaks in the $(HDL_{3a})_{gge}$ and $(HDL_{3b})_{gge}$ intervals (sizes at peak maxima: 8.55 ± 0.09 and 7.97 ± 0.02 nm, respectively), were similar to those (8.44 ± 0.07 and 7.88 ± 0.02 nm, respectively) observed in AI_M^-. The mean particle size of the major component in the $(HDL_{2b})_{gge}$ interval, however, was smaller (9.85 ± 0.02 vs. 10.34 ± 0.29 nm) in the AI_M^+ compared with that in the AI_M^-. Thus, the particle sizes of the major HDL_3 subpopulations in AI_M^+ were not significantly different from sizes of their counterparts in AI_M^-. It should be noted that the mean particle sizes of the major components of HDL in AI_M^- compared closely with those of a large number ($n = 191$) of subjects studied by us in the U.S.A. (8).

AI_M^+ HDL exhibited three characteristic gradient gel electrophoresis patterns (patterns I, II, and III, Fig. 2) that reflected the relative contributions of the two major peaks. Pattern I was characterized by a relatively sharp peak with maximum in the $(HDL_{3b})_{gge}$ interval together with a broader peak of lower amplitude; the latter peak was located within the $(HDL_{2a+3a})_{gge}$ interval with peak maximum in the $(HDL_{3a})_{gge}$ interval. In pattern II, the two major peaks, as noted in pattern I, were located within approximately the same HDL subpopulation intervals but now were of comparable amplitude. Pattern III showed a significantly greater amplitude of the broader peak (in the $(HDL_{2a+3a})_{gge}$ interval) when compared with the peak in the $(HDL_{3b})_{gge}$ interval. The main distinguishing feature among the three patterns was the relative content of the smaller and larger HDL subpopulations which had peak maxima in the $(HDL_{3b})_{gge}$ and $(HDL_{3a})_{gge}$ intervals, respectively. Pattern I had the highest relative content of smaller subspecies, and pattern III had the highest relative content of larger species. In addition, it should be noted that the group of AI_M^+ with pattern I exhibited the lowest mean HDL-C value (I: HDL-C, 9.3 ± 1.5 mg/dl) compared with that of AI_M^+ with patterns II and III (II: HDL-C, 14.6 ± 4.6 mg/dl, and III: HDL-C, 28.0 ± 9.9 mg/dl). Thus, it appears that as HDL-C levels are reduced, the particle size pattern becomes relatively enriched in the smaller HDL subpopulations. Such progressive relative enrichment of HDL patterns with species of smaller particle size as a function of decreasing plasma concentration of HDL-C was also observed in normal subjects. The correlation coefficient relating the percent of the total HDL pattern area in the particle size interval of the small subpopulation $(HDL_{3b})_{gge}$ vs. HDL-C was -0.79 ($p<0.001$) for normal male adults (age range: 35-59 yr; n = 91) (11). The correlation coefficient between the same parameters for an admittedly small sample of ten AI_M^+ subjects was -0.90 ($p<0.001$). The mean HDL-C plasma levels in the above ten AI_M^+ subjects was 15.7 ± 8.3 mg/dl, while the mean level in the 91 normal male subjects was 44.0 ± 11.6 mg/dl.

Furthermore, it is well established that low levels of HDL-C are frequently associated with elevated plasma triglyceride levels and this also appeared to be the case for AI_M^+. Thus, for 33 AI_M^+ (12), the correlation coefficient for plasma triglyceride level vs. HDL-C was -0.30 ($p=0.05$); for 91 normal males cited above, the

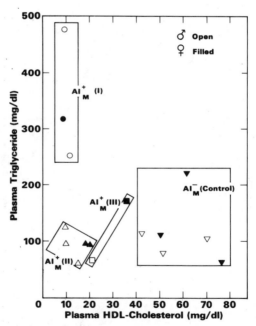

Fig. 4. Plot of triglyceride and HDL-cholesterol levels in plasma of AI_M^+ and AI_M^-. Data points for AI_M^+ of the same pattern type (I, II, and III) and for AI_M^- control are enclosed by solid lines. Sex of subjects is indicated. Subjects in this figure are those described in Table I and in Figs. 2 and 3.

correlation coefficient for the same variables was −0.49 (p<0.001). When values of plasma triglyceride (TG) and HDL-C were plotted for the ten AI_M^+ and six AI_M^- whose HDL were analyzed by electrophoresis, the group of AI_M^+ with pattern I exhibited the lowest mean HDL-C value and the highest mean TG value, relative to those of AI_M^+ with patterns II and III (Fig. 4). These data suggest that the pattern I distribution, in which the relative content of the smaller $(HDL_{3b})_{gge}$ subpopulation was increased, reflected the presence of both elevated plasma TG levels and very low levels of HDL-C. The observation of the relative enrichment of HDL with smaller sized particles in the presence of hypertriglyceridemia (222-2500 mg/dl) and reduced HDL-C levels (22-30 mg/dl) has been previously reported by Eisenberg et al. (13).

In conclusion, our investigation of HDL particles in AI_M^+ indicated the following: (1) the AI_M^+ HDL particle size distribution consists mainly of two major components, one broad peak (mean size, 8.55 nm) in the $(HDL_{2a+3a})_{gge}$ interval and one sharp peak (mean size, 7.97 nm) in the $(HDL_{3b})_{gge}$ interval; (2) the mean particle sizes of the major HDL_3 components are similar to those observed within the same HDL subpopulation intervals in AI_M^- and normal subjects; (3) three pattern types of HDL distribution can be identified in AI_M^+ that reflect the relative contribution of the two major HDL components; (4) the pattern type with greatest relative build-up of smaller HDL particles is observed in a group of AI_M^+ with highest mean TG and lowest mean HDL-C values; and (5) the statistical relationship between plasma TG and HDL-C levels in AI_M^+ is inverse as observed in normal and hypertriglyceridemic subjects.

ACKNOWLEDGEMENTS

This work was supported by NIH Program Project Grant HL 18574 from the National Heart, Lung, and Blood Institute of the National Institutes of Health.

REFERENCES

1. G. J. Miller, and N. E. Miller, Plasma high-density lipoprotein concentration and development of ischaemic heart-disease, Lancet 1:16 (1975).

2. T. Gordon, W. P. Castelli, M. C. Hjortland, W. B. Kannel, and T. R. Dawber, High density lipoprotein as a prtoective factor against coronary heart disease: the Framingham study, Am. J. Med. 62:707 (1977).

3. G. Assmann, P. N. Herbert, D. S. Fredrickson, and T. Forte, Isolation and characterization of an abnormal high density lipoprotein in Tangier disease, J. Clin. Invest. 60:242 (1977).

4. L. A. Carlson, Fish eye disease: a new familial condition with massive corneal opacities and dyslipoproteinemia, Eur. J. Clin. Invest. 12:41 (1982).

5. G. Franceschini, C. R. Sirtori, A. Capurso, K. H. Weisgraber, and R. W. Mahley, A-I$_{Milano}$ apoprotein: decreased high density lipoprotein cholesterol levels with significant lipoprotein modifications and without clinical atherosclerosis in an Italian family, J. Clin. Invest. 66:892 (1980).

6. K. H. Weisgraber, S. C. Rall, T. P. Bersot, R. W. Mahley, G. Franceschini, and C. R. Sirtori, Apolipoprotein AI$_{Milano}$: detection of normal AI in affected subjects and evidence for a cysteine for arginine substitution in the variant AI, J. Biol. Chem. 258:2508 (1983).

7. G. Franceschini, T. G. Frosi, C. Manzoni, G. Gianfranceschi, and C. R. Sirtori, High density lipoprotein-3 heterogeneity in subjects with the apo-AI$_{Milano}$ variant, J. Biol. Chem. 257:9926 (1982).

8. A. V. Nichols, P. J. Blanche, and E. L. Gong, Gradient gel electrophoresis of human plasma high density lipoproteins, in: "Handbook of Electrophoresis, Vol. III," L. A. Lewis, ed., CRC Press, Boca Raton, Florida (1983).

9. F. T. Lindgren, L. C. Jensen, and F. T. Hatch, The isolation and quantitative analysis of serum lipoproteins, in: "Blood Lipids and Lipoproteins," G. J. Nelson, ed., Interscience, New York (1972).

10. P. J. Blanche, E. L. Gong, T. M. Forte, and A. V. Nichols, Characterization of human high-density lipoproteins by gradient gel electrophoresis, Biochim. Biophys. Acta 665:408 (1981).

11. F. T. Lindgren, A. V. Nichols, P. D. Wood, G. L. Adamson, M. A. Austin, L. A. Glines, V. Martin, and R. M. Krauss, in preparation.

12. G. Franceschini, C. R. Sirtori, G. Gianfranceschi, A. Menotti, A. Cerrone, G. Orsini, and V. Gualandri, A-I$_{Milano}$ apoprotein: identification of the complete kindred and evidence of a dominant genetic transmission, Amer. J. Human Genetics, in press (1985).

13. S. Eisenberg, D. Gavish, Y. Oschry, M. Fainaru, and R. J. Deckelbaum, Abnormalities in very low, low, and high density lipoproteins in hypertriglyceridemia, J. Clin. Invest. 74:470 (1984).

APOLIPOPROTEIN A-I$_{MILANO}$: IN VIVO METABOLISM OF AN

APOLIPOPROTEIN A-I VARIANT

H.B. Brewer Jr., G. Ghiselli, E.J. Shaefer, L.A. Zech, G. Franceschini*, and C.R. Sirtori*,

Molecular Disease Branch, National Heart, Lung, and Blood Institute, National Institutes of Health, Bethesda, MD 20892
*Centro per lo Studio della Malattie Dismetaboliche Enrica Grossi Paoletti, Università degli Studi di Milano Milan, Italy 20129

INTRODUCTION

Apolipoprotein (apo) A-I$_{Milano}$ is a human apoA-I variant in which cysteine replaces arginine at position 173 (1). Subjects with apoA-I$_{Milano}$ have mild hypertriglyceridemia, reduced plasma high density lipoproteins (HDL), and slight elevations of low density lipoproteins (LDL) (2). Despite reduced levels of HDL these patients have no evidence of premature cardiovascular disease (2,3).

The presence of a cysteine residue in apoA-I$_{Milano}$ results in the formation of mixed protein disulfide dimers in plasma, the major forms include apoA-I$_{Milano}$ – apoA-I$_{Milano}$ and apoA-I$_{Milano}$ – apoA-II (2,3). The importance of apoA-I$_{Milano}$ in the reduced levels of plasma HDL, and the lipid binding properties of apoA-I$_{Milano}$ are evaluated in the present report.

MATERIALS AND METHODS

Isolation and Characterization of the Plasma Lipoproteins and ApoA-I$_{Milano}$

Plasma lipoproteins were isolated by preparative ultra-centrifugation from the proband of the family reported by Franceschini et al (2). Lyophilized HDL were delipidated (chloroform-methanol, 3:1, v/v), and the apoA-I$_{Milano}$ isolated by preparative NaDodSO$_4$ gel electrophoresis (0.1 % NaDodSO$_4$, 15%

95

acrylamide, and 0.05% bisacrylamide) in a Bio-Rad model 220 dual slab gel apparatus (0.3 x 10 x 14 cm, Bio-Rad, Richmond, CA). One mg of protein was loaded per gel, and following electrophoresis the zone corresponding to the electrophoretic position of apoA-I was cut out. This section was transferred to the top of a 0.5% agarose gel (low mr, Bio-Rad) containing 0.5 M Tris-HCl (pH 6.8). The sample was electrophorsed (200 mA, 3 hr), the zones corresponding to the ionic front removed, and the gel ultracentrifuged (40,000 rpm, 3 hrs). The isolated apoA-I$_{Milano}$ was freed from low molecular weight contaminates by fractionation on P-GDG, (Bio-Rad, 1.2 cm x 60 cm, 0.08% ammonium bicarbonate). ApoA-I from HDL isolated from a normal subject was prepared by the same procedures utilized for apoA-I$_{Milano}$.

ApoA-I Kinetic Studies

Normal apoA-I and apoA-I$_{Milano}$ were iodinated as previously reported (4). Kinetic studies were performed on three normal volunteers. One week prior to study, the volunteers were placed on a metabolic isocaloric diet containing 200 mg cholesterol/1000 cal, and 16% protein, and 2% fat, and 42% carbohydrate. Following injection of ^{125}I apoA-I$_{Milano}$ and normal ^{131}I-apoA-I blood samples were drawn at 10 min, 6 hrs, 12 hrs, and at 4, 7, 10, and 14 days. The radioactivity was quantitated in plasma, and isolated lipoprotein density fractions.

HDL protein and lipid, as well as apoA-I concentrations were determined as previously reported (4,5).

Lipid Binding Properties of ApoA-I$_{Milano}$

The lipid binding properties of apoA-I$_{Milano}$ were evaluated by quantitation of radiolabeled apoA-I$_{Milano}$ in plasma following separation of the plasma lipoproteins by ultracentrifugation and gel permeation chromatography on Sepharose CL-6B (Pharmacia Fine Chemicals AB, Uppsala, column 1.2 x 120 cm, buffer 0.85% NaCl, 0.1 M Tris-HCl, pH 7.4, and 0.01% EDTA).

RESULTS

Normal apoA-I and monomeric apoA-I$_{Milano}$ were isolated in homogeneous form by preparative NaDodSO$_4$ gel electrophoresis. Normal apoA-I and apoA-I$_{Milano}$ were radiolabeled with ^{131}I and ^{125}I, respectively.

Kinetic studies were performed in three normal subjects utilizing ^{125}I-apoA-I$_{Milano}$ and normal ^{131}I-apoA-I. The radioactivity decay curves within HDL for ^{125}I-apoA-I$_{Milano}$ and normal ^{131}I-apoA-I for one of the subjects is illustrated in Figure 1.

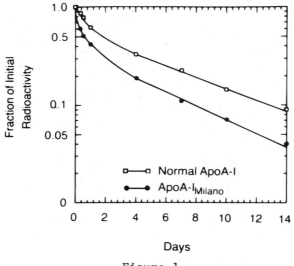

Figure 1

^{125}I-apoA-I$_{Milano}$ decayed at a faster rate than normal
^{131}I-apoA-I in both plasma and HDL. A faster decay of
^{125}I-apoA-I$_{Milano}$ was observed in all three subjects. The mean
residence times within HDL for ^{125}I-apoA-I$_{Milano}$ was 2.5 $\pm$ 0.7
days which was significantly shorter (p < 0.01) than for normal
^{131}I-apoA-I (4.1 $\pm$ 1.5 days).

The distribution of ^{125}I-apoA-I$_{Milano}$ within plasma at the
10 min point of the kinetic study was virtually identical to
normal ^{131}I-apoA-I. The percentages of radioactivity within the
< 1.063 g/ml, 1.063 - 1.21 g/ml, and > 1.21 g/ml density
fractions for ^{125}I-apoA-I$_{Milano}$ and normal ^{131}I-apoA-I were
5.5% $\pm$ 1.3 (mean $\pm$ 5.0), 88.3% $\pm$ 3.8, 6.2% $\pm$ 1.0 and 1.6% $\pm$ 1.0,
92.6% $\pm$ 13.7, and 5.8% $\pm$ 0.7 respectively. The distribution of
radioactivity of plasma ^{125}I-apoA-I$_{Milano}$ and normal ^{131}I-apoA-I
separated by Sepharose CL-6B chromatography were similar with
> 93% of the radioactivity within HDL.

DISCUSSION

Kinetic analysis of radiolabeled apoA-I$_{Milano}$ and normal
apoA-I in normal subjects revealed that apoA-I$_{Milano}$ is
catabolized at a faster rate than normal apoA-I. Normal subjects
were selected for these studies since the only variable would be
the apoA-I variant, and a direct comparison of the catabolism of
normal apoA-I and apoA-I$_{Milano}$ would be possible. An evaluation

of the kinetic behavior of apoA-I$_{Milano}$ can not be obtained in the proband since secondary changes in apolipoprotein-lipoprotein metabolism may be present in the subject with the dyslipo-proteinemia. The lipid binding properties of apoA-I$_{Milano}$ were evaluated by a comparison of the distribution of normal ^{131}I-apoA-I and ^{125}I-apoA-IMilano following separation of lipoproteins by gel permeating chromatography and ultra-centrifugation. No significant difference in the lipid binding properties of apoA-I$_{Milano}$ could be detected by these techniques.

The combined results from these studies indicate that apoA-I$_{Milano}$ does not differ significantly in lipid binding properties from normal apoA-I. ApoA-I$_{Milano}$, however, is catabolized at a faster rate than normal apoA-I. These results were interpreted as indicating that apoA-I$_{Milano}$ is kinetically abnormal, and is responsible for the reduced HDL levels present in the apoA-I$_{Milano}$ patients. These data are consistent with the concept that the cysteine modification in apoA-I$_{Milano}$ is of functional significance. These studies emphasize the important role of apoA-I in modulating HDL levels, and indicate that apoA-I variants may result in clinical hypoalphalipoproteinemias.

REFERENCES

1. Weisgraber, K.H., Rall, S.C. Jr., Bersot, T.P., Mahley, R.W., Franceschini, G., and Sirtori, C.R. (1983) Apolipoprotein A-I$_{Milano}$ detection of normal A-I in affected subjects and evidence for a cysteine for arginine substitution in the variant A-I. J. Biol. Chem. _258_, 2508-2513.

2. Francheschini, G., Sirtori, C.R., Capurso, A., Weisgraber, K.H., and Mahley, R.W. (1980) A-I$_{Milano}$ apoprotein, decreased high density lipoprotein cholesterol levels with significant lipoprotein modifications and without clinical atherosclerosis in an Italian family. J. Clin. Invest. _66_, 892-990.

3. Francheschini, G., Sirtori, M., Geanfranceschi, G., and Sirtori, C.R. (1981) Relation between the HDL apoprotein and A-I isoproteins in subjects with the A-I$_{Milano}$ abnormality. Metabolism _30_, 502-509.

4. Schaefer, E.J., Zech, L.A., Jenkins, L.L., Bronzert, T., Rubalcaba, E.A., Lindgren, F.T., Aamodt, R.L., and Brewer, H.B., Jr. (1982) Human apolipoprotein A-I and A-II metabolism. J. Lipid Res. _23_, 850-861.

5. Schaefer, E.J., Blum, C.B., Levy, R.I., Jenkins, L.L., Alaupovic, P., Foster, D.M., Brewer, H.B., Jr. (1978) Metabolism of high-density lipoprotein apolipoproteins in Tangier Disease. New Engl. J. Med. _299_, 905-910.

THE LIMONE SUL GARDA GENE

S.-H. Chen, G. Franceschini, C.R. Sirtori and L. Chan

Departments of Cell Biology and Medicine
Baylor College of Medicine, Houston, TX USA
and
Center E. Grossi Paoletti and Chemotherapy Chair
University of Milano, Via A. Del Sarto 21, 20129 Milano
Italy

High density lipoproteins (HDL) are a heterogeneous group of lipoproteins noted for their negative correlation with the incidence of atherosclerosis (Barr et al., 1951; Gofman et al., 1966; Miller & Miller, 1975; Gordon et al., 1977). The mechanism by which they confer protection against atherosclerosis is unclear. In vitro experiments involving isolated erythrocytes and cultured cells suggest that HDL may be involved in the delivery of cholesterol from the peripheral tissues to the liver for disposal (Glomset & Norum, 1973; Stein & Stein, 1973; Stein et al., 1976; Bates & Rothblat, 1974). Metabolic studies in man have suggested an inverse correlation between the size of the total body cholesterol pool and plasma HDL level (Miller et al., 1976). It is also possible that HDL may simply be a marker for a certain pattern of lipid transport and metabolism that confers protection against the development of atherosclerosis.

Apolipoprotein (apo)A-I is the major protein constituent of HDL. It is a 243 amino acid polypeptide (Baker et al., 1974; Brewer et al., 1978). It is a co-factor for lecithin-cholesterol acyltransferase, a plasma enzyme that catalyzes the conversion of cholesterol and phosphatidylcholine to cholesteryl esters and lysophosphatidylcholine (Fielding et al., 1972a,b). ApoA-I was found to be a necessary component in mixtures with phospholipid that can remove cholesterol from ascites cell membranes (Jackson et al., 1975). The plasma level of apoA-I is an even stronger predictor than HDL of protection against coronary artery disease (Maciejko et al., 1983).

99

ApoA-I is thus of pivotal importance in HDL metabolism. Its structure and function have been under investigation in various laboratories. The description of apoA-I$_{Milano}$ as the first mutant of human apolipoproteins provided an opportunity to examine the structure-function relationships of this protein (Franceschini et al., 1980; Weisgraber et al., 1980). The origin of the apolipoprotein variant has been traced to Limone Sul Garda, a small community in Northern Italy. The purpose of this communication is a description of some initial studies on the Limone Sul Garda gene, the variant apoA-I gene which is expressed as the A-I$_{Milano}$ phenotype.

Materials and Methods

Human ApoA-I cDNA. A full-length human apoA-I cDNA pA1-3 was isolated from a library of human liver cDNA clones by the technique of oligonucleotide hybridization. The details of the cDNA cloning and its complete sequence have been reported previously (Cheung & Chan, 1983).

Human Leukocyte DNA Isolation and Analysis. DNA was isolated from human leukocytes by the technique of Kan & Dozy (1978). It was digested with various restriction enzymes under conditions described by the suppliers. DNA fragments were fractionated by agarose gel electrophoresis, transferred to nitrocellulose paper, and hybridized to ^{32}P-labeled nick-translated pA1-3 DNA probe (Southern, 1975).

Results and Discussion

DNA was isolated from an A-I$_{Milano}$ carrier, his normal wife, two normal children, and one carrier child, as well as from normal Italians in the Milano area, and Caucasian Americans. Restriction mapping using 5 different enzymes (BamH1, PstI, EcoRI, HindIII, and HincII) showed no difference in the DNA patterns of the apoA-I gene between the A-I$_{Milano}$ carrier, his normal relatives, and normal Caucasian controls.

Our observation of a normal structural organization of the Limone Sul Garda gene is not unexpected. The A-I$_{Milano}$ protein is characterized by a single cysteine for arginine replacement at position 173 of apoA-I (Weisgraber et al., 1983). This change can be accounted for by a single base substitution.

The apoA-I gene has previously been localized to the long arm of human chromosome 11 (Cheung et al., 1984). It is closely linked to the apoC-III gene, which is located 2.6 Kb downstream from the 3' end of the apoA-I gene (Karathanasis et al., 1983; Protter et al., 1985). In our mapping studies, therefore, we have also studied the general structural organization of the apoC-III gene in an A-I$_{Milano}$ carrier, and found it to be normal.

Combining the observations from different laboratories, we can summarize our present understanding of the gene responsible for A-I$_{Milano}$ as follows: The Limone Sul Garda gene codes for a variant apoA-I mRNA which is, in turn, translated into a variant apoA-I protein. The mutation can be accounted for by a single base substitution, but this premise has to be confirmed. The gene is located on the long arm of chromosome 11. Its general structural organization is not different from that of normal apoA-I gene. The apoC-III gene in the carriers also appear grossly normal.

Future studies on the Limone Sul Garda gene will include a direct confirmation of the specific single-base substitution. Furthermore, we will look for restriction fragment length polymorphism involving the apoA-I gene in the population at Limone Sul Garda (Rees et al., 1983). If such polymorphism exists in this community, it should be possible to assign the Limone Sul Garda gene to a specific allele. These additional studies will enable us to more fully understand the genetic background for apoA-I$_{Milano}$, the first apolipoprotein variant described in man.

Acknowledgment

This work was partially supported by a grant from the March of Dimes Birth Defects Foundation.

References

Baker, H.N., Delahunty, T., Gotto, A.M., Jr., & Jackson, R.L. (1974) Proc. Natl. Acad. Sci. USA 71, 3631-3634.
Barr, D.P., Russ, E.M., & Eder, H.A. (1951) Am. J. Med. 11, 480-493.
Bates, S.R., & Rothblat, G.H. (1974) Biochem. Biophys. Acta 360, 38-55.
Brewer, H.B., Jr., Fairwell, T., LaRue, A., Ronan, R., Houser, A., & Bronzert, T.J. (1978) Biochim. Biophys. Res. Commun. 80, 623-630.
Cheung, P., & Chan, L. (1983) Nucleic Acids Res. 11, 3703-3715.
Cheung, P., Kao, F.T., Law, M.L., Jones, C., Puck, T.T., & Chan, L. (1984) Proc. Natl. Acad. Sci. USA 81, 508-511.
Fielding, C.J., Shore, V.G., & Fielding, P.E. (1972a) Biochem. Biophys. Res. Commun. 46, 1493-1498.
Fielding, C.J., Shore, V.G., & Fielding, P.E. (1972b) Biochim. Biophys. Acta 270, 513-518.
Franceschini, G., Sirtori, C.R., Capurso, A., Weisgraber, K.H., & Mahley, R.W. (1980) J. Clin. Invest. 66, 892-900.
Glomset, J.A., & Norum, K.R. (1973) Adv. Lipid Res. 11, 1-65.
Gofman, J.W., Young, W., & Tandy, R. (1966) Circulation 34, 679-697.

Gordon, T., Castelli, W.P., Hortland, M.C., Kannel, W.B., & Dawher, T.R. (1977) Am. J. Med. 62, 107-114.

Jackson, R.L., Gotto, A.M., Stein, O., & Stein, Y. (1975) J. Biol. Chem. 250, 7204-7209.

Kan, Y.W., & Dozy, A.M. (1978) Proc. Natl. Acad. Sci. USA 75, 5631-5635.

Karanthanasis, S.K., McPherson, J., Zannis, V.I., & Breslow, J.L. (1983) Nature (London) 304, 371-373.

Maciejko, J.J., Holmes, D.R., Kottke, B.A., Zinsmeister, A.R., Dinh, D.M., & Mao, S.J.T. (1983) New Engl. J. Med. 309, 385-389.

Miller, G.J., & Miller, N.E. (1975) Lancet 1, 16-19.

Miller, N.E., Nestel, P.J., & Clifton-Bligh, P. (1976) Atherosclerosis 23, 535-547.

Protter, A.A., Levy-Wilson, B., Miller, J., Bencen, G., White, T., & Seilhamer, J.J. (1984) DNA 3, 449-456.

Rees, A., Shoulders, C.C., Stocks, J., Galton, D.J., & Baralle, F.E. (1983) Lancet 1, 444-446.

Southern, E.M. (1975) J. Mol. Biol. 98, 503-517.

Stein, O., & Stein, Y. (1973) Biochim. Biophys. Acta 326, 232-244.

Stein, O., Vanderhoek, J., & Stein, Y. (1976) Biochim. Biophys. Acta 431, 347-358.

Weisgraber, K.H., Bersot, T.P., Mahley, R.W., Franceschini, G., and Sirtori, C.R. (1980) J. Clin. Invest. 66, 901-907.

Weisgraber, K.H., Rall, S.C., Bersot, T.P., Mahley, R.W., Franceschini, G., and Sirtori, C.R. (1983) J. Biol. Chem. 258, 2508-2513.

IMMUNOLOGICAL CHARACTERIZATION OF APOLIPOPROTEIN AI

FROM NORMAL HUMAN PLASMA: MAPPING OF ANTIGENIC DETERMINANTS

Peter Milthorp*, Philip K. Weech, Ross W. Milne
and Yves L. Marcel

Laboratory of Lipoprotein Metabolism, Clinical Research
Institute of Montreal, 110, Pine avenue west, Montreal
Quebec H2W 1R7, Canada

Apolipoprotein AI is the major apolipoprotein in normal human serum, where it is present within complex and heterogeneous populations of lipoproteins. Apo AI-containing lipoproteins may or may not contain apo AII[1-3], apo E [4] and their complexity is to date best shown by isoelectric focusing on agarose which demonstrates the presence of more than ten discrete fractions [5]. This heterogeneity of apo AI distribution in serum lipoproteins certainly contributed to the difficulties encountered in the definition of apo AI metabolism [6] and of apo AI immunological properties [7]. While it has been generally considered that apo AI does not always express all of its antigenic sites because of its amphipathic nature and its reaction with lipids[8-10], the effect of protein-protein interactions on apo AI configuration within complex lipoproteins could also be involved. Another important and sometimes overlooked factor which may affect the immunoreactivity of apo AI is the dynamic nature of intravascular lipid transport in which lipoprotein structure depends on the continual input and output of lipoproteins and on their interactions between themselves and with cell membranes and receptors. Because of its association with polydisperse lipoproteins and of its weak affinity for lipids relative to other apoproteins such as apo AII[11-12], apo AI distribution may be changed in vitro in serum samples resulting in a variation of its immunoreactivity.

---
*Present address: A-B Biologicals, Chedoke McMaster Hospitals, Southam Building, Sanatorium Road, Hamilton, Ontario L8N 3Z5, Canada.

103

For these reasons, the antigenic properties of apo AI must be defined both in its native state, that is in the form associated with lipoproteins, and in the isolated and purified state. Recently we have characterized three different antigenic determinants, referred to here as sites B, C and D, and which span respectively apo AI-CNBr fragments 1-2, 2 and 3 [13]. These determinants are recognized by a first series of monoclonal antibodies (series 1 MAB) which were generated by immunization and screening with purified apo AI [13]. Immunization of animals and screening of antibodies with purified apo AI may select MAB that react with determinants that are not normally expressed on the apolipoproteins associated with the native lipoproteins due to interaction with various lipids and apolipoproteins as reviewed above. To evaluate this possibility, we have generated a second series of MAB by immunization of mice with native HDL and by screening with both HDL and purified apo AI. We describe here the characterization of the determinants recognized by series 2 MAB and compare them to those reacting with series 1 MAB.

MATERIALS AND METHODS

Preparation of Sera and Lipoproteins

Sera were prepared from normolipidemic fasted subjects and stored at 4°C in sodium azide (0.02%). HDL was prepared from serum or plasma (without prestaining) by discontinuous density gradient centrifugation in a manner similar to that of Terpstra et al. [14]. HDL_3 was prepared by sequential centrifugation between the densities of 1.125 and 1.210 g/ml [13]. HDL and HDL_3 were dialysed, lyophilized, and delipidated with chloroform-methanol [15] to produce apo HDL or apo HDL_3. Apo AI was isolated from delipidated HDL_3 by preparative isoelectricfocusing [16]. Protein assays were performed by the method of Lowry et al. [17].

Monoclonal antibodies to apo AI

MAB to apo AI were produced by hybridomas resulting from the fusion of plasmacytoma SP2-0 and BALB/c mouse spleen cells. Production of series 1 MAB from mice immunized with purified apo AI have been described previously [13]. Series 2 MAB were produced by immunizing mice with freshly prepared HDL. This HDL was stored frozen at -20°C to minimize modification of apo AI immunogenicity. Series 2 MAB were selected by cloning cells that produced antibody reacting with fresh HDL, stored HDL and purified apo AI. Culture supernatants were used to determine the class and subclass of the MAB [18].

Iodination of antibodies

MAB were isolated from ascites fluid by selective elution of the appropriate subclass from protein-A Sepharose columns using a discontinuous pH gradient [19]. Iodination of the rabbit anti-mouse Ig and anti-apo AI MAB was performed according to Mellman and Unkeless [20] and has been described in detail elsewhere [21].

Antibody binding assay for the distinction of antigenic determinants

This method has been previously described by Stahli et al [22]. Immulon II wells (Dynatech Laboratories) were coated with apo HDL or HDL and were not saturated with ovalbumin as background binding was minimal. Reaction buffer (100 1; PBS pH 7.2, 0.05% Tween-20, 0.5% ovalbumin, 0.02% azide) containing a 1/250 dilution of the appropriate MAB was incubated in the well for 60 min at room temperature. This concentration of antibody was approximately four times that required to saturate all apo AI antigenic sites in the well. The wells were then washed three times with wash buffer (PBS containing 0.05% Tween-20 and 0.02% azide) and 50 1 (4-6 ng) of a second radiolabelled MAB (100,000 cpm) was added to each well. Wells were incubated for 60 min at room temperature and washed as above. The presence of equivalent MAB binding sites on apo AI was determined from the radioactivity bound to the wells.

Polyacrylamide gel electrophoresis, isoelectric focusing and immunoreaction of apo AI after electrophoretic transfer to nitrocellulose paper

The methods of Kane [23], Neville [24] and Warnick et al [25] were followed for alkaline-urea, SDS-polyacrylamide (15%) gel electrophoresis, and isoelectric focusing (pH 4-6), respectively. The separated proteins were transferred electrophoretically [26] to nitrocellulose paper which was then cut into strips corresponding to the lanes on the gel, some of which were stained with amido black to verify the transfer. The remaining strips were incubated with monoclonal ascitic fluid diluted 1/3000, and washed. The bound MAB was reacted with 1×10^6 cpm of ^{125}I-labelled rabbit anti-mouse Ig. The strips were washed, dried and autoradiographed on XAR-5 Kodak film with an intensifier screen (Cronex, DuPont).

RESULTS

The series of monoclonal antibodies reacting with apo AI which have been studied are identified as 5G6, 3D4, 5A6, and 6B8 for series 1 and 5F6, 4H1, 3G10, 2F1, 4F7 and 5C7 for series 2. In the latter series, four hybridomas secreted antibody of the IgG1 subclass (5F6, 4H1, 3G10, 2F1), one secreted IgG2a antibody (4F7), and one secreted IgM antibody (5C7).

Specificity of anti-apo AI monoclonal antibodies assessed by reaction with apo AI after gel electrophoresis and isoelectric focusing

Series 1 MAB have already been shown to react specifically with apo AI and apo AI-CNBr fragments that have been electrophoretically transferred to nitrocellulose paper[13]. In order to confirm that series 2 MAB reacted specifically with apo AI, either purified apo AI or apo HDL were separated by SDS-polyacrylamide gel electrophoresis. The protein bands were transferred electrophoretically to nitrocellulose paper and strips were then reacted individually with series 2 MAB. The autoradiograph demonstrated that all series 2 MAB reacted with a single band corresponding to a protein of about 28,000 daltons. To further document the specificity of the antibodies apo HDL was subjected to alkaline-urea polyacrylamide gel electrophoresis and treated as described above. All series 2 MAB reacted with one common band corresponding to the major isomorph of apo AI: AI-3, which segregates in this electrophoretic system.

Apo HDL was also separated by isoelectric focusing in the pH range 4 to 6 and the immunoreaction of the separated proteins showed that each MAB from series 2 reacted with all apo AI and pro apo AI isomorphs[27] as identified by their respective pI and by comparison with apo AI standards.

In summary, each MAB from series 2 reacted specifically with a protein, and all its isomorphs, that displayed the molecular weight and electrophoretic characteristics of apo AI, but we should note that antibodies 2F1 and 5C7 always displayed a weak reaction with the antigens transferred to nitrocellulose paper.

Mapping of antibody binding sites in apo AI

Binding sites were mapped by first reacting the solid phase antigen, either apo HDL or HDL, with a saturating concentration of one antibody and then with a trace amount of another antibody labelled with [125]I[22]. Maximal binding of labelled antibody indicates different binding sites for the two antibodies. No binding of labelled antibody indicates the same binding site. The same site in this case being defined as a single determinant or determinants close enough together to exclude simultaneous binding of their corresponding antibodies to the same molecule of apoAI. Greater than the expected maximal binding (enhancement) suggests that binding of one antibody stabilizes or induces a conformational form of the antigen which favours the binding of a second different antibody to a determinant located elsewhere on the same molecule of antigen.

An example of these experiments is shown in Figure 1 where

apo HDL is used as the solid phase antigen. As the quantity of 3D4 and 3G10 bound to the solid phase antigen approaches saturation, the binding of ^{125}I-labelled 3G10 is decreased proprotionately. On the other hand as the amount of 4H1 bound to the antigen approaches saturation no decrease in binding of ^{125}I-labelled 3G10 is evident. These results suggest that 3G10 and 3D4 bind at the same location on apo AI and that 4H1 binds at a site different from that recognized by 3G10.

The results of all mapping experiments are summarized in Table 1. These results are expressed as per cent inhibition of maximum binding of the labelled second MAB by the first MAB at saturating concentrations. Negative numbers indicate that in the presence of the first antibody, the binding of the second labelled antibody is enhanced. It should be noted that in all cases inhibition or enhancement of binding was proportional to the quantity of first antibody used in the experiments (Fig. 1).

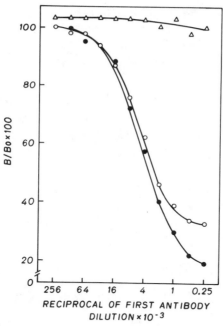

Figure 1: Cotitration of monoclonal antibodies. Cotitration was performed sequentially as described under methods. Initial dilution of the first unlabelled monoclonal antibodies 3G10 (o), 3D4 (●), 4H1 (▲) was 1/250. Concentration of the second labelled monoclonal antibody 3G10 was 0.16 g/ml. Each point represents the average of duplicate samples.

It can be seen that not all interactions were reciprocal or complete. Three major antigenic sites on apo AI had been mapped previously[13] with series 1 MAB (5G6, 3D4, 5A6 and 6B8); 5G6 reacts at a site B, 5A6 and 3D4 are located at the same site C, and 6B8 binds at site D. The present experiments confirm these results and extend them. Of the series 2 MAB, 3G10 maps next to site C, 5F6 maps at site D. Since neither 4H1 nor 2F1 inhibited the binding of the other very efficiently it is likely that they bind in the same region of apo AI but not at the same location. It can be seen that the IgM, 5C7, can block the binding of some of the MAB at all three major antigenic loci, however not all antibodies binding at these sites were blocked, 4F7 also behaved in an anomalous fashion. It should be noted that 4F7 did not block its own binding, but that binding of 3D4 or 5A6 at site C, or 6B8 or 5F6 at site D block the binding of 4F7 to apo AI. In contrast, binding of 3G10 caused enhanced binding of 4F7, and the binding of 4H1 to its determinant caused an even greater enhanced binding of 4F7 (Table 1).

Table 1: Summary of the cotitration of monoclonal anti-AI antibodies. Percent inhibition of binding.

First MAB	Radiolabelled second MAB						
	5F6	4H1	3G10	2F1	4F7	6B8	3D4
5F6	84	-4	1	-5	79	88	25
4H1	21	90	-6	38	-854	26	34
3G10	6	-24	68	2	-246	34	73
2F1	11	34	12	74	-67	35	28
4F7	2	23	-19	-5	-20	18	32
6B8	68	26	8	0	79	88	-12
3D4	15	17	80	3	80	4	95
5A6	8	19	60	2	68	-30	89
5C7	6	32	5	4	-43	51	61

Apo HDL was bound to the solid phase and the two MABs were bound sequentially.

a. % inhibition = $1 - \dfrac{\text{binding of labelled MAB with MAB}}{\text{binding of labelled MAB without MAB}} \times 100$

The magnitude of inhibition or enhancement was proportional to the quantity of first MAB used in the experiments (see text and Fig.1).

The results using HDL immobilized on the well as a solid phase antigen showed the same spatial relationship between the antigenic sites as described above (results not shown). Differences in conformation if any between free apo A-I and apo A-I in HDL are not, therefore, detected with these antibodies and by this technique.

Location of antigenic determinants on apo AI CNBr-fragments

The location of the individual antigenic determinants identified by series 2 MAB on apo AI-CNBr fragments was also determined. Apo AI-CNBr fragments were separated by alkaline-urea polyacrylamide gel electrophoresis and subsequently transferred to nitrocellulose paper for immunoblotting experiments, as described in detail in a previous study [13] . All the results were consistent with and defined further the conclusions of the mapping by competitive immunoassays as described above.

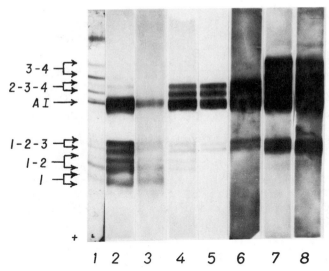

Figure 2: Autoradiography of antibody reaction with CNBr-cleaved fragments of apo AI. CNBr cleaved apo AI was electrophoresed on alkaline-urea polyacrylamide gel, electrophoretically transfered to nitrocellulose paper and individual strips were reacted with the different antibodies as identified. 1, amido black stain of the separated proteins. 2 to 8, autoradiography of the replica after reaction with individual antibodies: 4H1, 2F1, 3G10, 4F7, 5A6, 6B8, and 5F6.

Antibody 4H1 clearly identified a site different from all the other antibodies from either series 1 or 2, and reacted with CNBr fragments 1, 1-2, and 1-2-3, but not with fragment 2-3-4 (Fig. 2). Therefore 4H1 recognized a determinant which we identified as site A for further reference and which is located on CNBr fragment 1. Antibody 2F1 also reacted with the same fragments as 4H1 although as noted above 2F1 reactions in all immunoblots was generally weak. Thus 2F1 also recognized a determinant on CNBr fragment 1, but the lack of strong competition between 4H1 and 2F1 noted in radioimmunoassays indicated that the determinants for 4H1 and 2F1 are probably at different loci on CNBr fragment 1, and will be referred to as sites A and A' respectively (fig. 3).

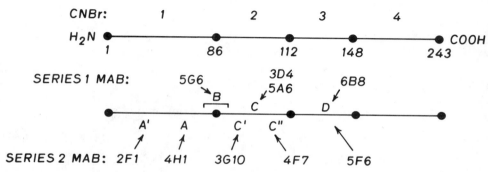

Figure 3:   A linear representation of the proposed spatial relationships of the antigenic determinants on apo AI recognized by the different MAB from series 1 and 2. The positions of the determinants have been assigned from the results of the reactions of antibodies with CNBr-fragments and of the competitive antibody assays.

4F7 reacted only with partial fragments 1-2-3 and 2-3-4 (Fig. 2) and thus recognized a determinant on fragment 2 or 3 (Fig. 3). Antibody 3G10 reacted with partial fragments 1-2, 1-2-3 and 2-3-4 but not with fragments 1, 3-4 or 4 (Fig. 2) and therefore recognized a determinant on fragment 2 but at a site different from that for 4F7 or 5A6 because the later 2 MAB do not react with partial fragment 1-2 . From this we concluded that 3G10 recognized a different determinant on CNBr-fragment 2 (Fig. 3).

Finally antibody 5F6 exhibited the same specificity as 6B8 from series 1 [13] and reacted only with partial fragments 1-2-3, 2-3-4 and 3-4 (Fig. 2) and therefore also reacted at site D on CNBr fragment 3 (Fig. 3) in agreement with the competition noted above between 5F6 and 6B8.

DISCUSSION

In the present studies we have been able to identify antigenic determinants present on apo AI associated with native HDL and to compare them with the determinants previously characterized on purified and isolated apo AI [13]. The antibodies from series 2 like those from the first series react with proteins with the molecular weight and the pI described for apo AI. All the MAB react with each isomorph of apo AI including those of pro apo AI [27] which demonstrates that the determinants are present on apo AI molecules independently of their polymorphic nature.

Series 2 MAB were produced by immunization with HDL and screening with both HDL and apo AI. This was done in an attempt to produce MAB that reacted with exposed apo AI determinants on HDL. This approach was partially successful as four of our series 2 MAB (4H1, 3G10, 5F6 and 4F7) were found to react equally well with apo AI in sera, HDL, apo HDL and in its pure form, and because various delipidating and denaturing treatments failed to modify their reaction with sera (Milthorp, Weech, Milne and Marcel, manuscript in preparation). This suggests that these MAB react with non-cryptic sites in HDL and that these sites are not degraded during the purification of apo AI.

The methods of determination of apo AI antigenic determinants by solid phase radioimmunoassay [22] and reaction of MAB with CNBr fragments of apo AI have located a total of seven binding sites for the nine MAB mapped (Fig. 3). CNBr fragment 1 (residues 1 to 86) contains the binding sites for 4H1 and 2F1. These two MAB interact weakly on cotitration and 2F1 reacts only poorly with material transferred to nitrocellulose paper. We therefore suggest that 2F1 does not bind to the same determinant (site A') as 4H1 (site A). As noted previously 5G6 appears to bind at a site B located on the boundary of CNBr fragments 1 and 2 [13]. CNBr fragment 2 (residues 86-112) binds four of the nine monoclonal antibodies studied.

MAB 3G10 interacted strongly with 3D4 and 5A6 in cotitration experiments indicating identity of binding sites. However binding to CNBr fragments indicates that although 3G10 binds to CNBr fragment 2, its specificity is different in that it binds partial fragment 1-2 whereas 5A6 and 3D4 which react at a site C do not. Therefore we attributed to 3G10 a binding site C' on fragment 2 which is different from site C. The binding pattern of 4F7 to

CNBr fragments indicated that it could react to either fragment 2 or 3. However it does not react with either partial fragments 1-2 or 3-4 and therefore its binding site could be close to the cleavage points at residues 86 or 112 or 148. But because in cotitration experiments, 4F7 binding is enhanced by 4H1 and 3G10 while being inhibited by both 3D4, 5A6 and 5F6, 6B8, we concluded that 4F7 should be mapped at a site C" located on fragment 2 and close to residue 112. (Fig. 3). MAB 5F6 interacts strongly with 6B8 in cotitration experiments and both MAB react identically with CNBr fragments. The binding site (D) of these two MAB is on CNBr fragment 3 (residues 112 to 148). The fact that determinants for series 2 MAB 4H1, 3G10 and 5F6 are located on the first three CNBr fragments (residues 1-148) suggests that this portion of the apo AI molecule is exposed on the surface of HDL. The lack of selection of any MAB for determinants on the C-terminal end of the apo AI molecules suggests that residues 148 to 243 are poorly antigenic in the mouse.

The enhanced binding of 4F7 by prior binding of either 4H1 or 3G10 to apo HDL is unusual but has been noted before for other pairs of MAB directed against antigens other than apo AI[28-30]. The fact that 4F7 is unable to compete with itself in sequential cotitration experiments suggests that it binds poorly to apo AI although this is not apparent when using 4F7 in solid phase RIA or in its reaction with apo AI transferred electrophoretically to nitrocellulose paper. A possible explanation for these unusual results may be that the 4F7 antigenic determinant is present in an unstable region of apo AI. Binding of 4H1 at site A or 3G10 at site C' may change apo AI conformation and stabilize the molecule thus enhancing the binding of 4F7 at site C. Therefore if theory and interpretation of the results are correct, these inhibitions and enhancements between pairs of antibodies also suggest that all these antigenic sites are found on the same molecule, and not on different apo AI molecules.

If we consider the secondary structure of apo AI as predicted by Chou and Fasman rules[31-32] from the apo AI sequence[33], we observe that a large number of B-turns are located toward the N-terminus of the molecule and consequently the chain from residues 1 to 148 represents a densely packed region where α-helices and β-sheets are positioned next to one another (Fig. 4). This packing within the molecule in the N-terminal region, where all the antigenic determinants identified by MAB from series 1 and 2 are located, explains how binding of antibodies to determinants seemingly remote on the primary structure but closer on the secondary structure may result in partial inhibition or in enhanced binding.

The fact that MAB from 2 different immunization procedures and from 2 different fusions identify determinants that are localized on CNBr-fragments 1, 2 and 3 toward the N-terminal of the molecule indicate that this region is the most antigenic in the mouse. Our results are in agreement with those of Schonfeld and colleagues who characterized MAB that react with determinants localized on CNBr-fragments 1 and 3 of human apo AI [34]. In contrast, in earlier studies using polyclonal antibodies to human apo AI raised in the rabbit, the same group had observed a different specificity, namely that the carboxy-terminal fragment of apo AI was the most antigenic [9,35]. It is likely that these opposite results are related to species specificity and reflects the different antigenicity of human apo AI in the mouse and in the rabbit. Thus because CNBr-fragments 1, 2 and 3 on the N-terminal region of apo AI are antigenic in the mouse, it is unlikely that the N-terminal region is masked by lipids, as proposed earlier for the interpretation of results with antisera raised in the rabbit[35].

In conclusion, we have characterized seven distinct antigenic determinants on apo AI which span CNBr-fragments 1, 2 and 3 on the N-terminal side. By virtue of the screening strategy which we adopted most of the antibodies from series 2 react with determinants whose expression is independent of the presence of lipids.

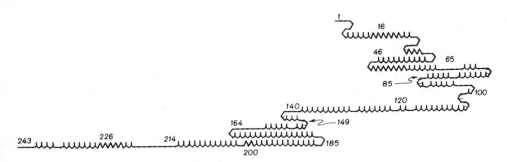

Figure 4:   Secondary structure of apo AI as predicted by Chou and Fasman rules. (Reprinted with permission of Pergamon Press Ltd from ref. 36).

REFERENCES

1. M.C. Cheung, J.J. Albers, Characterization of lipoprotein particles isolated by immunoaffinity. Particles containing AI and AII and particles containing AI but no AII. J. Biol. Chem. 259: 12201 (1984).

2. P.I. Norfeldt, S.O. Olofsson, G. Fager, and G. Bondjers, Isolation and characterization of the lipoprotein families A and AI from high density lipoproteins of human serum. Eur. J. Biochem. 118:1 (1981).

3. A.C. Nestruck, P.D. Niedman, H. Wieland, and D. Seidel, Chromatofocusing of human high density lipoproteins and isolation of lipoproteins A and AI. Biochim. Biophys. Acta 753: 65 (1983).

4. Y.L. Marcel, C. Vézina, D. Emond, and G. Suzue, Human high density lipoprotein heterogeneity presence of lipoproteins with and without apo E and their roles as substrates for lecithin:cholesterol acyltransferase. Proc. Natl. Acad. Sci. USA 77: 2969 (1980).

5. Y.L. Marcel, P.K. Weech, T.-D. Nguyen, R.W. Milne, and W.J. McConathy, Apolipoproteins as the basis for heterogeneity in high density lipoprotein$_2$ and high density lipoprotein$_3$. Studies by isoelectricfocusing on agarose films. Eur. J. Biochim. 143; 467 (1984).

6. S. Eisenberg, High density lipoprotein metabolism. J. Lipid Res. 25: 1017 (1984).

7. K.K. Steinberg, G.R. Cooper, S.R. Graiser, and M. Rosseneu, Some considerations of methodology and standardization of apoprotein AI immunoassays. Clin. Chem. 29: 415 (1983).

8. G. Schonfeld, and B. Pfleger, The structure of human high density lipoprotein and the levels of apolipoprotein AI in plasma as determined by radioimmunoassay. J. Clin. Invest. 54: 236 (1974).

9. G. Schonfeld, J.S. Chen, and R.G. Roy, Use of antibody specificity to study the surface disposition of apoprotein AI in human high density lipoproteins. J. Biol. Chem. 252: 6655 (1977).

10. S.J.T. Mao, J.P. Miller, A.M. Gotto Jr., and J.T. Sparrow, The antigenic structure of apolipoprotein AI in human high density lipoproteins. Radioimmunoassay using surface-specific antibodies. J. Biol. Chem. 255: 3448 (1980).

11. P.A. Lagocki, and A.M. Scanu, In vitro modulation of the apolipoprotein composition of high density lipoprotein. J. Biol. Chem. 255: 3701 (1980).

12. C. Edelstein, M. Halari, and A.M. Scanu, On the mechanism of the displacement of apolipoprotein AI by apolipoprotein AII from the high density lipoprotein surface. Effect of concentration and molecular forms of apolipoprotein AII. J. Biol. Chem. 257: 7189 (1982).

13. P.K. Weech, R.W. Milne, P. Milthorp, and Y.L. Marcel, Apolipoprotein AI from normal human plasma. Definition of three distinct antigenic determinants. Biochim. Biophys. Acta, in press, 1985.

14. A.H.M. Terpstra, C.J.H. Woodward, F.J. Sanchez-Muniz, Improved techniques for the separation of serum lipoproteins by density gradient ultracentrifugation. Visualization by prestaining and rapid separation of serum lipoproteins from small volumes of serum. Anal Biochem 111: 149 (1981).

15. S.-O. Olofsson, W.J. McConathy, and P. Alaupovic, Isolation and partial characterization of a new acidic apolipoprotein (apolipoprotein F) from high density lipoproteins of human plasma. Biochemistry 17: 1032 (1978).

16. A.C. Nestruck, G. Suzue, and Y.L. Marcel, Studies on the polymorphism of human apolipoprotein A-I. Biochim. Biophys. Acta 617: 1210 (1980).

17. O.H. Lowry, M.J. Rosebrough, A.L. Farr, and R.J. Randall, Protein measurement with the Folin phenol reagent. J. Biol. Chem. 193: 265 (1951).

18. M.P. Chalon, R.W. Milne, and J.P. Vaerman, In vitro immunosuppressive effect of serum from orally immunized mice. Eur. J. Immunol. 9: 747 (1979).

19. P.L. Ey, S.J. Prowse, and C.R.Jenkin, Isolation of pure IgG1, IgG2a and IgG2b immunoglobulin from mouse serum using protein A Sepharose. Immunochem 15: 429 (1978).

20. I.S. Mellman, and J.C. Unkeless, Purification of a functional mouse Fc receptor through the use of a monoclonal antibody. J. Exp. Med. 152: 1048 (1980).

21. R.W. Milne, R. Théolis Jr., R.B. Verdery, and Y.L. Marcel, Characterization of monoclonal antibodies against human low density lipoprotein. Arteriosclerosis 3: 23 (1983).

22. C. Stahli, V. Miggiano , J. Stocker, Th. Staehlin, P. Haring, and B. Takacs, Distinction of epitopes by monoclonal antibodies. Methods in Enzymology 92: 242 (1983).

23. J.P. Kane, A rapid electrophoresis technique for identification of subunit species of apoproteins in serum lipoproteins. Anal. Biochem. 53: 350 (1973).

24. D.M. Neville, Molecular weight determination of protein dodecyl sulphate complexes by gel electrophoresis in a discontinuous buffer system. J. Biol. Chem. 246: 6328 (1971).

25. G.R. Warnick, C. Mayfield, J.J. Albers, and W.R. Hazzard, Gel isoelectric focusing method for specific diagnosis of familial hyperlipoprotinemia type III. Clin. Chem 25: 279 (1979).

26. H. Towbin, T. Staehelin, and J. Gordon, Electrophoretic transfer of proteins from polyacrylamide gels to nitrocellulose sheets: procedure and some applications. Proc. Natl. Acad. Sci. USA 76: 4350 (1979).

27. V.I. Zannis, J.L. Breslow, and A.J. Katz, Isoproteins of human apolipoprotein A-I demonstrated in plasma and intestinal organ culture. J. Biol. Chem. 255: 8612 (1980).

28. R. Tosi, N. Tanigaki, R. Sorrentino, R. Accolla, and G. Corte, Binding of one monoclonal antibody to human Ia molecules can be enhanced by a second monoclonal antibody. Eur. J. Immunol. 11: 721 (1981).

29. P.H. Ehrlich, W.R. Moyle, Z.A. Moustafa, and R.E. Canfield, Mixing two monoclonal antibodies yields enhanced affinity for antigen. J. Immunol. 128: 2709 (1982).

30. N.J. Holmes, and P. Parham, Enhancement of monoclonal antibodies against HLA-A2 is due to antibody bivalency. J. Biol. Chem. 258: 1580 (1983).

31. P.Y. Chou, and G.D. Fasman, Conformational parameters for amino acids in helical B-sheets and random coil regions calculated from proteins. Biochemistry 13: 211 (1974).

32. P.Y. Chou, and G.D. Fasman, Prediction of protein conformation. Biochemistry 13: 222 (1974).

33. H.B. Brewer Jr., T. Fairwell, A. LaRue, R. Ronan, A. Houser, T.J. Bronzert, The amino acid sequence of human apo AI, an apolipoprotein isolated from high density lipoproteins. Biochem. Biophys. Res. Commun. 80: 623 (1978).

34. G. Schonfeld, T. Kitchens, R. Dargar, Site specific anti human apo AI monoclonal antibodies. Arteriosclerosis 4, 566a (1984).

35. G. Schonfeld, R.A. Bradshaw, J.-S. Chen, Structure of high density lipoproteins. The immunologic reactivities of the COOH and NH_2-terminal regions of apolipoprotein AI. J. Biol. Chem. 251: 3921 (1976).

36. Y.L. Marcel, P.K. Weech, P. Milthorp, F. Tercé, C. Vézina and R.W. Milne. Monoclonal antibodies and characterization of apolipoprotein structure and function in Progress in Lipid Research, vol. 23, part 3, R.T. Holman, ed., Pergamon Press Ltd, Oxford, in press.

ACKNOWLEDGEMENTS

We are indebted to Dr. H.B. Brewer Jr. for his generous gift of purified apo AI-CNBr fragments, to T.D. N'guyen for her technical assistance and to Drs. A. Fuks and G. Price for helpful discussions. Louise Lalonde gave excellent secretarial help.

These studies were supported by grants from the Medical Research Council of Canada (PG-27) and the Quebec Heart Foundation. Dr. P. Milthorp is a recipient of an Industrial Research Fellowship (Natural Sciences and Engineering Research Council of Canada) with A-B Biological Supplies Inc., Hamilton, Ontario. Dr. R.W. Milne is a scholar of the Fondation de la Recherche en Santé du Québec.

LIPID BINDING PROPERTIES OF HUMAN APO A1 MUTANTS

M. Rosseneu[1], H. De Loof[1], G. Assmann[2], U. Jabs[2], and M. Phillips[3]

Dept. of Clinical Biochemistry, A.Z. St-Jan, Brugge, Belgium
Zentr. Labo. Univ. Munster. Munster, Germany
Medical College of Pennsylvania, Philadelphia, PA 19129

INTRODUCTION

Since the first apo A1 mutant, called apo A1 Milano, was reported by Franceschini et al (1,2), several other apo A1 mutants have been discovered and characterized (3,4).
As these mutants were detected by isofocusing, they all involve one or more mutations at charged residues. These mutations occur at different locations in the apoprotein sequence so that some of them might influence the apoprotein-lipid association. We have studied the lipid binding properties of several of these apo A1 mutants, isolated in Munster in the course of a screening program, and report on a comparison of their association properties with synthetic lipids, to those of normal apo A1. Such data should provide information about the structure-function relationship in apo A1 and other related apoproteins.

MATERIALS AND METHODS

Apoprotein isolation and characterization

The apo A1 isoforms in the mutants were identified by analytical gel isofocusing in a 4-6 pH gradient and isolated by preparative isofocusing under the same experimental conditions (5). The purity of the isolated isoforms was verified by analytical isofocusing and by amino acid analysis.
The apo A1 mutants were further characterized by peptide mapping and tryptic digestion. The peptides were isolated by HPLC and the mutations localized and identified by sequence analysis of the particular segment (4).

The study of the apo AI-lipid association was carried out with synthetic dimyristoyl lecithin liposomes, prepared by sonication (6,7). It involved complex isolation by density-gradient ultracentrifugation and gel chromatography (7), monitoring of the tryptophanyl fluorescence emission,of the fluorescence polarisation after labeling with diphenyl hexatriene (8) and measurement of circular dichroism.All fluorescence studies were carried out on a Aminco SF 5000 spectrofluorimeter and the circular dichroism was measured on a Jasco spectropolarimeter.Protein concentrations were assayed by amino acid analysis.

Table 1. Amino acid substitutions in the apo AI variants.

APO AI VARIANT	MUTATION
MUNSTER 2	ALA158-GLU
MUNSTER 2	LYS106-0
MUNSTER 3	PRO4-ARG
MUNSTER 3	ASP103-ASN
MUNSTER 3	PRO3-HIS
MUNSTER 3	ASP213-GLY
MUNSTER 4	GLU198-LYS
MARBURG	LYS 107-0
GIESSEN	PRO143-ARG
MILANO	ARG173-CYS

RESULTS

1-Complex isolation and characterization

The apo AI mutations identified in the Munster population are summarized in table 1. The Munster 2, 3, 4 notation correspond to the position of the variant on the isofocusing gel. The pI differences can be due to either the introduction of a negative charge or the deletion of a positive residue (Munster 2 variant). The Munster 3 variant has one negative charge less than the normal isoform, while there is a difference of two charge units between the normal and variant isoforms of the subject with the Munster 4 pattern.The complexes between these isoforms and unilamellar DMPC liposomes were fractionated in a salt gradient at densities between 1.05 and 1.15 (6,9), fig 1A. As previously reported for normal apo AI (6), two complexes could be resolved by this technique. A lipid-rich complex was fractionated at a density around 1.09, while a protein-rich complex floated at a density of 1.11 g/ml. In all apo AI mutants, both the normal and the variant isoforms could recombine with lipids (table 2). The Munster 2 variant with the Ala 158-Glu substitution, behaved differently as three complexes could be separated by isopycnic ultracentrifugation (fig.1B). The third complex at a density of 1.13 g/ml contained about 40% of the apoprotein present in the original mixture. This protein-rich complex had a mean

120

composition of 57 mol DMPC/mol apo AI, compared to 237 and 107 mol/mol for the two other complexes. After gel chromatography on a Sepharose 6B-CL column, complexes of similar composition could also be isolated between DMPC and the mutant apo AI proteins.

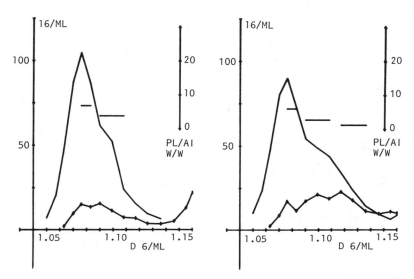

Fig. 1. Isolation of the complexes formed between DMPC and the ALA158-GLU mutant. A:normal isoform; B:variant isoform.

Table 2.Density and percentage of protein in the complexes formed between DMPC and apo AI normal and variant isoforms.

MUTATION	ISO-FORM	COMP.1		COMP.2		COMP.3	
		D g/ml	%PR	D g/ml	%PR	D g/ml	%PR
ALA158-GLU	M	1.08	26.6	1.10	32.3	1.13	41.2
	N	1.08	41.1	1.10	58.9		
ASP213-GLY	M	1.09	72.3	1.11	27.7		
	N			1.10	100		
LYS107-0	M	1.09	64.7	1.11	35.3		
	N	1.09	52.6	1.11	47.4		
ASP103-ASN	M	1.09	42.3	1.11	57.7		
	N	1.09	53.6	1.11	46.4		
GLU198-LYS	M			1.10	100		
	N	1.09	54.2	1.11	45.8		
PRO4-ARG	M	1.09	44.7	1.11	56.3		
	N	1.09	62.8	1.11	38.2		
NORMAL APO AI		1.09	43.4	1.11	56.6		

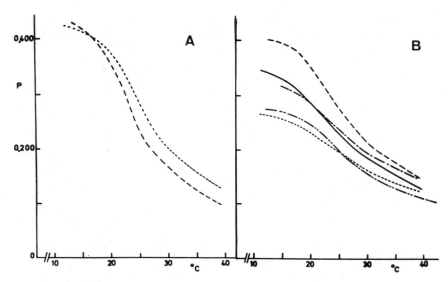

Fig 2. Fluorescence polarisation ratio of apo AI-DMPC complexes labeled with diphenyl hexatriene. A: DMPC(-----); DMPC +normal apo AI (-----).   B: DMPC(-----); DMPC +apo AI variant Ala158-Glu after 1h(———); 2h(-----); 3h(-----); 4h(-----) incubation.

2-Fluorescence properties of the apo AI mutants and of the apo AI-DMPCcomplexes

The intensity of the maximum of the trytophanyl fluorescence emission was measured both in the native protein and the apo AI-DMPC complexes. Lipid binding to apo AI was accompanied by a blue shift of about 5 nm and an increase in the intensity of the trytophanyl emission of 20-25%.

Fluorescence polarization, after labeling with diphenyl hexatriene (DPH), was applied to the monitoring of the fluidity of the lipid phase of the complexes. In agreement with previous observations on DMPC and DMPC-cholesterol complexes with apo AI, most of the apo AI mutants decreased the lipid fluidity, upon their association with the phospholipid (fig 2A). In contrast, the mutant protein with the Ala158-Glu substitution, increased the fluidity of DMPC (fig 2B) and this effect increased with the incubation time. Similar data were obtained with cholesterol-DMPC mixtures at ratios up to 20 mol%. As a consequence of the increased fluidity in the complex, the transition of the phospholipid was shifted toward lower temperatures, compared to that of pure DMPC or DMPC-cholesterol mixtures.

3-Circular dichroism of apo AI mutants and of the apoprotein-lipid complexes

The helical content of the normal and variant isoforms of the Ala158-Glu apo AI mutant was not significantly different from that of the corresponding isoform of apo AI. An increase in helical content by about 15% was observed upon association of the mutant apo AI isoforms with DMPC, a value close to that measured with normal apo AI (10).

4-Stability of the apo AI mutants and of the lipid complexes

The stability of both the normal and variant isoforms of the apo AI mutants was followed by monitoring the trytophanyl emission, as protein unfolding is accompanied by a red shift and a decreased intensity of the trytophanyl emission (8). Exposure of the apo AI mutants isoforms to increasing pH induced a protein conformational change around pH 10.5 to 11. In the presence of lipids, the transition was shifted to pH 11.5 to 12, due to the protective effect of the lipids (9) .With GdmCl, denaturation occurs at concentrations around 1mol/L for the native protein and 3 to 4 mol/L for the apo AI-DMPC complexes.
These denaturation profiles were similar for all mutants and for the apoprotein-lipid complexes.

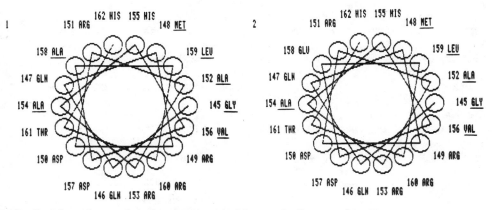

Fig 3. Edmundson-wheel representation of the apo AI helical segment between residues 145-162, in 1: normal apo AI. 2:Ala158-Glu apo AI variant. Apolar residues are underlined.

Table 3.Influence of the mutations on the hydrophobic moment $\langle\mu_i\rangle$ and hydrophobicity $\langle H_i\rangle$ of the helical segments of apoAI.

Mutation	Segment	$\langle\mu_i\rangle$	$\langle H_i\rangle$
	103-119	.37	-.45
LYS107-0	103-119	.27	-.39
	125-139	.43	-.36
PRO143-ARG	125-162	.42	-.47
	143-162	.39	-.39
ALA158-GLU	143-162	.36	-.46
	167-181	.21	-.31
ARG173-CYS	167-181	.21	-.12

5-Prediction of the lipid-protein binding zones in apo AI

The apo AI protein, in analogy with other apoproteins, such as apo AII and apo CIII, has a high helical content which increases upon association with phospholipids (10). Using the theoretical calculations of Chou and Fasman (11), one can predict the most probable location of these helical segments. Seven helical segments, with a minimal length of 11 residues, could be identified in a region between residues 74 and 238. Most of these helical segments are located within the repetitive sequences identified in apo AI (12).
Among the apoAI mutants listed in table 1, most of the mutations did not significantly affect the helical content of apo AI, predicted theoretically. This agrees with the experimental observations on the Ala158-Glu mutant. The apo AI Giessen mutant, with a Pro143-Arg mutation has a significantly higher helical content in the region around the mutation, as the proline residue in the normal apoAI has a strong helix-breaking capacity. There is however no report about the lipid-binding properties of this particular mutant protein. The helical segments, predicted in apo AI can be further characterized by their hydrophobicity $\langle H_i\rangle$ and their mean helical moment $\langle\mu_i\rangle$, as proposed by Eisenberg et al. (13) and by Krebs and Phillips (14). These values are summarized in table 3, showing that the Ala158-Glu mutation increases the hydrophilic character of this segment and slightly decreases its hydrophobic moment. Other significant changes appear with the mutations: LYS107-0, PRO143-ARG and ARG173-CYS.
The configuration of the helical segment between residues 146 and 163 is illustrated on fig 3 in the normal and (Ala158-Glu)

mutant protein. The segregation of the polar and apolar
residues on each side of the helix and the amphipathic
character of this segment is illustrated on this
Edmundson-wheel representation.
Segrest et al (15), have proposed that apoprotein-lipid
association most likely involves amphipathic helical
segments,such as the one depicted on fig 3. It is not clear
however,whether all or only some of these segments are involved
in lipid binding.
The segments, most likely to associate with lipids should have
the following features:an average to high hydrophobicity,be
adjacent to a segment with a coil structure, as this structure
requires least energy to become helicoidal and have a high
hydrophobic moment corresponding to a pronounced amphipathic
character.
Within apo AI, helical segments fulfilling such criteria are :
74-85, 103-119, 125-139, 143-162, 167-181, 186-205, 220-243.
Among the mutations described above, none of the amino acid
substitutions or deletions would prevent meeting the
requirements postulated for lipid binding, in any of the
helical segments.

DISCUSSION

In this paper we compared the lipid binding properties of the
normal and mutant isoforms of several apo AI mutants to those
of normal apo AI and tried to develop a semi-theoretical basis
for the prediction of lipid binding segments in apo AI and in
these mutants.
The physico-chemical properties of the mutant proteins did not
significantly differ from those of normal apo AI, and the same
was observed with the DMPC complexes. Only the Ala158-Glu
mutation affected both the composition and the lipid fluidity
of the complex. A protein-rich complex was isolated with this
particular mutant with a lipid fluidity higher than that of the
pure lecithin. As this mutation increases the hydrophilic
character of this helical segment , the variant protein might
preferentially interact with the surface of the lipid.The
insertion of protein segments between the phospholipid head
groups, would account for the increased fluidity in contrast
with an impaired mobility of the fatty acyl chains reported
previously for normal apo AI-phospholipid association.
Theoretical calculations on the most probable location of the
helical segments in apo AI, together with an analysis of their
hydrophobicity and hydrophobic moment enabled a temptative
location of the lipid-binding segments in apo AI. A comparison
of the data obtained for normal apo AI and for the mutants
predicts that the mutations identified in the Munster
population should not significantly affect the lipid binding

properties of the apo AI protein. These theoretical
calculations are therefore supported by the "in vitro"data
reported in this paper as well as by the HDL levels of the
probands, in whom the mutations were identified (4). The study
of new mutants of apo AI and of other apoproteins should enable
a better correlation between structural and functional
properties of the plasma apoproteins.

REFERENCES
1.G.Franceschini,C.R.Sirtori, A.Capurso, K.H.Weisgraber, and
R.W.Mahley.A-I Milano Apoprotein.Decreased high density
lipoprotein cholesterol levels with significant lipoprotein
modifications and without clinical atherosclerosis in an
italian family.J.Clin.Invest.66:892 (1980).
2.K.Weisgraber, T.P.Bersot, R.W.Mahley, G.Franceschini, and
C.R.Sirtori .A-I$_{Milano}$ Apoprotein.Isolation and
characterization of a cysteine-containing variant of the A-I
protein from human high density lipoproteins.
J.Clin.Invest.66:901 (1980).
3.G.Utermann, A.Steinmetz, R.Paetzold, J.Wilk, G.Feussner,
H.Kaffarnik, C.Mueller-Eckhardt, D.Seidel, K-H Vogelberg, and
F.Zimmer.Apolipoprotein AI$_{Marburg}$.Studies on two kindreds with
a mutant of apolipoprotein AI.Hum.Genet 61:329 (1982).
4.H-J.Menzel, G.Assmann, S.C.Rall, K.H.Weisgraber, and
R.W.Mahley. Human apolipoprotein A-I polymorphism :
identification of amino acid substitutions in three
electrophoretic variants of the Munster-3 type.
J.Biol.Chem. 259:3070 (1984).
5. H-J.Menzel, R-G.Kladetzky, and G.Assmann. One-step screening
method for the polymorphism of apolipoproteins A-I, A-II, and
A-IV. J.Lipid Res.23:915 (1982).
6.70 P.Van Tornout, H.Caster, M.J.Lievens, M.Rosseneu and
G.Assmann."In vitro" interaction of human HDL with
apolipoprotein AII.Synthesis of AII-rich HDL.
Biochim.Biophys.Acta 663:630 (1981)
7.M.Rosseneu, P.Van Tornout, M.J.Lievens and G.Assmann.
Displacement of the human apoprotein AI by the human apoprotein
AII from complexes of (apoprotein AI)
-phosphatidylcholine-cholesterol. Eur.J.Biochem .117:347 (1981)
8..M.Rosseneu, P.Van Tornout, M.Lievens, H.Caster, and
G.Assmann. Dissociation of the apo AI protein from
apoprotein-phospholipid complexes and from HDL.A fluorescence
study. Eur.J.Biochem. 128:455 (1982).
9.M.Rosseneu, G.Schmitz, M.J.Taveirne and G.Assmann. Lipid
binding properties of the Tangier apo AI protein and of its
major isoproteins. J.Lipid Res. 25:111 (1984).
10.R.L.Jackson, J.D.Morrisett and A.M.Gotto. Lipoprotein
structure and metabolism. Physiol.Rev. 56:259 (1976).
11.P.Y.Chou, and G.D.Fasman. Conformational parameters for
amino acids in helical,beta-sheet and random coil regions
calculated from proteins. Biochemistry 13:211 (1974).

12.A.D.McLachlan. Repeated helical pattern in apolipoprotein A-I. Nature 267:465 (1977).

13.D.Eisenberg. Three-dimensional structure of membrane and surface proteins. Ann.Rev.Biochem. 53:595 (1984).

14.K.E.Krebs and M.Phillips. The contribution of alpha-helices to the surface activities of proteins.FEBS Lett. 175:263 (1984).

15.J.P.Segrest, R.L.Jackson, J.D.Morrisett, and A.M.Gotto. A molecular theory of lipid-protein interactions in the plasma lipoproteins. FEBS Lett. 38:247 (1974).

RECENT STUDIES ON THE METABOLIC DEFECT IN TANGIER DISEASE

Brewer, H.B., Jr., Bojanovski, D., Gregg, R.E., and
Law, S.W.

Molecular Disease Branch, National Heart, Lung, and
Blood Institute National Institutes of Health
Bethesda, MD. 20892

INTRODUCTION

Tangier disease is a rare familial dyslipoproteinemia characterized by hypocholesterolemia, moderate hypertriglyceridemia, abnormal chylomicron remnants, low levels of low density lipoproteins (LDL), and a marked deficiency of high density lipoproteins (HDL) (1-4). Clinically these patients are characterized by hepatosplenomegaly, recurrent transient neuropathy, lymphadenopathy, and orange tonsils (1-4). The characteristic apolipoprotein profile present in Tangier disease is a severe reduction in apolipoproteins (apo) A-I and apoA-II. Previous studies have established that the reduced plasma levels of apoA-I and apoA-II in Tangier disease are due to increased catabolism rather than reduced synthesis of the A-I and A-II apolipoproteins (5). In the present report, we will review our recent studies on the molecular defect in Tangier disease.

MATERIALS AND METHODS

Isolation of Lipoproteins and Apolipoproteins

Plasma lipoproteins were isolated by preparative ultracentrifugation from normal subjects and patients with Tangier disease as previously described (6). The pro and mature isoforms of apoA-I were isolated by preparative isoelectrofocusing as previously reported (7). The individual isoforms were analyzed for purity by amino acid analysis, NaDodSO$_4$ gel electrophoresis, and analytical isoelectrofocusing (6,7).

129

Cloning of cDNA for apoA-I$_{Tangier}$

The cDNA for apoA-I$_{Tangier}$ was cloned from mRNA isolated from liver from a patient with Tangier disease obtained during elective surgery. The preparation of the mRNA and the cloning of the cDNA in pBR322 has been previously reported (8). The clones were screened utilizing probes for normal apoA-I (8). Primer extension was used to complete the cDNA sequence of apoA-I$_{Tangier}$ not present in the pBR322 clones. DNA sequences were determined by the Maxam and Gilbert procedure using 8% or 20% urea polyacrylamide gels (9).

Kinetic Studies of Tangier ApoA-I Isoforms

ApoA-I kinetic studies were performed in normal subjects and patients with Tangier disease. Subjects were placed on a diet (42% fat, 42% carbohydrate, and 16% protein, cholesterol 200 mg/1000 calories, P/S ratio 0.2). One week prior to the initiation of the study, proapoA-I and mature apoA-I were radiolabeled with ^{125}I and ^{131}I respectively as previously described (7). The radioactivity among the apoA-I isoforms was determined following separation by preparative isoelectrofocussing.

Blood samples were collected in EDTA (0.1%) and the radioactivity quantitated in plasma, isolated lipoprotein fractions, and apoA-I isoforms. Plasma residence times for injected apolipoproteins were computed utilizing the SAAM 27 programs (10) on a VAX 11/780 Computer.

RESULTS

Initial studies from our laboratory have established that the reduced plasma level of HDL in Tangier disease is due to increased catabolism of the A-I and A-II apolipoproteins (5). Of particular interest was the observation of the increase in the plasma pro-apoA-I isoform in Tangier disease (11-12). Detailed kinetic studies have been performed on the metabolism of the pro and mature apoA-I isoforms in normal man (13). In normal subjects apoA-I is secreted almost exclusively as the pro isoform which is then rapidly converted to mature apoA-I. ProapoA-I and mature apoA-I have residence times of 0.23 and 6.5 days respectively. The kinetics of ^{125}I proapoA-I$_{Tangier}$ and ^{131}I mature apoA-I$_{Tangier}$ were studied in Tangier patients. The residence times of both ^{125}I-proapoA-I and mature ^{131}I-apoA-I were the same, and very rapid (residence time <0.15 days). The rate of conversion of proapoA-I to mature apoA-I was normal, which was consistent with the conversion of proapoA-I to mature apoA-I analyzed in vitro (7). The relative increase in proapoA-I in Tangier disease is due to the rapid catabolism of the proapoA-I isoform which is faster than the rate of conversion of proapoA-I to mature apoA-I. As indicated above the rate of catabolism of mature apoA-I is

130

rapid, and similar to proapoA-I. These results establish that the
rate of conversion of proapoA-I to mature apoA-I in Tangier
disease is not abnormal, and not the molecular defect in the
disease.

In order to definitively establish the structure of
apoA-I$_{Tangier}$, we have cloned apoA-I$_{Tangier}$ and determined the
complete cDNA and derived amino acid sequence. The amino acid
sequence of preproapoA-I$_{Tangier}$ is identical to normal preproapoA-I except for an isosteric replacement of an aspartic acid for
glutamic acid at position 120. These data definitively established that apoA-I in Tangier disease is normal.

DISCUSSION

During the last several years major advances have been made
in our understanding of the metabolic and molecular defect in
Tangier disease. Initial studies revealed that the defect was due
to increased catabolism of the A-I apolipoprotein, rather than a
defect in synthesis. The evaluation of plasma apoA-I from Tangier
patients revealed a marked increase in proapoA-I which has now
been shown to be due to the increased rate of catabolism of
proapoA-I with no defect in conversion of proapoA-I to mature
apoA-I. The complete amino acid sequence of preproapoA-I from a
Tangier patient has been completed utilizing molecular biology
techniques, and shown to be identical to normal apoA-I except for
a single isosteric amino acid substitution. The combined results
reviewed here are interpreted as indicating that the defect in
Tangier disease is a post-translational defect in apoA-I processing. The defect in processing may be either extracellular and
involve proteolytic processing or cellular - intracellular traffic-
king of the apolipoprotein following reaction with the punative
HDL receptor. Additional studies will be required to further
define the catabolic pathway(s) for apoA-I metabolism, and to
elucidate the specific defect in lipoprotein metabolism present in
Tangier disease.

REFERENCES

1.   Fredrickson, D.S., Altrocchi, L.V., Avoili, Goodman, D.S.,
     and Goodman, H.C. (1968) Tangier disease. Ann. Intern. Med.
     27. 165-174.
2.   Herbert, P.M., Gotto, A.M., Jr., and Fredrickson, D.S. (1978)
     Familial Lipoprotein Deficiency. In the Metabolic Basis of
     Inherited Disease. 4th edition, J.B. Stanbury, J.B.
     Wyngaarden, and D.S. Fredrickson, editors. McGraw-Hill Book
     Co., New York, pp. 544-588.
3.   Assmann, G. (1979) Tangier disease and the possible role of
     high density lipoproteins in atherosclerosis. In. A.M. Gotto
     and R. Paoletti (Eds)., Atherosclerosis Reviews, Raven Press,
     New York, pp. 1-28.

4. Schaefer, E.J., Zech, L.A., Schwartz, D.E., and Brewer, H.B., Jr. (1980) Coronary heart disease prevalence and other clinical features in familial high density lipoprotein deficiency (Tangier Disease). Ann. Int. Med. $\underline{93}$, 261-266.

5. Schaefer, E.J., Blum, C.R., Levy, R.I., Jenkins, L.L., Alaupovic, P., Foster, D.M., and Brewer, H.B., Jr. (1978) Metabolism of high-density lipoprotein apolipoproteins in Tangier disease. New Engl. J. Med. $\underline{299}$, 905-910.

6. Kay, L.L., Ronan, R., Schaefer, E.J., and Brewer, H.B., Jr. (1982) Tangier disease: A structural defect in apolipoprotein A-I (apoA-I$_{Tangier}$). Proc. Natl. Acad. Sci. U.S.A. $\underline{79}$, 2485-2489.

7. Bojanovski, D., Gregg, R.E., and Brewer, H.B., Jr. (1984) Tangier Disease. In vitro Conversion of ProapoA-I$_{Tangier}$ to Mature apoA-I$_{Tangier}$. J. Biol. Chem. $\underline{259}$, 6049-6051.

8. Law, S.W. and Brewer, H.B., Jr. (1984) Nucleotide sequence and the encoded amino acids of human apolipoprotein A-I mRNA. Proc. Natl. Acad. Sci. U.S.A. $\underline{81}$, 66-70.

9. Maxam, A.M. and Gilbert, W. (1977) A new method for sequencing DNA. Proc. Natl. Acad. Sci. U.S.A. $\underline{74}$, 560-564.

10. Berman, M. and Weiss, M.F. (1978) SAAM Manual. U.S. DHEW publication 75-180, National Institutes of Health.

11. Zannis, V.I., Lees, A.M., Lees, R.S., and Breslow, J.L. (1982) Abnormal apoA-I isoprotein composition in patients with Tangier disease. J. Biol. Chem. $\underline{257}$, 4978-4986.

12. Brewer, H.B., Jr., Fairwell, T., Meng, M.S., Kay, L., and Ronan, R. (1983) Human proapoA-I$_{Tangier}$: Isolation of proapoA-I$_{Tangier}$ and amino acid sequence of the peptide. Biochem. Biophys. Res. Commun. $\underline{113}$, 934-940.

13. Bojanovski, D., Gregg, R.E., Ghiselli, G., Schaefer, E.J., Light, J.A., and Brewer, H.B., Jr. (1985) Human apolipoprotein A-I isoprotein metabolism: ProapoA-I conversion to nature A-I. J. Lipid Res. $\underline{26}$, 185-193.

APOLIPOPROTEIN A-I AND A-II METABOLISM IN SUBJECTS WITH CORONARY HEART DISEASE (CHD)

Ghiselli, G., Beigel, Y. and Gotto, A.M., Jr.

Department of Medicine, Baylor College of Medicine
and The Methodist Hospital, Houston, TX   77030

A number of epidemiological studies replicated in various laboratories have established that the incidence of coronary heart disease (CHD) is correlated with the concentration of certain lipoprotein classes and apolipoproteins in plasma (1). High levels of low density lipoprotein (LDL) and plasma apoB have been associated to an increased risk of developing CHD (2-4). High density lipoprotein (HDL) cholesterol levels in plasma are negatively correlated to CHD and appear to represent an independent risk factor (5). ApoA-I and apoA-II are the major protein constituents of HDL. Plasma levels of apoA-I and apoA-II have been reported to be lower in subjects with CHD in comparison with controls in a number of studies (1,6).

ApoA-I is an activator of LCAT reaction in plasma. ApoA-II is thought to be a specific activator of the hepatic lipoprotein lipase (7). Both apolipoproteins are polymorphic in plasma. The apoA-I plasma polymorphic system consists of a proform, designated proapoA-I (A-I$_1$ of the polymorphic scale), and a series of mature isoproteins designated A-I$_3$, A-I$_4$ and A-I$_5$, which differ by one unit of charge (8). The polymorphic pattern of apoA-I in plasma is illustrated in Figure 1. ProapoA-I constitutes approximately 3% of the total apoA-I circulating mass. A-I$_3$ is the prominent apoA-I isoprotein in plasma. _In vivo_ turnover studies have demonstrated that proapoA-I is the only form of apoA-I secreted by the liver and intestine and that it is completely converted in plasma to A-I$_3$ soon after secretion (9). Further investigations (10) have revealed that A-I$_3$ is then slowly converted in plasma to A-I$_4$ and to A-I$_5$ by a process with the kinetic characteristics of deamidation. More than 80%

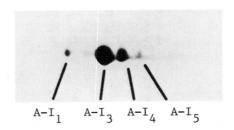

$$A-I_1 \quad A-I_3 \quad A-I_4 \quad A-I_5$$

Figure 1: Apolipoprotein A-I polymorphism in plasma.
In this two-dimensional gel electrophoretogram are illustrated
the different isoproteins of the apoA-I polymorphic system in
plasma. $A-I_1$ corresponds to proapoA-I and $A-I_3$, $A-I_4$ and $A-I_5$
are the mature isoproteins. The relative abundance of the different isoproteins is: $A-I_1$, 3.2%; $A-I_3$, 81.4%; $A-I_4$, 13.0% and
$A-I_5$, 2.4% (see reference 10).

of the catabolism of apoA-I occurs through $A-I_3$; thus, deamidation is not a necessary step for apoA-I catabolism. ApoA-II
polymorphism is less complex than that seen for apoA-I, and only
a major apoA-II isoprotein is present in plasma; the minor isoforms possibly resulting from deamidation (11).

    In spite of the frequently observed decreased levels of
apoA-I and apoA-II in subjects with premature coronary atherosclerosis, no data are as yet available on the metabolic basis
of such an abnormality. In a series of in vivo turnover
studies, we have determined the metabolic parameters of apoA-I
and apoA-II in subjects with CHD and compared the results with
those obtained in a group of normal volunteers. Subjects with
CHD were recruited from patients undergoing diagnostic characterization for anginal syndrome or previous myocardial infarction. The subjects were male caucasians in the age range of 42
to 69. Normal subjects were recruited from the local medical
school population for comparative studies. Lipids, HDL cholesterol, apoA-I and apoA-II plasma concentrations were measured by
automated technique or specific radioimmunoassays, and the results are presented in Table I. No statistical differences in

the plasma lipid and LDL cholesterol levels were detected between the two groups of subjects. HDL cholesterol, however, was significantly reduced in subjects with CHD. ApoA-I and apoA-II levels were also decreased. <u>In vivo</u> turnover studies were performed in five CHD subjects with low apoA-I and apoA-II levels and in seven normal volunteers. Apolipoproteins were isolated from normal plasma; mature apoA-I constituted 95% of the apoA-I preparation. The apolipoproteins were radioiodinated by the iodine monochloride method and tested for the ability to reassociate to lipoprotein prior to injection (9). Turnover studies were conducted following an inpatient protocol for the CHD subjects and an outpatient protocol for the normal volunteers. Metabolic steady state conditions were ascertained by the fact that lipids, HDL cholesterol, apoA-I and apoA-II plasma levels and body weight remained constant throughout the study. The plasma radioactivity decay curves for apoA-I and apoA-II in CHD and control subjects are shown in Figure 2. Kinetic analysis revealed that both apoA-I and apoA-II were catabolized at a significantly faster rate in the CHD subjects as compared to the

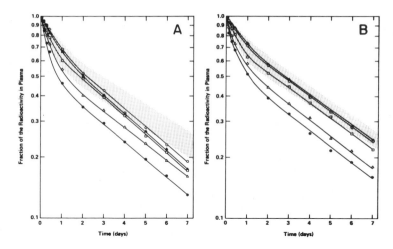

Figure 2: Plasma radioactivity disappearance curves after injection of ^{125}I-ApoA-I (Panel A) and ^{131}I-ApoA-II (Panel B) in controls and CHD subjects.

Radioiodinated apoA-I and apoA-II were injected simultaneously in 7 control and 5 CHD subjects and blood samples collected at 10 min, 3, 6 and 9 hours and thereafter daily up to the 7th day. Plasma aliquots were counted for the associated radioactivity. The radioactivity decay curves shown are those observed in CHD subjects. The decay curves in normal volunteers fall within the shaded area.

TABLE I

LIPIDS AND APOLIPOPROTEIN LEVELS IN CONTROLS AND CHD SUBJECTS

Subjects	Plasma Concentration (mg/dl)					
	Chol	TG	LDL Chol	HDL Chol	ApoA-I	ApoA-II
Control (18)	186 ± 9[+]	94 ± 10	118 ± 7	41 ± 2	113 ± 11	29 ± 2
CHD (65)	192 ± 4	109 ± 4	129 ± 4	33 ± 1	89 ± 3*	23 ± 2*

+ Mean ± SE
* $p < 0.05$ v.s. Control

TABLE II

MEAN RESIDENCE TIME IN PLASMA OF APOA-I AND APOA-II IN CONTROLS AND CHD SUBJECTS

Subjects	Mean Residence Time (days)	
	ApoA-I	ApoA-II
Control (7)	4.6 ± 0.4[+]	5.3 ± 0.5
CHD (5)	3.6 ± 0.5*	4.3 ± 0.5

+ Mean ± SE
* $p < 0.05$ v.s. Control

controls. The residence time of apoA-I and apoA-II averaged 4.6 days and 5.3 days in the controls and 3.6 days and 4.3 days in the CHD subjects respectively. ApoA-I and apoA-II absolute catabolic rates, however, remained in the normal range.

The metabolic defect underlying hypoalphalipoproteinemia in subjects with CHD is not known. HDL are thought to facilitate reverse cholesterol transport between the peripheral tissues and the liver (12). The data presented are consistent with the view that apoA-I and apoA-II synthesis is normal in CHD subjects. On the other hand the plasma residence time of these apolipoproteins is decreased, implying faster catabolism. The mechanism and the sites of catabolism of apoA-I, apoA-II are not fully known. While evidence exists (13,14) that HDL may bind specifically to liver cells, subsequent catabolism through internalization and lysosomal degradation has yet to be demonstrated. In fact in vivo turnover studies in rats suggest that apoA-I is actively catabolized by the liver and the kidney; but, in these tissues, apoA-I catabolism appears to be dissociated from that of the HDL lipid components (15). These studies, however, point out potential sites of modulation of apoA-I and apoA-II levels in plasma. Since the synthesis of apoA-I and apoA-II in CHD hypoalphalipoproteinemic subjects is normal, low levels of these apolipoproteins in plasma must be maintained by an adjustment of the apoA-I and apoA-II catabolic pathways to a lower concentration level. This may imply up regulation of the HDL cellular receptor or perhaps compositional changes of HDL in CHD subjects so as to allow a more rapid catabolism. Further studies will be necessary to test these hypotheses.

REFERENCES

1) G. Heiss and H.A. Tyroler, Are apolipoproteins useful for evaluating ischemic heart disease? A brief overview of the literature, in "Proceedings of the Workshop on Apolipoprotein Quantification," K. Lippel, ed., NIH Publ. No. 83-1266, Bethesda (1983).
2) S.M. Grundy, Recommendation for the treatment of hyperlipidemia in adults, Arteriosclerosis 4:443A (1984).
3) P.W. Wilson, R.J. Garrison, W.P. Castelli, et al., Prevalence of coronary heart disease in the Framingham Offspring Study: Study of lipoprotein cholesterols, Am. J. Cardiol. 46:649 (1980).

4) P. Avogaro, G. Bittolo Bon, G. Cazzolato et al., Plasma
    levels of apolipoprotein A-I and apolipoprotein B in human
    atherosclerosis, Artery 4:385 (1978)

5) T. Gordon, W.P. Castelli, M.C. Hyortland et al., High
    density lipoprotein as a protective factor against coronary
    heart disease: The Framingham Study, Am. J. Med. 62:707
    (1977).

6) G. Fager, O. Wiklund, S-O. Olofsson et al., Multivariate
    analysis of serum apolipoproteins and risk factor in
    relation to acute myocardial infarction. Arteriosclerosis
    1:273 (1981)

7) S. Eisenberg, High density lipoprotein metabolism, J. Lipid
    Res. 25:1017 (1984).

8) G. Ghiselli, E.J. Schaefer, J.A. Light and H.B. Brewer,
    Jr., Apolipoprotein A-I isoforms in human lymph: effect of
    fat absorption, J. Lipid Res. 24:731 (1983).

9) G. Ghiselli, A.M. Gotto Jr., S. Tanenbaum and B.C.
    Sherrill, Proapolipoprotein A-I conversion kinetics in vivo
    in human and in rat, Proc. Natl. Acad. Sci. USA 82: 874
    (1985)

10) G.Ghiselli, M.F. Rohde, S. Tanenbaum et al., Origin of
    apolipoprotein A-I polymorphism in plasma, J. Biol. Chem.
    260:15662 (1985).

11) G. Schmitz, K. Ilsemann, B. Melnik and G. Assmann,
    Isoproteins of human apolipoprotein A-II: isolation and
    characterization, J. Lipid Res. 24:1021 (1983).

12) J.A. Glomset and K.R. Norum, The metabolic role of lecithin
    cholesterol acyltransferase: perspective from pathology,
    Adv. Lipid Res. 11:1 (1973)

13) P.S. Bachorik, F.A. Franklin, D.G. Virgil and P.O.
    Kwiterovich, High-affinity uptake and degradation of
    apolipoproteinE free high-density lipoprotein and low-
    density lipoprotein in cultured porcine hepatocytes,
    Biochemistry 21:5675 (1982).

14) J.M. Hoeg, S.J. Demosky, S.B. Edge et al., Characterization
    of a human hepatic receptor for high density lipoproteins,
    Arteriosclerosis 5:228 (1985).

15) C. Glass, R.C. Pittman, D.B. Weinstein and O. Steinberg,
    Dissociation of tissue uptake of cholesterol ester from
    that of apoprotein A-I of rat plasma high density
    lipoprotein: Selective delivery of cholesterol ester to
    liver, adrenal and gonad, Proc. Natl. Acad. Sci. USA,
    80:5435 (1983).

AN APOPROTEIN AII GENE POLYMORPHISM AND HYPERLIPIDAEMIA

G.A.A. Ferns, S.C. Shelley*, A. Rees, J. Stocks,
and D.J. Galton

Medical Professorial Unit, St Bartholomew's Hospital
West Smithfield, London EC1 and *Sir William Dunn
School of Pathology, University of Oxford

There is a considerable degree of allelic variation in
human populations.   Some variants have deleterious consequences
for the individual possessing them, and selective forces
strongly oppose their spread in populations.   Other genetic
variants may have been of selective advantage in the past and
consequently their frequencies have increased in the population.
However, due to possible changes in environment, these variants
may now be neutral or slightly disadvantageous for the
individual.   Such variants may provide the genetic basis for
the common metabolic diseases such as type II diabetes mellitus
and the hyperlipidaemias.   They would be expected to occur at
the same frequency as the disease (at frequencies greater than
1-2% in the population) and would therefore fall within the
definition of a genetic polymorphism[1].

Two possible examples of such polymorphic variants are the
hypervariable DNA sequences adjacent to the 5'-end of the human
insulin gene on the short arm of chromosome 11, and a point
mutation in the fourth exon of the apoprotein CIII gene on
the long arm of chromosome 11 that creates a new cleavage site
for the restriction enzyme SstI.   The former polymorphism is
due to variable insertions of a 14bp oligonucleotide repeat
sequence ranging in length between 0-2500bp.   The role of this
polymorphic locus is not known; however individuals who are
homozygous for large insertion sequences occur quite rarely in
healthy Caucasians (less than five per cent), whereas the
frequency of this genotype has been found to be up to 30% in
patients with glucose or lipid intolerance[2,3].   In the latter
example of allelic variants, the polymorphic SstI site is found
in approximately 5% of healthy Caucasians, but is observed in

TABLE 1

Distribution of the Msp1 DNA polymorphism adjacent to the apoprotein AII gene in racial and hypertriglyceridaemic groups

Group	Genotype Distribution			Allelic Frequencies	
	$M_{3.1}$ $M_{3.1}$	$M_{3.1}$ $M_{3.7}$	$M_{3.7}$ $M_{3.7}$	$M_{3.1}$	$M_{3.7}$
normotriglyceridaemic Caucasians n=23	18	5	0	0.89 (41/46)	0.11 (5/46)
normotriglyceridaemic Japanese n=20	12	8	0*	0.80 (32/40)	0.20 (8/40)*
hypertriglyceridaemic Caucasians n=14	8	5	1*	0.75 (21/28)	0.25 (7/28)*
hypertriglyceridaemic Japanese n=30	14	16	0+	0.73 (44/60)	0.27 (16/60)+

*p > 0.05 when compared with the normotriglyceridaemic Caucasian group in a 2x2 contingency table.
+p > 0.05 when compared with the normotriglyceridaemic Japanese group in a 2x2 contingency table.
8µg of leucocyte DNA was digested with the enzyme MspI, restricted fragments separated on a 1% agarose gel, Southern blotted onto a nitrocellulose filter and hybridised to a ^{32}p labelled cDNA apoprotein AII gene probe. Filters were washed and hybridisation bands visualised by autoradiography at -70°C.

about 30% of hypertriglyceridaemic subjects with a type IV or V phenotype[4].

In a search for other possible apoprotein gene variants that may relate to hyperlipidaemia, we have investigated a MspI polymorphism close to the 3' end of the apoprotein AII gene, on chromosome 1[5]. The polymorphic MspI restriction site occurs within the Alu sequence approximately 175bp from the 3' end of the apoprotein AII gene. Another MspI cleavage site is in the 5' flanking region of the gene. Restriction enzyme analysis demonstrates two allelic variants, one of about 3.1 Kbp and one of about 3.7 Kbp. Since there is a report that this polymorphism relates to plasma levels of apoprotein AII[6] it is of obvious importance to establish whether there is any disease association. Previous studies have shown that genetic polymorphisms that demonstrate disease association may also show assymmetrical distribution in racial groups[7,8].

We have therefore also studied the distribution of the allelic and genotypic frequencies in different racial groups (Table 1). As can be seen this polymorphism appears to be uniformly distributed between the groups we have investigated, showing no racial or disease associated differences. Thus the MspI polymorphism of the apoprotein AII gene appears to be neutral, similar to a previously reported TaqI polymorphism adjacent to the apoprotein CII gene on chromosome 19[9]. However it may still be of use as a genetic marker for the parental origin of a particular apoprotein AII gene in family studies.

Acknowledgements

This work was supported by the Wellcome Trust (to GAF) and to the Fritz-Thyssen Foundation. Grateful thanks to Dr F E Baralle for permission to use the apoprotein AII gene probe.

REFERENCES

1. D.J.Galton, "Molecular Genetics of Common Metabolic Disease" publ. E. Arnold, London (1968).
2. P.S. Rotwein, J. Chirgwin, M. Province, W.C. Knowler, D.J.Pettit, B. Cordel, H.M. Goodman and M.A. Permutt, The 5' flanking region of the human insulin gene : a genetic marker for non-insulin dependent diabetes. N. Engl. J. Med. 308:65 (1983).
3. N.I. Jowett, L.G. Williams, G.A. Hitman and D.J. Galton Diabetic hypertriglyceridaemia and a related 5' flanking polymorphism of the human insulin gene. Br.Med.J. 288:96 (1984).

4. A.Rees, J. Stocks, C.C. Shoulders, D.J. Galton and
    F.E. Baralle, DNA polymorphism adjacent to the human
    apoprotein A-1 gene : relation to hypertriglyceridaemia.
    Lancet i : 444 (1983).
5. T.J. Knott, R.L. Eddy, M.E. Robertson, L.M. Priestley,
    J. Scott and T.B. Shows, Chromosome localization of the
    human apoprotein C-1 gene and of a polymorphic apoprotein
    A-II gene. Biochem. Biophys. Res. Comm. 125:299 (1984).
6. J. Scott, L.M. Priestley, T.J. Knott, M.E. Robertson,,
    G. Kostner, G.J. Miller and N.E. Miller, High density
    lipoprotein composition is altered by a common DNA
    polymorphism adjacent to the apoprotein A-II gene in Man.
    Lancet i:771 (1985).
7. L.G. Williams, N.I. Jowett, M.A. Vella, S. Humphries and
    D.J. Galton, Allelic variation adjacent to the human insulin
    and apoprotein C-II genes in different ethnic groups.
    Human Genetics (in press).
8. A. Rees, J. Stocks, C.R. Sharpe, M.A. Vella, C.C. Shoulders,
    J. Katz, N.I. Jowett, F.E. Baralle and D.J. Galton,
    DNA polymorphism in the apo A1/CIII gene cluster :
    association with hypertriglyceridaemia. J. Clin. Invest.
    (in press).
9. S. Humphries, N.I. Jowett, L.G. Williams, A. Rees,
    M.A. Vella, O. Myklebost, A Lydon, M.Seed, D.J. Galton,
    R. Williamson, A DNA polymorphism adjacent to the human
    apolipoprotein C-II gene. Molec. Biol and Med. i:463 (1983).

ANALYSIS OF APOLIPOPROTEIN A-I SYNTHESIZED IN VITRO

FROM CHICK INTESTINAL mRNA

St. Ferrari[*], P. Tarugi, R. Battini[*],
M. Ghisellini and S. Calandra

Istituto di Chimica Biologica[*] e Patologia
Generale dell'Università di Modena
Modena, Italy

INTRODUCTION

In man and in many laboratory animals including the
chick apolipoprotein A-I (apo A-I) is the main constituent peptide of plasma high density lipoproteins (HDL)
(1-5). In all species examined so far apo A-I is synthesized in liver and intestine (6-8) as a precursor molecule (pre-proapo A-I) which is characterized by an aminoacid extension at its NH_2 terminal end (signal peptide).
Part of this sequence is cleaved co-translationally to
originate the intracellular precursor of apo A-I (proapolipoprotein A-I) (9-15). In man and rat the latter is
secreted into the blood stream where is converted to the
mature extracellular form by the action of some plasma
protease(s) (16-19). It has been reported that in man
(20-25), rat (25), mouse (24), rabbit (25) and chick (15)
plasma apo A-I consists of a family of isoforms which
have the same molecular weight, react equally well with
anti apo A-I antiserum, but have different isoelectric
points. The relative content of each isoform spans over
a wide range (from 1-2% for the minor isoforms to 60-70%
for the major ones) and shows a high degree of species
difference (25).
The presence of many isoforms in plasma raises several questions with regard to their origin. Isoforms may
represent the product of: 1) different sequences coding

143

for apo A-I which are translated at a different rate in those tissues capable of secreting plasma lipoproteins or 2) post-translational modifications of the product of a single coding sequence. The present study was aimed to ascertain: a) whether the primary translation product of apo A-I produced in vitro by chick intestine mRNA existed as single or multiple forms; b) how the isoform pattern was affected by co-translational processing and c) the difference between the isoform pattern of in vitro synthesized apo A-I and apo A-I present in plasma HDL.

RESULTS

In vitro translation of apo A-I intestinal mRNA

We have investigated the ability of chick intestinal RNA to program the cell-free synthesis of apo A-I. Fig.1 (lane a) shows that the primary translation product immunoprecipitated by specific anti chick apo A-I rabbit IgG migrates as a single Mr 28,000 protein in monodimensional gel electrophoresis. By comparing the intensity of the band corresponding to apo A-I relative to the other polypeptides synthesized in the cell free system it emerges that apo A-I mRNA represents a quantitatively prominent species (about 5%) in the mRNA population of chick intestine (Fig. 2). Since apo A-I is a secretory protein it is expected that the in vitro primary translation product contains an aminoacid extension at its NH_2 terminal end (signal peptide). Indeed incubation of the cell free translation mixture with dog pancreas membranes results in the partial conversion (about 50%) of the primary translation product to a lower molecular weight species (Mr 27,000) which is still efficiently immunoprecipitated by anti apo A-I antibodies (Fig 1, lane b).

Isoforms of the primary translation product of apo A-I

In order to ascertain whether the multiple isoforms of plasma apo A-I (ref. 15 and Fig. 4) were originated as discrete primary translation products or were the results of post-translational/post-secretorial modifications, the translation products of chick intestine mRNA were separated by two dimensional gel electrophoresis. The fluorogram of this gel shows the presence of three

144

discrete spots in the molecular weight region corresponding to apo A-I preprotein (Mr 28,000), suggesting the
existence of isoforms (Fig. 2). To corroborate this finding in vitro synthesized apo A-I was immunoprecipitated
and subjected to 2-D gel electrophoresis. We observed the
presence of three isoforms whose isoelectric points were
6.2, 6.0, and 5.9 respectively (Fig. 3 panel A). Visual-
ly the relative ratio of the three species (indicated by
the number 1-3 from the more basic to the more acidic) is
approximately 5:2:1. The addition of dog pancreas membranes to the translation mixture has a clear effect on the
isoform pattern (Fig. 3, panel B). As expected from the
data obtained by the monodimensional electrophoretic analysis we observed about 50% conversion of the primary
translation products to lower molecular species (26,000).
Furthermore the products of co-translational processing
are represented by two species having slightly more acidic pI than the parental primary translation products
(Fig. 3, panel B, spots 4 and 5).

Apo A-I isoforms in chick plasma

In chick plasma apo A-I consists of a family of at
least 4-5 isoforms (numbered 1-5 from the more basic to
the more acidic in fig.4). Isoform 3 (pI 5.7) is the
major one accounting for about 70% of total apo A-I mass.
The relative content of the various isoforms appears to
be unstable as incubation of plasma at 37°C leads to a
pronounced change of the isoform distribution. The latter
consists of a decrease of isoform 3 and a concomitant increase of isoform 4 (pI 5.6) and 5 (pI 5.5).

DISCUSSION

In the present study we confirmed that apo A-I is a
major protein produced by chick intestine (15) and that
in a cell free system apo A-I is synthesized as a prepeptide which is processed co-translationally in the presence of endoplasmic reticulum membranes. We show further
by high resolution two dimensional gel electrophoresis
that newly synthesized apo A-I exists in at least three
isoforms. Co-translational processing leads to the appearance of two more acidic isoforms which have a lower molecular weight as compared to the primary translation
product.

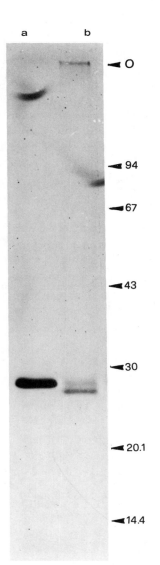

a b

◄ O

◄ 94

◄ 67

◄ 43

◄ 30

◄ 20.1

◄ 14.4

Fig.1
SDS-PAGE fluorogram showing co-translational processing of chick intestinal apo A-I. Chick intestinal poly(A)+ RNA was tranlated in reticulocyte lysates either in the absence or in the presence of dog pancreas microsomal membranes. The translation products were immunoprecipitated from the translation mixture by anti chick apo A-I IgG and subjected to polyacrylamide gel electrophoresis in the presence of SDS. The pattern is shown of immunoprecipitable products translated in the absence (lane a) or in the presence (lane b) of endoplasmic reticulum membranes. The origin (O) and M_r values (x 10^3) of protein markers run in a parallel lane are indicated.

The existence of several isoforms of the primary translation product of chick apo A-I is in agreement with a recent observation that apo A-I synthesized in vitro by translation of RNA isolated from several rooster tissues

exists as a family of isoforms (15). Moreover the presence of multiple forms of the primary translation product
of apo A-I appears to be a specific feature of this polypeptide as this property pertains also to apo A-I encoded by mRNA isolated from both mouse (23-24) and rat liver.   The origin of isoforms is unclear at present. It
seems unlikely that is due to artifacts generated in the
translation system since the same pattern was observed
using both reticulocyte lysate and wheat germ extracts.

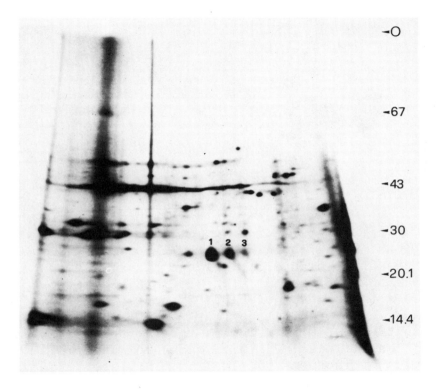

Fig. 2

Two dimensional gel electrophoresis of in vitro translation products encoded by chick intestinal poly(A)+ RNA.
The pattern is shown of the polypeptides translated in
vitro and subjected to two-dimensional gel electrophoresis. Numbers (1-3) placed on top of the spots indicate
the position of apo A-I isoforms from the basic (left)
to the acidic site (right).

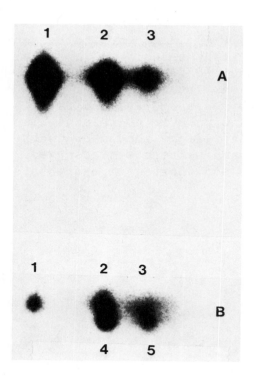

Fig. 3

Two dimensional gel electrophoresis of apo A-I translated in vitro in the presence of dog pancreas microsomal membranes. The fluorograph shows the isoform pattern of immunoprecipitated apo A-I translated in vitro in the absence (panel A) and in the presence (panel B) of microsomal membranes. Numbers (1-5) identify the A-I spots observed. Basic side is on the left, acidic on the right.

Variations in the charge of a family of polypeptides might be due to minute differences in their primary sequence. Such differences might reflect the existence of several mRNAs either generated by post-transcriptional modification of a single primary transcript or encoded by a multigene family. Studies are in progress to test these possibilities. Whatever mechanism underlays the formation of isoforms our findings indicate that pre-apo A-I is sinthesized as multiple forms and that the isoform pattern of in vitro translated apo A-I is profoundly affected by the presence of endoplasmic reticulum membranes. This idea is in agreement with a previous report where we showed that apo A-I isolated from HDL present in rat liver Golgi apparatus exists already as multiple isoforms (19).

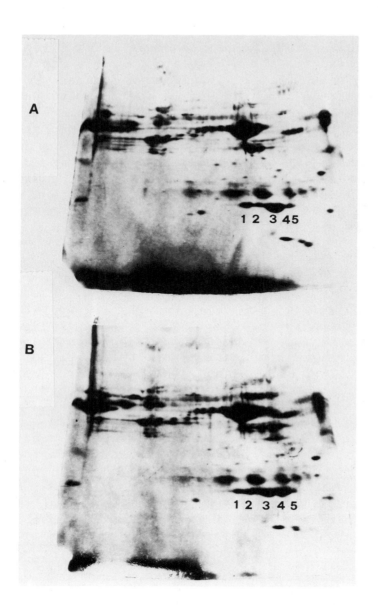

Fig. 4

Two dimensional gel electrophoresis of chick plasma before (panel A) and after (panel B) incubation at 37°C for
72 h. Numbers (1-5) indicate apo A-I isoforms. During the
incubation the relative content of isoform 3 decreases
whereas that of isoforms 4 and 5 increases.

Chick plasma apo A-I consists of at least 5 isoforms. In fresh plasma and freshly isolated HDL the major one is isoform 3 (about 70% of total apo A-I mass). We suggest that the more acidic isoforms 4 and 5 derive from the intravascular transformation of isoform 3 since, following plasma incubation at 37°C, we observed a decrease of isoform 3 and a concomitant increase of the more acidic isoforms 4 and 5. In conclusion the group of apo A-I isoforms represent a complex family of peptides which originate early in the synthetic pathway of apo A-I and undergo several changes during their intracellular transit and residence in plasma.

REFERENCES

1. Eisenberg, S., 1984, High density lipoprotein metabolism, J. Lipid Res. 25: 1017
2. Chapman, M.J., 1980, Animal lipoproteins: chemistry, structure and comparative aspects, J. Lipid Res.21:789
3. Kruski, A.W., and Scanu, A.M., 1975, Properties of rooster serum high density lipoproteins, Biochim. Biophys. Acta, 409:26
4. Jackson, R.L., Lin, H.Y.H., Chan, L., and Means, A.R. 1976, Isolation and characterization of the major apolipoprotein from chick high density lipoproteins, Biochim. Biophys. Acta, 420: 342
5. Kelley, J.L., Schjeide, O.A., Schjeide, S., Milius, R. and Alaupovic, P., 1980, Quantification of the major apolipoproteins in chicken and turkey serum during embryonic development, Comp. Biochem. Physiol.,65B:239
6. Marsh, J.B., 1976, Apoproteins of the lipoproteins in a nonrecirculating perfusate of rat liver, J. Lipid Res., 17:85
7. Green, P.H.R., and Glickman, R.M., 1981, Intestinal lipoprotein metabolism, J. Lipid Res., 22:1153
8. Bisgaier, C.L., and Glickman, R.M., 1983, Intestinal synthesis, secretion and transport of lipoproteins. Ann. Rev. Physiol. 45:625
9. Stoffel, W., Blobel, G., and Walter, P., 1981, Synthesis in vitro and translocation of apolipoprotein A-I across microsomal vesicles, Eur. J. Biochem., 120: 519

10. Gordon, J.I., Smith, D.P., Andy, R., Alpers, D.H., Schonfeld, G., and Strauss, .W., 1982, The primary translation product of rat intestinal apolipoprotein A-I mRNA is an unusual preproprotein, J. Biol. Chem. 257: 971

11. Zannis, V.I., Kurnit, D.M., and Breslow, J.L., 1982, Hepatic apo A-I and apo E and intestinal apo A-I are synthesized in precursor isoprotein forms by organ cultures of human fetal tissues, J. Biol. Chem., 257: 536

12. Stoffel, W., Kruger, E., and Deutzmann, R., 1983, Cell free translation of human liver apolipoprotein A-I and A-II mRNA processing of primary translation products, Hoppe-Seylers' Z. Physiol. Chem. , 364:227

13. Zannis, V.I., Karathanasis, S.K., Keutmann,H.T., Goldberger, R.G., and Breslow, J.L., 1983, Intracellular and extracellular processing of human apolipoprotein A-I; secreted apolipoprotein A-I isoprotein 2 is a propeptide Proc. Natl. Acad. (USA), 80: 2574

14. Gordon, J.I., Sims, H.F., Lentz, S.R., Edelstein,C., Scanu, A.M., and Strauss, A.W., 1983, Proteolytic processing of human preproapolipoprotein A-I, J. Biol. Chem. 258:4037

15. Blue, M.L., Ostapchuk, P., Gordon, J.S., and Williams, D., 1982, Synthesis and apolipoprotein A-I by peripheral tissues of the rooster, J. Biol. Chem., 257: 11151

16. Stoffel, W., Knyrim, K., and Bode, C., 1983, A serum proteinase converts proapolipoprotein A-I secreted by rat hepatocytes to the mature apolipoprotein, Hoppe-Seyler's Z. Physiol. Chem., 364:1631

17. Edelstein, C., Gordon, J.I., Toscas, K., Sims, H.F. Strauss, A.W., and Scanu, A.M., 1983, In vitro conversion of proapoprotein A-I to apoprotein A-I, J. Biol. Chem. 258:11430

18. Sliwkowski, M.B., and Windmueller, H.G., 1984, Rat liver and small intestine produce proapolipoprotein A-I which is slowly processed to apolipoprotein A-I in the circulation, J. Biol. Chem. 259:6459

19. Tarugi, P., Ghisellini, M., Pecorari, M., Brugni, N. and Calandra, S., 1985, Isoforms of rat apolipoprotein A-I isolated from the lipoproteins of hepatic Golgi apparatus and plasma, Atheroslerosis (in press).

20. Nestruck, A.C., Suzue, G., and Marcel, Y.L., 1980, Studies on the polymorphism of human apolipoprotein A-I. Biochim. Biophys. Acta, 617:110
21. Zannis, V.I., Lees, A.M., Lees, R.S., and Breslow, J. Abnormal apoprotein A-I isoprotein composition in patients with Tangier disease, 1982, J. Biol. Chem. 257:4978
22. Ghiselli, C., Schaefer, E.J., Light, J.A., and Brewer, B.H., 1983, Apolipoprotein A-I isoforms in human lymph; effect of fat absorption, J. Lipid Res. 24:731
23. Ertel-Miller, J.C., Barth, R.K., Shaw, P.H., Elliot, R.W., and Hastie, N.D., 1983, Identification of a cDNA clone for mouse apoprotein A-I (apo A-I) and its use in characterization of apo A-I mRNA expression in liver and small intestine, Proc. Natl. Acad. Sci. (USA) 80:1511
24. O'Donnell, K.A., and Lusis, A.J., 1983, Genetic evidence that the multiple apolipoprotein A-I isoforms are encoded by a common structural gene, Biochim. Biophys. Res. Commun. 114:275
25. Calandra, S., Tarugi, P., and Ghisellini, M., 1984 Separation of the isoprotein forms of apoprotein A-I of rat, rabbit and human HDL by combined isoelectrofocusing and SDS-polyacrylamide gel electrophoresis Atherosclerosis, 50:209

ACKNOWLEDGEMENT

This work was supported by the " Progetto Finalizzato Ingegneria Genetica e Basi Molecolari delle Malattie Ereditarie " of the Consiglio Nazionale delle Ricerche (CNR) of Italy.
Correspondence should be addressed to dr. S. Calandra Istituto di Patologia Generale, Università di Modena, via Campi 287, 41100 MODENA

VERSATILE E.coli EXPRESSION-MODIFICATION VECTORS AS TOOLS FOR STRUCTURE-FUNCTION STUDIES OF APOLIPOPROTEIN A1

Lucia Monaco, Rolando Lorenzetti, Alessandro Sidoli,
Marco Soria

Laboratory of Molecular Biology, Farmitalia Carlo Erba
24 Viale E. Bezzi, 20146 Milano, Italy

INTRODUCTION: THE pFCE4 SYSTEM

Recent efforts by several laboratories have focused on the development of recombinant vectors that allow efficient expression of eukaryotic genes in E.coli (reviewed by Harris, 1983). One such vector, pAS1, contains the strong, regulatable phage lambda promoter, P_L, two sites for N utilization, (Nut_L and Nut_R), and the ribosome binding site and initiation codon of the cII gene (Rosenberg et al., 1983). More recently, a derivative of pAS1 was described having the transcription termination signal t_o positioned beyond the Bam H1 cloning site: this plasmid was named pOTS (Devare et al., 1984).

A series of plasmids suitable for cloning and site-directed mutagenesis, the pEMBL family (Dente et al., 1983), was recently described having the intragenic region of the filamentous phage f1 inserted in pUC plasmids (Vieira and Messing, 1982). This region contained all the cis-acting elements required for replication and morphogenesis of the circular single-stranded viral genomic DNA (Dotto et al., 1981; Dotto and Horiuchi, 1981). Besides all the features of pUC plasmids, pEMBL plasmids had the property of being encapsidated as single-stranded DNA (ssDNA) upon infection with f1, so that virions released in the medium contained either f1 or pEMBL ssDNA in about equivalent amounts.

We have employed a similar approach to construct derivatives

153

of the expression vector pOTS, such that single stranded copies
of the recombinants could be obtained and employed directly for
DNA sequencing by the dideoxy chain termination method (Messing,
1983) and/or oligonucleotide-directed mutagenesis (Zoller and
Smith, 1983). These expression-modification vectors were named
pFCE4$^+$ and pFCE4$^-$ (Lorenzetti et al., 1985a). An outline of the
construction and of the resulting plasmids is shown in Figure 1.

The orientation of the f1 origin of replication determines
which of the two filaments is encapsidated into the viral
particles: the sense (coding) strand in pFCE4$^+$, and the antisense
strand in pFCE4$^-$. ssDNA from pFCE4$^+$ could be used as template for
oligonucleotide-primed DNA synthesis from the P_L promoter towards
the Bam HI site; conversely, DNA synthesis using ssDNA from
pFCE4$^-$ could be primed in the reverse orientation, from the Bam HI
site towards the P_L promoter.

CONSTRUCTION OF RECOMBINANT VECTORS

Because of the versatility of these vectors we decided to
subclone a cDNA fragment containing the sequence coding for the
mature human apolipoprotein A1 (apoA1, Sharpe et al., 1984) into
pFCE4$^+$. The apoA1 coding sequence had been reconstructed at its
5' end in order to express the mature protein in E.coli, with a
resulting "portable" gene having two BamHI sites at its extremities
and the sequence coding for the mature protein immediately
preceded by an ATG start codon (Lorenzetti et al., 1985b).

The BamHI fragment containing the modified apoA1 gene was
purified and subcloned into the BamHI site of pFCE4$^+$. The
resulting construction with the correct orientation of the insert
was verified by the dideoxy chain termination sequencing (Fig. 2A).
This plasmid was named pLS66.

Using this strategy, the ApoA1 gene was inserted out of frame
with respect to the ATG start codon already present in the vector.
Thus, the next step was to restore the reading frame by
positioning the apoA1 gene immediately after this ATG codon.

IN-FRAME POSITIONING

A useful opportunity afforded by pFCE4 is site-directed
gene deletion: in-frame positioning of the cloned gene can be
performed using "bridge" oligonucleotides, having sequences
complementary to the stretches of bases flanking the region to be
deleted on either side (Adelman et al., 1983; Singh et al., 1984;
Sollazzo et al., 1985).

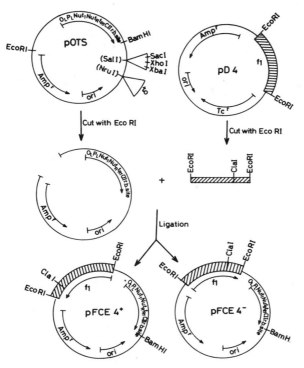

Fig. 1. Construction of pFCE4⁺ and pFCE4⁻. A 1300 bp fragment,
containing the origin of replication of phage f1 flanked
by eco RI linkers (Dotto and Horiuchi, 1981), was excised
from plasmid pD4 (Dotto et al., 1981) by Eco RI digestion
and then ligated to che plasmid vector pOTS (Devare et al.,
1984) linearized with Eco RI.

For this purpose, we synthesized, by the phosphotriester
method (Crea and Horn, 1980), a single-stranded oligonucleotide
having the following sequence: 5'-CTTACATATGGACGAGCC-3'.

This oligonucleotide should anneal with its 5' end to the
region immediately preceeding and including the ATG of the vector
(nucleotides 1 to 10), and with its 3' end to the first 8
nucleotides of the apoA1 gene, thus looping out the 8 extra
nucleotides present in pLS66 (Fig. 2). The ssDNA of pLS66 was
prepared as described (Kunkel, 1985) using E.coli RL841 as host.

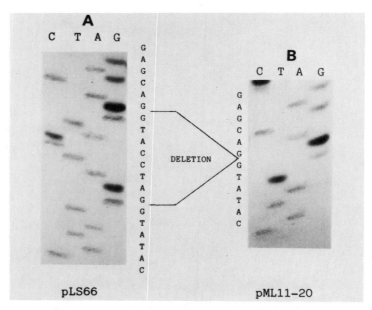

Fig. 2. Nucleotide sequence of pLS66 and pML11-20. The sequences
show the junction between the ATG start codon of pFCE4[+]
and the beginning of the apoA1 gene before (pLS66, A) and
after the deletion (pML11-20, B).

This bacterial strain is a derivative of E.coli RZ1032 containing
plasmid pCI857 (M. Zabeau, unpublished) which produces a
temperature sensitive repressor of the P_L promoter present in
pFCE4.

Using this protocol, the ssDNA produced by this strain
contained several uracil residues in place of thymine, thus acting
as a normal functional template "in vitro" but not being
biologically active upon transformation into a wild-type (ung[+])
E.coli 71/18CI[ts] strain, which is the normal host for these
plasmids.

0.1 pmoles of pLS66 ssDNA were annealed with 2 pmoles of
kinased mutagenic oligonucleotide (a 20 fold excess) at 56°C for
30 min in 15 mM Tris-Cl, pH 8.5, and 15 mM $MgCl_2$. After cooling
at room temperature the elongation-ligation mixture was added and
the reaction was continued at 15°C overnight. The elongation
reaction mixture was as follows (final concentrations): 10 mM

Tris-Cl, pH 8.5; 10 mM MgCl$_2$; 0.5 mM ATP; 0.05 mM dNTPs; 5 mM DTT; 1 unit of DNA polimerase, Klenow fragment, and 1.5 units of T4 DNA ligase.

After incubation the reaction mixture was phenol extracted, isopropanol and ethanol precipitated; 71/18 CI^{ts} competent cells were transformed and plated on selective medium containing 0.1 mg/ml of ampicillin. In order to identify clones that contained the desired deletion, 150 colonies were picked, grown on ordered plates and transferred onto nitrocellulose filters. The hybridization was performed at room temperature in 6x SSC and 10x Denhardt's using the mutagenic oligonucleotide as a probe. The filters were then washed in 6x SSC and 0.1% SDS at two different temperatures: the first time at room temperature, to check the hybridization efficacy, and then at 50°C, i.e. 4°C below the theoretical melting temperature. This was calculated according to the following formula, Tm = 4xGC + 2xAT, where GC and AT are the numbers of pairings formed by the oligonucleotide with the mutagenized template (Norrander et al., 1983). After each washing the filters were exposed with X-ray sensitive films. Candidate mutant colonies, yielding positive signals also at a stringent temperature, were confirmed by dideoxy chain-termination sequencing (Fig. 2B). The efficiency of this protocol is rather high, about 50% (R. Lorenzetti, unpublished). pFCE4$^+$ with the apo A1 gene correctly positioned in frame was named pML11-20.

EXPRESSION

In preliminary experiments, pML11-20 was unable to efficiently express mature apoA1. This should not be due to the pFCE4 vector, which was capable to express other eukaryotic genes like the one coding for human alpha-2 interferon (Lorenzetti et al., 1985a). These negative results might be due to a transcriptional and/or translational blockade in the expression of the apoA1 gene or to rapid degradation of the apolipoprotein inside the bacterial cell. That a transcriptional blockade might be ruled out was suggested by experiments in which a similar construction with a different promoter was fused to a downstream bacterial Gal K gene having its own ribosomal binding site and AUG initiator. Assays for the expression of Gal K revealed that efficient transcription of the polycistronic mRNA was taking place (Lorenzetti et al., 1985b). That rapid degradation was affecting expression of apoAI was indicated by a pulse labelling experiment, where a protein of the

expected molecular weight was present only in heat induced
cultures of pML11-20 after a pulse of 30 sec (Fig. 3). After a
pulse of 2 min the same protein was no longer recognizable, as if
very rapid degradation had diluted out this protein while the other
proteins continued to be labelled and accumulated. ApoA1 could not
be detected in the induced cultures by enzyme immunoassay or by
western blot analysis (M. Casati and R. Palomba, unpublished).

To overcome these problems, a fusion recombinant was obtained
between the gene coding for beta-galactosidase and the apoA1 gene.
Other Lac fusions have been successfully employed for the
expression of highly labile proteins in E.coli (Germino et al.,
1983; Germino and Bastia, 1984). We observed that the fused beta-
galactosidase apoA1 gene product was expressed efficiently, about
18% of total cellular proteins (Lorenzetti et al., 1985b).

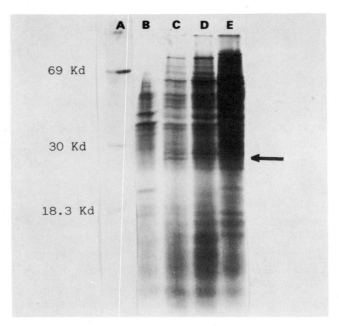

Fig. 3. Pulse labelling of pML11-20. 15% SDS-PAGE of bacterial
cultures after 30 sec pulse with 35S-methionine.
A) Molecular weight markers: albumin , carbonic anhydrase
and lactoglobulin A. B) Cells harboring pFCE4+ induced at
42°C for 40 min. From C to E cells harboring pML11-20 not
induced (lane E) or induced at 42°C for 20 min (lane D)
or 40 min (lane C). The arrow indicates the protein of
about 28 Kd which is present only in pML11-20 induced
cultures (lanes C and D).

Although this method allowed us to overcome the barrier(s) to efficient expression, more work remains to be done to separate the apoA1 moiety from its fused beta-galactosidase counterpart, e.g. introducing appropriate recognition sites for protease cleavage. The availability of the pFCE4-apoA1 recombinants will permit obtaining specific mutants by the oligonucleotide-directed mutagenesis method we described. This will enable the study of the relationships between structure and biological activity of the apoA1 protein, which plays a central role in the regulation of lipid metabolism.

ACKNOWLEDGEMENTS

The work leading to the engineering of pFCE4 was initiated in the laboratory of Drs M. Rosenberg and A. Shatzman at Smith, Kline and French Laboratories, Swedeland, PA. We acnowledge the help of Dr. Sonia Levi in performing some of the experiments.

REFERENCES

Adelman, J., Hayflick, J., Vasser, M., and Seeburg, P., 1983, In vitro deletional mutagenesis for bacterial production of the 20000-dalton form of human pituitary growth hormone, DNA, 2:183-193.

Crea, R., and Horn, T., 1980, Synthesis of oligonucleotides on cellulose by a phosphotriester method, Nucleic Acids Res., 8:2331-2348.

Dente, L., Cesareni, G., and Cortese, R., 1983, pEMBL: a new family of single stranded plasmids, Nucleic Acid Res., 11:1645-1655.

Devare, S., Shatzman, A., Robbins, K., Rosenberg, M., and Aaronson, S., 1984, Expression of the PDGF-related transforming protein of simian sarcoma virus in E.coli, Cell, 36:43-49.

Dotto, G., Enea, V., and Zinder, H., 1981, Functional analysis of bacteriophage intergenic region, Virology, 114:463-473.

Dotto, G., and Horiuchi, K., 1981, Replication of a plasmid containing two origins of bacteriophage f1, J. Mol. Biol., 153:169-176.

Germino, J., and Bastia, D., 1984, Rapid purification of a cloned gene product by genetic fusion and site-specific proteolysis, Proc. Natl. Acad. Sci. USA, 81:4692-4696.

Germino, J., Gray, J.G., Charbonneau, H., Vanaman, T., and Bastia, D., 1983, Use of gene fusions and protein-protein interaction in the isolation of a biologically active regulatory protein: The replication initiato protein of plasmid R6K, Proc. Natl. Acad. Sci. USA, 80:6848-6852.

Harris, T.J.R., 1983, Expression of eukaryotic genes in E. coli, in: "Genetic Engineeting 4", R. Williamson, ed., Academic Press, London.

Kunkel, T.A., 1985, Rapid and efficient site-specific mutagenesis without phenotypic selection, Proc. Natl. Acad. Sci. USA, 82:488-492.

Lorenzetti, R., Dani, M., Lappi, D.A., Martineau, D., Casati, M., Monaco, L., Shatzman, A., Rosenberg, M., and Soria, M., 1985a, pFCE4: a new system of E. coli expression-modification vectors, Submitted.

Lorenzetti R., Sidoli, A., Palomba, R., Monaco, L., Martineau, D., Lappi, D.A., and Soria, M., 1985b, Expression of the human apolipoprotein A1 gene fused to E. coli beta-galactosidase, Submitted.

Messing, J., 1983, New M13 vectors for cloning, Methods Enzymol., 101:20-78.

Norrander, J., Kempe, T., and Messing, J., 1983, Construction of improved M13 vectors using oligodeoxynucleotide-directed mutagenesis, Gene , 26:101-106.

Rosenberg, M., Ho, Y., and Shatzman, A., The use of pKC30 and its derivatives for controlled expression of genes, Methods Enzymol., 101:123-138.

Sharpe, C.R., Sidoli, A., Shelly, C.S., Lucero, M.A., Shoulders, C.C. and Baralle, F.E., 1984, Human apolipoproteins AI, AII, CII and CIII. cDNA sequences and mRNA abundance, Nucl. Acids. Res., 12:3917-3932.

Singh, A., Lugovoy, M.J., Kohr, W.J. and Perry, L.J., 1984, Nucl. Acids Res., 12:8927-8938.

Sollazzo, M., Frank, R. and Cesareni, G., 1985, High level expression of RNAs and proteins: the use of synthetic oligonucleotides for the precise fusion of coding sequences to regulatory sequences, Gene, in press.

Vieira, J. and Messing, J., 1982, The pUC plasmids, an M13mp7-derived system for insertion mutagenesis and sequencing with synthetic universal primers, Gene, 19:259-268.

Zoller, M. and Smith, M., 1983, Oligonucleotide-directed mutagenesis of DNA fragments cloned into M13 vectors, Methods Enzymol., 100:468-500.

160

SELECTION OF MONOCLONAL ANTIBODIES AS PROBES FOR THE

STUDY OF GENETIC POLYMORPHISM OF LDL APO B.

Yves L. Marcel, Allan Sniderman*, Philip K. Weech and
Ross W. Milne

Laboratory of Lipoprotein Metabolism, Clinical Research
Institute of Montreal, and *Cardiovascular Research Unit
Royal Victoria Hospital, Montreal, Quebec, Canada

The liver synthesizes a large apolipoprotein identified as apo B or B-100, which is primarily involved in the transport of the most hydrophobic lipids, triglycerides and cholesteryl esters. Whereas the lipids and apolipoproteins that constitute the different lipoproteins represent a dynamic set of molecules which exchange and transfer amongst the different particles, apo B is unique in that it appears to remain always associated with the same lipoprotein. However from its entry in the circulation as a nascent VLDL, the components of the lipoprotein containing apo B will undergo continuous and complex transformations. As the lipolytic pathway proceeds, the VLDL are depleted of their triglycerides but they also acquire cholesteryl esters from HDL and ultimately become cholesteryl ester-rich particles as LDL. This pathway is most active with nascent VLDL [1] and the ability of the apo B containing lipoproteins to acquire cholesteryl esters decreases progressively from the newly secreted particle to the circulating VLDL [1,2] to the mature LDL and at that latter stage, there is only exchange of cholesteryl esters between HDL and LDL particles but no net transfer [3]. This process may still be further complicated by the exchange of cholesteryl ester and triglycerides that can take place between LDL and VLDL particles [4], as these reactions appear to be mediated by the concentration gradients of these respective molecules in the donor and acceptor lipoproteins [5].

These pathways may be in part responsible for the production of a spectrum of LDL particles of different sizes in a given individual and this together with genetic differences accounts for the variation in mean hydrated density or size of the LDL that are found in different subjects be they normal [6] or abnormal. In familial hypercholesterolemia for example, LDL concentration is

161

increased but these particles are characterized by a lower than normal mean hydrated density and are cholesteryl ester enriched [7]. In contrast in hyperapobetalipoproteinemia, the LDL that accumulate have a higher mean hydrated density and are small particles that have a decreased cholesteryl ester to apo B ratio [8]. While these differences may result from the overproduction of cholesterol and triglycerides in familial hypercholesterolemic and hyperapobetalipoproteinemia respectively, other factors, such as genetic mutations of apo B may also be involved.

Structural differences in LDL apo B can be studied with the precise probes that are the monoclonal antibodies (MABS). We have described over the past few years a battery of MABS which can be applied to the study of apo B-containing lipoproteins whether in terms of their metabolic heterogeneity or in terms of genetic polymorphism. We shall review here briefly their properties and evaluate how they can be applied to population studies of LDL apo B.

The MABS initially obtained proved to be very useful because they identified at least two distinct structural and functional domains on apo B, that is on the one hand, the region which is common to the hepatic (B-100) and intestinal (B-48) forms of apo B, and on the other hand the region which coincides or overlap with the binding site of apo B with its receptor and which is present or expressed exclusively on B-100 [9,10]. The identification of the latter domain was based on the direct evidence that antibodies 3F5, 4G3, 3A8, 3A10 and 5E11 or their Fab fragments could block both the binding of ^{125}I-LDL to the LDL receptor of cultured human fibroblasts and the LDL-mediated suppression of cholesterol synthesis [9]. A secondary evidence for the identification of this binding domain of apo B which is presumably a limited portion of the molecule, is that the 5 antigenic determinants were spatially grouped together in cotitration experiments [9].

In contrast antibodies 1D1 and 2D8 which reacted with both the hepatic and intestinal forms of apo B [10], identified antigenic determinants which were distant from each other and from the cluster of determinants cited above [9], and neither 1D1 nor 2D8 inhibited binding of LDL to its receptor [9]. These results are compatible with sequence homologies between B-48 and B-100 and led us to propose that all or parts of B-48 sequence is contained within that of B-100. This concept is supported by the antigenic cross-reaction of the 2 proteins also reported by other groups [11,13] In addition, repeated attempts to obtain MABS specific for B-48 by immunization and screening with either B-48- containing chylomicrons or with purified B-48 failed to yield antibodies that would not cross-react with B-100 (Milne and Marcel, unpublished observations). The existence of antigenic determinants that are exclusive for B-100 was also exploited to isolate lipoproteins that contain B-48 as their sole apo B species: apo B-48-containing VLDL were prepared from VLDL of type III [14] and type IV [15] hyperlipoproteinemic subjects using 4G3 and 5E11 coupled to Sepharose as immunoadsorbant columns. These apo B-48-VLDL were both enriched in apo E but the enrichment in cholesteryl esters seen in the fraction isolated from type III was not observed in that isolated from type IV, probably reflecting the longer intravascular half-life of the apo B-48-VLDL in type III. An observation which is in agreement with the demonstration that apo B-48 by itself does not contribute to the binding of these particles to apo E or apo B/E receptors [16].

The antigenic determinants identified by our different MABS on apo B were found to have diverse lipid requirements for their expression [17]. Only MAB 1D1 reacted with delipidated and solubilized apo B, but the immunoreactivity with 2D8 could be recovered upon incorporation of the solubilized apo B into phosphatidyl choline-cholesterol liposomes. In contrast the antigenicity of the other determinants was not restored by incorporation in these liposomes but required the association of apo B with microemulsions consisting of phosphatidylcholine and cholesteryl oleate. These latter recombinant microemulsions, which structurally mimic LDL in having a neutral cholesteryl ester core surrounded by amphipathic lipids, reacted with MAB 3F5, 4G3 and 5E11. We believe that it is highly significant, in terms of apo B tertiary structure that the determinants which have the most stringent lipid requirements are those that are close to the receptor binding domain of apo B. For the recognition of apo B by the LDL receptor, this domain may also require a highly ordered tertiary structure which is a function of its lipid environment.

In summary, these studies demonstrate that LDL apo B of a given normolipemic subject is characterized by three types of antigenic determinants such as those expressed independently of lipids (1D1), those requiring amphipathic lipids (2D8) and finally those which necessitate a hydrophobic core surrounded by amphipathic lipids (3F5, 4G3 and 5E11). Having distinguished these types of determinants in single donors, we could then proceed to evaluate how the expression of each of them varied within LDL subfractions and between LDL of individual subjects of defined populations. A group of patients with hyperapobetalipoproteinemia and of normolipemic subjects was selected for the initial studies[18] and the LDL of each donor were further fractionated according to their densities into LDL-1 (the most buoyant), LDL-2 (the intermediate) and LDL-3 (the densest). These 3 LDL subclasses from the patients and control subjects had an LDL cholesterol to LDL protein ratio ranging from about 0.7 to 1.8 and allowed us to evaluate the relationships between particle size or lipid load of the particle and the immunoreactivity of individual antigenic determinants. Three of the MABS (1D1, 5E11 and 3A10) did not discriminate significantly between the LDL subfractions, whereas 3 other antibodies (2D8, 4G3 and 3F5) were significantly more reactive with LDL-1 and least reactive with LDL-3 [18]. Further the immunoreactivities of antibodies 2D8, 4G3 and 3F5 were highly correlated with the cholesterol to protein ratio of all LDL subfractions of each subject taken together as a group with r values of 0.727, 0.870 and 0.898 respectively [18]. Therefore the expression of each of these 3 determinants is affected in a predictable manner by the LDL cholesterol to protein ratio which is an index of the size of the particles.

When the individual values (inverse of immunoreactivity) for each LDL subfraction of each subject are identified and plotted for each antibody (Figure 1), additional observations can be made: although the immunoreactivities of 3F5 and 4G3 are both highly correlated with the LDL cholesterol to protein ratio, 3F5 immunoreactivity varies by more than 500% over the range of LDL size in contrast to 4G3 immunoreactivity which vary only by about 50%. Therefore antibody 3F5 could prove to be interesting to identify subjects whose LDL particles have a relatively low or high hydrated density. It has been shown in effect that normal subjects are characterized by LDL of different mean hydrated densities and that this parameter remains constant with time for a given individual ; however it is still unknown whether this parameter is under genetic control and related to apo B. Compared to the others, the antigenic determinant recognized by 1D1 is minimally affected by parameters related to size or lipid load of LDL and consequently significant variations in the expression of this determinant would be related to other unknown parameters and thus possibly to genetic modifications.

The opposite reasoning can be held with respect to the determinants identified by antibodies 3A10 and 5E11 as their expression varies greatly and equally within each group of LDL subfractions: the immunoreactivity of these determinants changes significantly but in a manner that is unrelated to the cholesterol to protein ratio of the LDL particles. However when the results are considered on a donor basis, it appears that the reactivities of most sets of LDL subfractions are elevated or decreased simultaneously. Therefore it is possible that the variations in 3A10 and 5E11 immunoreactivities are related to the individual subject and could be under genetic control.

In summary, in each subject, LDL represent a spectrum of particles of different sizes mostly characterized by different ratio of lipids to protein and in addition, the modal hydrated density or size of the LDL can vary from subject to subject. Because we have shown that these parameters will directly influence the expression of certain antigenic determinants but not that of others, it is essential that each determinant be completely

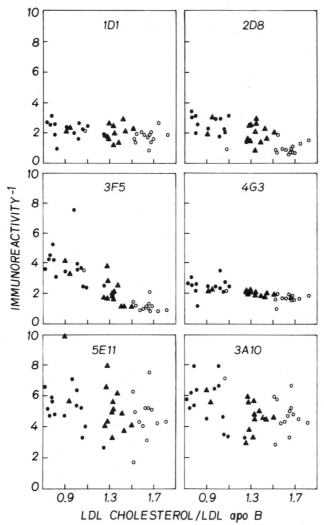

Fig. 1: Immunoreactivity of low density lipoproteins of different density and composition. Individual LDL-1 (o), LDL-2 (▲) and LDL-3 (●) are defined as a function of their cholesterol to protein ratio and the immunoreactivity measured the ability of each fraction to compete with a standard LDL in radioimmunoassays with given MABS (adapted from ref. 18).

characterized before undertaking population studies aimed at the evaluation of the relationships between antigenic expression and genetic polymorphism in apo B.

References

1. S.P. Noël, R. Dupras, C. Vézina and Y.L. Marcel, Comparison of very low density lipoproteins isolated from rat liver perfusate, rat serum and human plasma as acceptors for cholesteryl ester transfer. Biochim. Biophys. Acta 796: 277 (1984).

2. Y.L. Marcel, C. Vézina, B. Teng and A. Sniderman, Transfer of cholesterol esters between human high density lipoproteins and triglyceride-rich lipoproteins controlled by a plasma protein factor. Atherosclerosis 35: 127 (1980).

3. A. Sniderman, B. Teng, C. Vézina and Y.L. Marcel, Cholesterol ester exchange between human plasma high and low density lipoproteins mediated by a plasma protein factor. Atherosclerosis 31: 327 (1978).

4. R.J. Deckelbaum, S. Eisenberg, Y. Oschry, E. Butbul, I. Sharon and T. Olivecrona, Reversible modification of human plasma low density lipoproteins toward triglyceride-rich precursors. A mechanism for losing excess cholesterol esters. J. biol. Chem. 257: 6502 (1982).

5. C.J. Fielding, G.M. Reaven, G. Lin and P.E. Fielding, Increased free cholesterol in plasma low and very low density lipoproteins in non-insulin dependent diabetis mellitus: its role in the inhibition of cholesteryl ester transfer. Proc. Natl. Acad. Sci. USA 81: 2512 (1984).

6. W.R. Fisher, M.G. Hammond, M.C. Mengel and G.L. Warmke, A genetic determinant of the phenotypic variance of the molecular weight of low density lipoprotein. Proc. Natl. Acad. Sci. USA 72: 2347 (1975).

7. B. Teng, G.R. Thompson, A.D. Sniderman, T.M. Forte, R.M. Krauss and P.O. Kwiterovich Jr, Composition and distribution of low density lipoprotein fractions in hyperapobetalipoproteinemia, normolipidemia and familial hypercholesterolemia. Proc. Natl. Acad. Sci. USA 80, 6662 (1983).

8. A.D. Sniderman, S. Shapiro, D. Marpole, B. Skinner, B. Teng and P.O. Kwiterovich Jr, Association of coronary atherosclerosis with hyperapobetalipoproteinemia (increased protein but normal cholesterol levels in human plasma low density (B) lipoproteins). Proc. Natl. Acad. Sci. USA 77: 604 (1980).

9. R.W. Milne, R. Théolis Jr., R.B. Verdery and Y.L. Marcel, Characterization of monoclonal antibodies against human low density lipoproteins. Arteriosclerosis 3:23 (1983).

10. Y.L. Marcel, M. Hogue, R. Théolis Jr. and R.W. Milne, Mapping of antigenic determinants of human apolipoprotein B using monoclonal antibodies against LDL. J. Biol. Chem. 257: 13165 (1982).

11. L.K. Curtiss and T.S. Edgington, Immunochemical heterogeneity of human plasma apolipoprotein B. I. Apolipoprotein B binding of mouse hybridoma antibodies. J. Biol. Chem. 257: 15213 (1982).

12. M.J. Tikkanen, R. Dargar, B. Pfleger, B. Gonen, J.M. Davie and G. Schonfeld, Antigenic mapping of human low density lipoprotein with monoclonal antibodies. J. Lipid Res. 23: 1032 (1982).

13. M.J. Tikkanen, T.G. Cole, K.S. Hahm, E.S. Krul and G. Schonfeld, Expression of apolipoprotein B epitopes in very low density lipoprotein subfractions. Studies with monoclonal antibodies. Arteriosclerosis 4: 138 (1984).

14. R.W. Milne, P.K. Weech, L. Blanchette, J. Davignon, P. Alaupovic and Y.L. Marcel, Isolation and characterization of apolipoprotein B-48 and B-100 very low density lipoprotein from type III hyperlipoproteinemic subjects. J. Clin. Invest. 73: 816 (1984).

15. F. Tercé, R.W. Milne, P.K. Weech, J. Davignon and Y.L. Marcel, Apolipoprotein B-48 and B-100 very low density lipoproteins. Comparison in dysbetalipoproteinemia (type III) and familial hypertriglyceridemia (type IV). Arteriosclerosis 5: 201 (1985).

16. D.Y. Hui, T.L. Innerarity, R.W. Milne, Y.L. Marcel and R.W. Mahley, Binding of chylomicron remnants and B-very low density lipoproteins to hepatic and extrahepatic lipoprotein receptors. A process independent of apolipoprotein B-48. J. Biol. Chem. 259: 15060 (1984).

17. Y.L. Marcel, M. Hogue, P.K. Weech and R.W. Milne, Characterization of antigenic determinants on human solubilized apolipoprotein B. Conformational requirements for lipids. J. Biol. Chem. 259: 6952 (1984).

18. B. Teng, A. Sniderman, R.M. Krauss, P.O. Kwiterovich Jr., R.W. Milne and Y.L. Marcel, Modulation of apolipoprotein B antigenic determinants in human low density lipoprotein subclasses. J. Biol. Chem. 260: 5067 (1985).

STRUCTURE-FUNCTION STUDIES OF APOLIPOPROTEIN B100 AND THE SEARCH FOR MUTANTS

M. John Chapman, P. Forgez, and Thomas L. Innerarity*

INSERM U-9, Hopital de la Pitié, 75651 PARIS Cedex 13, France and *Gladstone Foundation Laboratories for Cardiovascular Disease, Cardiovascular Research Institute, Departments of Pathology and Medicine, University of California, San Francisco, Calif. 94110

The major carrier of cholesterol in the plasma of man and certain mammals is apolipoprotein (apo-) B.[1] This complex and specialized protein is found primarily in and represents the principal protein component of low density lipoproteins (LDL).[2] Apolipoprotein B is currently the focus of much interest in view of the apparent role of LDL in atherosclerosis.[3]

Apolipoprotein B100, the hepatic form of apo-B in man,[4] is the component of LDL that embodies the binding domain for interaction with the apo-B,E(LDL) receptor on cell surface membranes of hepatic and extrahepatic tissues.[5] It is a glycoprotein of variable (up to 10% by weight) carbohydrate content; the sugar moiety is organized into high mannose chains and at least two groups of complex oligosaccharides featuring N-acetylglucosamine, mannose, galactose, fucose, and sialic acid.[6,7] A potential role for such carbohydrate chains may be the protection of certain regions of the B protein sequence from proteases, although other roles, such as stabilization of particle surface organization through ionic and Van der Waal's interactions, cannot be excluded.

Studies of the apo-B100 protein have been hampered by the extreme insolubility and intractability of the protein upon delipidation. These problems have been compounded by the protein's marked sensitivity to oxygen-mediated degradation and proteolytic cleavage and by its tendency to form aggregates.[8-12] Stringent conditions must therefore be adhered to in studies of apo-B100 structure. Both the lipoprotein particles containing this protein and the delipidated apo-B must be effectively protected from both bacterial contamination and peroxidation.[8-10],[13],[14] Protective measures should also be applied to the initial serum or plasma from which apo-B-containing lipoproteins are isolated; moreover, lipoprotein separation should be initiated rapidly to avoid malondialdehyde formation and thence LDL modification.[14]

Practical difficulties in handling apo-B may explain in large part the disparate estimates of its molecular weight and subunit structure and have prompted studies of apo-B in the presence of strong detergents or denaturants.[15] Most recent hydrodynamic studies in which guanidine chloride was used attribute a $M_r \sim$ 400,000 to apo-B100.[16] The influence of the multiple carbohydrate side chains and six intramolecular disulfide bonds[17] on estimates of molecular weight is unknown at present. The very large molecular weight of apo-B100 suggests that there is one apo-B100 protein per molecule of LDL, which is consistent with data from monoclonal antibody studies suggesting the presence of one copy of each epitope per LDL particle.[18]

Strong evidence favoring a high molecular weight for apo-B of hepatic origin has been obtained recently by Knott et al.[19] The nucleotide sequence of complementary DNA that codes the carboxyl-terminal 30% of human apo-B100 was determined. The primary amino acid sequence deduced from the cDNA sequence contained 1,455 amino acids. The apo-B100 message was about 19 kilobases in length, which is sufficient to code for a 400,000- to 550,000-dalton protein. The apo-B100 message was found primarily in liver and, to a lesser extent, in small intestine, but in no other tissues.

Clearly, the protein chemist's direct, classic approaches to the determination of the primary structure of apo-B100 are impractical; the complete sequence of apo-B100 will have to be determined by the molecular biological approach. However, for some problems, the structure of the protein must be studied more directly. One approach has been to do limited proteolysis of apo-B100 either in the native LDL particle or after lipoprotein denaturation in the presence of detergents such as sodium dodecyl sulfate (SDS).[20],[21] This type of approach has made it possible to isolate and sequence small fragments of human apo-B100.[19-21] Such sequences are valuable in the confirmation of the structure obtained for apo-B100 from sequencing of the corresponding cDNA clones.[19]

One of the major features of the limited proteolysis of apo-B100 in native LDL involves the cleavage of this protein into a series of large fragments whose solubilities in aqueous buffers are frequently greater than that of holo-apo-B100.[22],[23] Indeed, when treated with trypsin under defined conditions, LDL-apo-B100 is cleaved into a series of core fragments ranging in molecular weight from ~10,000 to 100,000.[22-25] Such proteolysis occurs concomitantly with selective destruction of certain epitopes on LDL[23] and reduction in the α-helical content of its protein moiety.[26] This latter modification may be largely accounted for by the liberation of soluble, low-molecular-weight peptides (T-peptides) from LDL particles to yield a trypsin-modified molecule (T-LDL) deficient in surface protein.[22,24-26]

Despite loss of surface-exposed protein and extensive cleavage of apo-B100, T-LDL retains the capacity to bind to apo-B,E(LDL) receptors on cultured human skin fibroblasts[24] and porcine adrenocortical membranes,[27] albeit some two- to fourfold less efficiently than its native counterpart. Such proteolyzed particles therefore provide an approach to the identification of segments of apo-B100 possessing biological activity, and particularly of the fragments corresponding to the receptor binding domain. The identification of these fragments is clearly of considerable importance, since mutations in the binding domain of apo-B100 might lead to major perturbations of LDL and cholesterol homeostasis.

Our approach to the identification of receptor-binding fragment(s) in apo-B100 from the LDL of normolipidemic subjects comprised the following steps: 1) cleavage of apo-B100 present in native LDL with TPCK-trypsin,[22,25] 2) isolation of the protein-deficient proteolyzed LDL (T-LDL) and delipidation of the protein moiety with sodium deoxycholate at pH 10,[28] 3) subfractionation of the lipid-free tryptic core fragments by gel filtration chromatography on a Sephacryl S-300 column in deoxycholate-containing buffer, 4) reconstitution of T-LDL by making recombinants either of unfractionated T-LDL protein or isolated fragments with microemulsions of phospholipids and cholesteryl esters,[29] and 5) comparison of the apo-B,E(LDL) receptor binding activity of the protein-lipid recombinants with that of native LDL and of the initial T-LDL in the cultured fibroblast system.[24]

For this strategy to be successful, three criteria had to be fulfilled: 1) the fragmentation pattern of apo-B100 by trypsin should be reproducible, 2) the apo-B100 fragments should be soluble in aqueous buffers after delipidation, and 3) the binding domain of apo-B100 should be preserved in the fragments, and not destroyed by the cleavage treatment. Our earlier studies provided data to satisfy these criteria.[22,24,25]

The recombinants made from the protein moiety of T-LDL showed biological activity in our binding assay, although about 10-fold more recombinant T-LDL than native T-LDL protein was needed to displace 50% of the native ^{125}I-labeled LDL from the apo-B,E(LDL) receptors. The successful recombination of the total, cleaved apo-B100 protein with microemulsion particles suggests the potential of this experimental approach for both the identification of the binding site segment(s) and for the biological screening of segments of apo-B100 synthesized from its cDNA nucleotide sequence.

Monoclonal antibodies that inhibit the receptor binding of LDL should be useful in identifying the binding domain in apo-B100. We therefore screened a series of monoclonal antibodies against human serum LDL (d = 1.02-1.05 g/ml) and observed that antibody 18C4 inhibited ~80% of the direct binding of ^{125}I-labeled LDL to fibroblast apo-B,E(LDL) receptors. This antibody similarly blocked the direct binding of trypsinized LDL (Fig. 1), a finding consistent with our previous observation[24] that the receptor binding domain was maintained in the proteolyzed particles.

To identify more precisely the fragment(s) of apo-B100 that binds to the apo-B,E(LDL) receptor, we performed an immunoblotting of the tryptic polypeptides in T-LDL after electrophoresis in an SDS-polyacrylamide gel. Two bands were identified with antibody

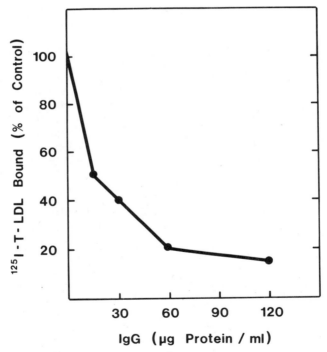

Fig. 1. Graph depicting the inhibition of the binding of ^{125}I-T-LDL to the apo-B,E(LDL) receptor on human fibroblasts. (IgG, immunoglobulin G)

18C4. They had molecular weights of ~22,000 and ~24,000, respectively (Fig. 2). The detection of two bands may be accounted for by the partial cleavage of a trypsin-susceptible peptide bond in the 24,000-dalton polypeptide; partial tryptic cleavages of peptide bonds in apo-B100 have been previously reported.[20],[25] Present studies are aimed at the purification of receptor-binding fragments, determination of their amino acid sequence, and identification of those amino acid residues active in the receptor-binding reaction.

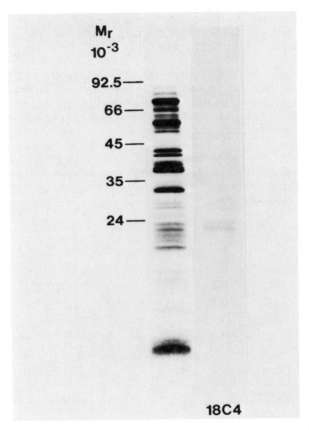

Fig. 2.   Electroimmunoblot of apo-T-LDL with monoclonal antibodies. Apolipoprotein T-LDL was electrophoresed on SDS-polyacrylamide gradient gel (10 to 20%), electrophoretically transferred to nitrocellulose paper, and incubated with monoclonal antibody 18C4. The paper was washed and then incubated with an antibody to mouse immunoglobulin G that was conjugated to peroxidase. On the left is the Coomassie blue-stained electrophoretic pattern of apo-T-LDL, and on the right is the corresponding colorimetric immunoblot after reaction with 18C4.

There are now strong indications from both physicochemical and molecular biological studies that apo-B100 is a high-molecular-weight apolipoprotein,[15] probably ~400,000 to 500,000 daltons, which is equivalent to ~4,000 amino acids. As such, it is 10-fold larger than any of the non-B apolipoproteins characterized to date.[15] In view of its size, molecular variants of apo-B100 would be expected to occur more frequently than those of the other proteins in the apolipoprotein family. The genetic polymorphism of LDL has been described in man,[30] and in a number of animal species, including rabbit, monkey, cow, sheep, pig, and mink.[31] Furthermore, the dysfunction of the apo-B100 gene and the absence of apo-B100 from plasma in abetalipoproteinemia and normotriglyceridemic abetalipoproteinemia have been described.[32]

How might molecular variants of apo-B100 be detected? Two basic approaches may be taken: 1) mutations affecting the biological activity of apo-B100 may be detected either by the screening of LDL in a simplified apo-B,E(LDL) receptor-binding assay[27] or by screening in an enzyme immunoassay using a panel of well-characterized monoclonal antibodies to LDL, and 2) mutations affecting both functional and non-functional regions of apo-B100 may be detected by evaluating the proteolytic cleavage pattern generated with different proteases. At the present time, progress has been made with both approaches.

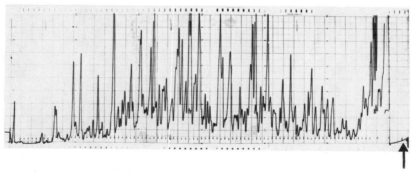

Fig. 3. Elution profile obtained from the fractionation of high-pressure liquid chromatography of a low-molecular-weight, tryptic peptide mixture derived from LDL-apo-B100. The peptide mixture was applied to a C4 reverse phase column and eluted with a gradient of 0 to 35% acetonitrile containing 0.1% trifluoroacetic acid. The eluate was monitored at 214 nm, with a full-scale detection of 0.3 absorbance units. The arrow indicates the point of sample injection.

Schumaker et al.[33] and Young et al.[34] employed the first approach and used monoclonal antibodies to apo-B100 to probe the polymorphism of apo-B. Young et al.[34] used the monoclonal antibody MB19 and a quantitative assay and found three distinct patterns of immunoreactivity: strong, weak, and intermediate. Family studies showed that the three MB19 binding patterns result from codominant transmission of two common apo-B alleles, each coding for an allotype with different affinity for MB19.

Easley et al.[35] employed the second approach and observed distinct tryptic and V8 protease cleavage patterns in LDL from different subjects. This approach has also been pursued in our laboratory, but we have focused on the mapping of hydrosoluble peptides liberated from the surface of LDL by trypsin.[22,25] By use of high-pressure liquid chromatography under suitable conditions, a highly reproducible profile of low-molecular-weight, tryptic peptides may be obtained (Fig. 3). About 200 components have been detected and will be purified and characterized in more detail.

The detection of apo-B100 variants may also be approached at the cDNA and mRNA levels. However, the large size of the genomic DNA and messenger RNA makes a sequencing approach impractical on a routine basis. On the other hand, polymorphisms in restriction fragment length, caused by digestion of genomic DNA from different subjects with restriction endonucleases, provide a simplified and direct method for the identification of deletions, insertions, or more complex rearrangements of the DNA.[36] The eventual application of such a practical approach awaits our further knowledge of the apo-B100 gene.

ACKNOWLEDGMENTS

Part of this work was completed during the tenure of M. J. Chapman as a Visiting Scientist at the Gladstone Foundation Laboratories for Cardiovascular Disease. P. Forgez was supported by a Research Fellowship from ICI-Pharma. We thank Kay Arnold and Shellie Jacobson for their technical assistance, Al Averbach and Sally Gullatt Seehafer for editorial assistance, and Kerry Humphrey for typing the manuscript.

REFERENCES

1. M. J. Chapman, Animal lipoproteins: chemistry, structure, and comparative aspects, J. Lipid Res. 21:789 (1980).
2. L. C. Smith, H. J. Pownall, and A. M. Gotto, Jr., The plasma lipoproteins: structure and metabolism, Annu. Rev. Biochem. 47:751 (1978).

3. R. W. Mahley, Development of accelerated atherosclerosis: concepts derived from cell biology and animal model studies, Arch. Pathol. Lab. Med. 107:393 (1983).

4. J. P. Kane, Apolipoprotein B: structural and metabolic heterogeneity, Annu. Rev. Physiol. 45:637 (1983).

5. R. W. Mahley and T. L. Innerarity, Lipoprotein receptors and cholesterol homeostasis, Biochim. Biophys. Acta 737:197 (1983).

6. N. Swaminathan and F. Aladjem, The monosaccharide composition and sequence of the carbohydrate moiety of human serum low density lipoproteins, Biochemistry 15:1516 (1976).

7. P. Lee and W. C. Breckenridge, Isolation and carbohydrate composition of glycopeptides of human apo low-density lipoprotein from normal and type II hyperlipoproteinemic subjects, Can. J. Biochem. 54:829 (1976).

8. M. J. Chapman and J. P. Kane, Stability of the apoprotein of human serum low density lipoprotein: absence of endogenous endopeptidase activity, Biochem. Biophys. Res. Commun. 66:1030 (1975).

9. K. V. Krishnaiah and H. Weigandt, Demonstration of protease-like activity in human serum low density lipoprotein, FEBS Lett. 40:265 (1974).

10. J. Schuh, G. F. Fairclough, Jr., and R. H. Haschemeyer, Oxygen-mediated heterogeneity of apo-low-density lipoprotein, Proc. Natl. Acad. Sci. USA 75:3173 (1978).

11. J. C. H. Steele, Jr., and J. A. Reynolds, Characterization of the apolipoprotein B polypeptide of human plasma low density lipoprotein in detergent and denaturant solutions, J. Biol. Chem. 254:1633 (1979).

12. S. Margolis and R. G. Langdon, Studies on human serum β_1-lipoprotein. III. Enzymatic modifications, J. Biol. Chem. 241:485 (1966).

13. D. M. Lee, A. J. Valente, W. H. Kuo, and H. Maeda, Properties of apolipoprotein B in urea and in aqueous buffers: the use of glutathione and nitrogen in its solubilization, Biochim. Biophys. Acta 666:133 (1981).

14. D. M. Lee, Malondialdehyde formation in stored plasma, Biochim. Biophys. Res. Commun. 95:1663 (1980).

15. R. W. Mahley, T. L. Innerarity, S. C. Rall, Jr., and K. H. Weisgraber, Plasma lipoproteins: apolipoprotein structure and function, J. Lipid Res. 25:1277 (1984).

16. J. Elovson, J. C. Jacobs, V. N. Schumaker, and D. L. Puppione, Molecular weights of apoprotein B obtained from human low-density lipoprotein (apoprotein B-PI) and from rat very low density lipoprotein (apoprotein B-PIII), Biochemistry 24:1569 (1985).

17. A. D. Cardin, K. R. Witt, C. L. Barnhart, and R. L. Jackson, Sulfhydryl chemistry and solubility properties of human plasma apolipoprotein B, Biochemistry 21:4503 (1982).

18. R. W. Milne and Y. L. Marcel, Monoclonal antibodies against

human low density lipoprotein: stoichiometric binding studies using Fab fragments, FEBS Lett. 146:97 (1982).

19. T. J. Knott, S. C. Rall, Jr., T. L. Innerarity, S. F. Jacobson, M. S. Urdea, B. Levy-Wilson, L. M. Powell, R. J. Pease, R. Eddy, H. Nakai, M. Byers, L. M. Priestley, E. Robertson, L. B. Rall, C. Betsholtz, T. B. Shows, R. W. Mahley, and J. Scott, Human apolipoprotein B: structure of carboxyl-terminal domains, sites of gene expression, and chromosomal localization, Science 230:37 (1985).

20. W. A. Bradley, M. F. Rohde, and A. M. Gotto, Jr., Studies on the primary structure of apolipoprotein B. Ann. NY Acad. Sci. 348:87 (1980).

21. R. C. LeBoeuf, C. Miller, J. E. Shively, V. N. Schumaker, M. A. Balla, and A. J. Lusis, Human apolipoprotein B: partial amino acid sequence, FEBS Lett. 170:105 (1984).

22. M. J. Chapman, S. Goldstein, and G. L. Mills, Limited tryptic digestion of human serum low-density lipoprotein: isolation and characterization of the protein-deficient particle and of its apoprotein, Eur. J. Biochem. 87:475 (1978).

23. K.-S. Hahm, M. J. Tikkanen, R. Dargar, T. G. Cole, J. M. Davie, and G. Schonfeld, Limited proteolysis selectively destroys epitopes on apolipoprotein B in low density lipoproteins, J. Lipid Res. 24:877 (1983).

24. M. J. Chapman, T. L. Innerarity, K. S. Arnold, and R. W. Mahley, In vitro apo-B,E receptor binding and in vivo catabolism of trypsin-modified low-density lipoproteins, in "Latent Dyslipoproteinemias and Atherosclerosis," J. L. de Gennes et al., eds., Raven Press, New York (1984).

25. M. J. Chapman, A. Millet, D. Lagrange, S. Goldstein, Y. Blouquit, C. E. Taylaur, and G. L. Mills, The surface-exposed, trypsin-accessible segments of apolipoprotein B in the low-density lipoprotein of human serum: fractionation and characterisation of the liberated peptides, Eur. J. Biochem. 125:479 (1982).

26. G. C. Chen, M. J. Chapman, and J. P. Kane, Secondary structure and thermal behavior of trypsin-treated low-density lipoproteins from human serum, studied by circular dichroism, Biochim. Biophys. Acta 754:51 (1983).

27. M. J. Chapman, F. Y. M. Loisay, P. Forgez, and H. Cadman, Characterisation of heterologous and homologous low-density lipoprotein binding to apolipoprotein B,E receptors on porcine adrenal cortex membranes: enhanced binding of trypsin-modified human low density lipoprotein. Biochim. Biophys. Acta 835:258 (1985).

28. A. Helenius and K. Simons, Removal of lipids from human plasma low-density lipoproteins by detergents, Biochemistry 10:2542 (1971).

29. M. T. Walsh and D. Atkinson, Solubilization of low-density lipoprotein with sodium deoxycholate and recombination of apoprotein B with dimyristoylphosphatidylcholine, Biochemistry

22:3170 (1983).

30. G. M. Kostner, Lp(a) lipoproteins and the genetic polymorphisms of lipoprotein B, in "Low-Density Lipoproteins," C. E. Day and R. S. Levy, eds., Plenum Press, New York (1976).

31. M. J. Chapman, Comparative analysis of mammalian plasma lipoproteins, in "Methods in Enzymology," J. Segrest and J. J. Albers, eds., Academic Press, Orlando, Florida, in press.

32. M. J. Malloy, J. P. Kane, D. A. Hardman, R. L. Hamilton, and K. B. Dalal, Normotriglyceridemic abetalipoproteinemia: absence of the B-100 apolipoprotein, J. Clin. Invest. 67:1441 (1981).

33. V. N. Schumaker, M. T. Robinson, L. K. Curtiss, R. Butler, and R. S. Sparkes, Anti-apoprotein B monoclonal antibodies detect human low density lipoprotein polymorphism, J. Biol. Chem. 259:6423 (1984).

34. S. G. Young, S. J. Bertics, L. K. Curtiss, D. C. Casal, J. L. Witztum, Monoclonal antibody MB19 detects genetic polymorphism in human apolipoprotein B, J. Biol. Chem., in press.

35. C. W. Easley, B. W. Patterson, and W. R. Fisher, A comparative study of enzymatic digestion profiles of apolipoprotein B from four human subjects, Biochim. Biophys. Acta 751:145 (1983).

36. D. L. Williams, Molecular biology in arteriosclerosis research, Arteriosclerosis 5:213 (1985).

IMMUNOBLOT ANALYSIS OF THE DIFFERENT APOLIPOPROTEIN B SPECIES

Carlo Gabelli*, Richard E. Gregg**, H. Bryan Brewer Jr.**

*Dept. of Internal Medicine, University of Padua, Padova
Italy and ** Molecular Disease Branch, NHLBI, National
Institutes of Health, Bethesda, MD, U.S.A.

INTRODUCTION

During the last two decades a great effort to understand the
structure of apolipoprotein B (apoB) has been made, however despite the relative ease of isolation, the detailed physico-chemical
characteristics of this protein are still unknown due to its large
apparent molecular weight and insolubility in aqueous buffers after
delipidation. The function of apoB is only partially known. In LDL.
apoB is the predominant apolipoprotein and is the protein ligand for
binding to the high affinity LDL receptor[1]. Genetic absence of apoB
is associated to severely impaired lipid transport[2]. In addition, it
is now known that there are multiple forms of apoB with different
molecular weights in the rat[3-5] and in man[6]. In man there are two
major forms, the larger apolipoprotein being designated apoB-100
and the small one apoB-48[6-8]. ApoB-100 is of hepatic origin and is
present on VLDL, IDL, and LDL. ApoB-48 is of intestinal origin and
is found predominantly on chylomicrons and on chylomicrons remnants
within VLDL and IDL[6-8].

The separation of the two forms of apoB coupled with immunoblot
techniques can be successfully used for separation and detection of
low amounts of these proteins as well as in the analysis of structure and metabolism of apoB-48 and apoB-100 by monoclonal antibodies.

Separation of the two B apolipoprotein is the first step for
further protein blotting and immunological assay.

ApoB-48 and apo-100 can be seperated by gel permeation chromatography in Sodium dodecylsulfate(NaDodSo$_4$)[9]: however, this method

179

is time consuming and it is difficult to isolate and quantitate small samples of protein. An alternative approach for separation of the B apolipoproteins is by 3% NaDodSO$_4$-PAGE[6],[10]. However, at this concentration of acrylamide, the gel matrix is very weak and handling becomes difficult. In addition, because of the weakness of the gel matrix, vertical slab gel electrophoresis is not feasible.

We have developed a modification of a method originally used for separation of ribonucleic acid, utilizing agarose-acrylamide gel electrophoresis, the resulting gel has the characteristic of being able to separate large molecular weight proteins while being of sufficient strenght to be utilized in a vertical slab gel apparatus and the gel immunoblotted or autoradiographed.

MATERIAL AND METHODS

Materials and Reagents

Acrylamide, bisacrylamide, TEMED, ammonium persulfate, NaDodSO$_4$, electrophoresis purity agarose (low gel temperature), bromphenol blue, and Coomassie brillant blue R-250 were purchased from Bio-Rad Laboratories. DTT was obtained from Schwarz-Mann, ultrapure Tris from Bethesda Research Laboratories. Inc., boric acid from Mallinckrodt, and certified ACS potassium bromide and EDTA from Fisher Scientific. A buffer containing 0.89 M Tris (pH 8.3) and 0.89 M boric acid (ten times the working concentration) was prepared filtered, and stored in a glass bottle at room temperature. A one percent NaDodSO$_4$ solution (ten times the working concentration)was kept as a stock solution at room temperature. Ten percent ammonium persulfate was kept at 4°C and made fresh weekly.

Sample preparation

Blood was collected in Na$_2$EDTA (1 mg/ml) and the plasma was quickly separated by centrifugation (2000 rpm) for 30 min at 4°C. Sodium azide (0.05%) and aprotinin (1000 KIU/ml) (Boeringer-Manheim) were added to the plasma. Lipoprotein fractions were obtained by ultracentrifugation in a Beckman 40.3 rotor at 39,000 rpm and 4°C [12]. Lipoproteins were isolated by tube slicing, dialyzed against 0.01 M EDTA containing 0.05% NaN$_3$ (pH 8.0),lyophilized, and delipidated with chloroform-methanol, 2:1 (v/v)[13]. Due to the insolubility of apoB-100 and apoB-48 in aqueous solutions, a tecnique was developed for dissolving the protein pellets in the sample buffer after delipidation. A small quantity of chloroform-methanol

(200-300 μl) was left in the bottom of the tube after delipidation. Tubes were warmed briefly (approximately 5 sec) in a 100°C oil bath. Fifty to 200 μl (depending on the thickness of the gel being used) of 1X Tris-borate buffer containg 3% NaDodSo$_4$ and 1.2% DTT was added while wortexing. The remaing chloroform-methanol was imme- diately volatilized with a nitrogen stream while still vortexing. To increase the denaturation of the apolipoproteins, sample were left at room temperature for 1 hour and then heated to 100°C for 3 min. One or two drops of 0.1% bromophenol blue in glycerol-water 1:1 (v/v) were added to each sample.

Agarose-Acrylamide Gel Electrophoresis

Agarose (1%) was dissolved in double distilled H$_2$O in a reflux apparatus (round bottom flask and condenser), which was heated just to boiling with a heating mantle. Crystalline acrylamide and bis- acrylamide were dissolved in 2X Tris-borate buffer containing 0.2% NaDodSO$_4$ to give final concentrations of 4% and 0.21%, respectively, and stirred in a water bath at 40°C. The agarose solution was then cooled to 40°C (with stirring) under a stream of tap water. The agarose and acrylamide solutions were mixed 1:1 and stirred at 40°C. The final concentrations were 2% acrylamide, 0.5% agarose, 0.105% bisacrylamide, and 0.1% NaDodSO$_4$ in 1X Tris-borate buffer (0.089% M). Ammonium persulfate (0.5 ml of 10% solution) and TEMED (33 ul) were added per 100 ml of agarose-acrylamide solution just prior to pouring. The solution was then quickly poured into 12 x 14 cm gels in a ver- tical slab gel apparatus (Hoefer SE 500,San Francisco, CA) which were cooled with circulating water at 20°C. Well formers cooled to 4°C were inserted and the gels left to polymerize overnigth at 20°C. A 1X Tris-borate buffer (pH 8.3) containing 0.1% NaDodSO$_4$ was utilized as a running buffer in both the upper and lower buffer chambers. Before electrophoresis the gels were cooled to 4°C and the electrophoreis performed at a constant voltage of 200 V at 4°C until the tracking dye reached the bottom of the gel (approximately 1.5 hours). Gels were either stained with Coomassie Blue for protein or used for transfer of protein to nitrocellulose[14]. When the gels were stained they were poured in methanol-water-acetic acid (10:10:1 v/v) containing 0.1% Coomassie brilliant blue R-250 for 30 minutes and destained in 5% methanol-7.5% acetic acid.

Immunoblotting

Proteins were tranferred to nitrocellulose paper (Schleicher-

Schuell 0.45 μm) at either 80 V for 2 h, 4°C, or at 30 V overnight at 4°C using a tranfer buffer containing 25 mM Tris-HCl, pH 8.3, 192 mM glycine, and 20% methanol.

After transfer protein binding sites on the nitrocellulose were blocked by incubation in 3% gelatine in TBS (20 mM Tris, 500 mM NaCl, pH 7.5) for 1h. The nitrocellulose paper was then incubated for 16-20 h with different monospecific policlonal antibodies raised in rabbit and in goat or with monoclonal antibodies obtained in mice. Usual dilution was for policlonal antibodies from 1:500 to 1:2000 and for monoclonal antibodies from 1:200 to 1:50. After incubation the nitrocellulose was washed three times for 15 min in TBS and incubated 4-6 h in 1% gelatin in TBS containing a 1:2500 dilution of an affinity purified horseradish peroxidase conjugated second antibody (anti-rabbit or goat or mice IgG) (Bio-Rad). The paper was rinsed again in TBS three times for 15 min and peroxidase was detected with a color reagent (Bio-Rad) according with the manufacturer's specifications.

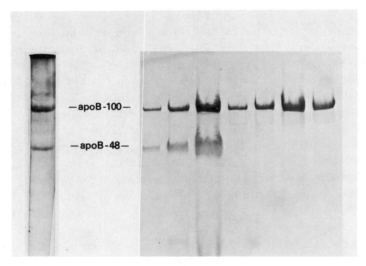

Fig. 1.   Tube and slab gel electrophoresis of apoB-100 and apoB-48. Left: 70 ug of VLDL protein from an apoE deficient patient separated by acrylamide NaDodSO$_4$ gel electrophoresis in a tube gel (7 x 100 mm). Right: lanes (left to right) contain 10 μg, 25 μg and 50 μg of VLDL protein isolated from a patient with apoE deficiency, the last four lanes contain 10 μg, 25 μg, 40 μg and 30 μg of normal VLDL protein separated by agarose-acrylamide slab gel electrophoresis.

RESULTS AND DISCUSSION

The polymorphic forms of apoB have previously been separated by 3% acrylamide NaDodSO$_4$-PAGE[6], but a difficulty with this system is the fragility of the polymerized gel. The tube gels break easly and the gel matrix is not of sufficient strenght to be utilized in vertical slab gel electrophoresis. To overcome this problem, we have adapted the agarose-acrylamide gel electrophoresis system of Peacock and Dingman[11-15] to separate the different forms of ApoB; Fig. 1 illustrates the sepraration of apoB forms from VLDL of a normal subject with predominately apoB-100 and an apoE deficient subject with both apoB-100 and apoB-48. There is good sepration between apoB-100 and apoB-48 even in the lanes in which the gel was markedly overloaded with protein (40-50 µg), and the separation is comparable to that obtained with 3% acrylamide tube gel electroporesis (Fig. 1).

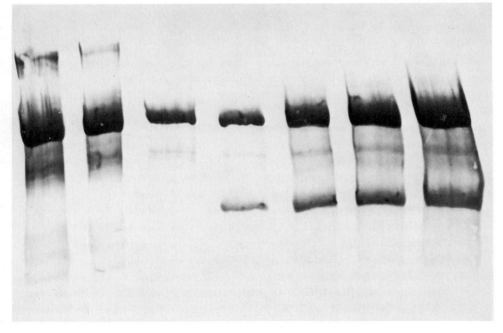

Fig. 2.   Immunoblot of VLDL; from left to right 10,5,2, µg of normal
          VLDL protein and 2,5,10,20 µg VLDL protein from an apo E
          deficient patient. In the first two lanes a band above apoB
          100 band is evident. Immunoblot was developed with a rabbit
          polyclonal anti-apoB antiserum

The agarose-acrylamide gel method together with the immuno-blotting technique greately enhances the possibility to detect small amounts of apoB species. Good immunoreactivity was obtained using only 2 μg of total VLDL protein where we extimated apoB accounted for about 25% (∿0.5 μg) (Fig. 2). Moreover this method allows to study the different affinity of monoclonal antibodies for the different apoB species. Monoclonal antibodies however generally shows lower affinity for the protein and for some of them a sligtly different protocol must be used for detection at the antibody-antigen complexes[16]. A band of apparent higher apparent molecular weight than apoB-100 can be detected in some samples (Fig. 2); it has been our experience that this band greately decreases or disappears after prolonged treatment (3 h) with DTT at 37°C, and it may rappresent an apoB-apo(a) complex.

In conclusion, we have found that agarose-acrylamide gel electrophoresis coupled with immunoblotting increase the possibility to detect small amounts of apoB protein and may facilitate the investigation apoB structure.

ACKNOWLEDGEMENTS

This work was partially supported by the National Research Council of Italy (C.N.R. Progetto Bilaterale 84.0185.04)

REFERENCES
1. M. S. Brown, P.T. Kovanen, and J.L. Goldstein, 1981, Regulations of plasma cholesterol by lipoprotein receptors, Science 212: 628-635
2. P. H. Herbert, G. Assmann, A. M. Gotto, Jr., D.D. Fredrickson, 1983, Familial lipoprotein deficiency: abetalipoproteinemia, hypobetalipoproteinemia, and Tangier disease, In the Metabolic Basis of Inherited Disease, J. B. Stambury, J. B. Wyngaarden, D. D. Fredrickson, J. L. Goldstein, and M. S. Brown, editors, McGraw-Hill, New York, 5th ed. 589-621
3. K. V. Krishnaiah, L. F. Walker, K. Borensztjn, G. Schonfeld, and G. S. Getz, 1980, Apolipoprotein B variant derived from rat intestine, Proc. Natl. Acad. Sci. USA, 77:3806-3810
4. J. Elovson, Y. O. Huang, N. Baker, and R. Kannan, 1981, Apolipoprotein B is structurally and metabolically heterogenous in the rat, Proc. Natl. Acad. Sci USA, 78:157-161
5. C. E. Sparks, and J. B. Marsh, 1981, Metabolic heterogeneity of apolipoprotein B in the rat, J. Lipid Res. 22:519-527

6. J. P. Kane, D. A. Hardman, and H. E. Paulus, 1980, Heterogeneity of apolipoprotein B: Isolation of a new species from human chylomicrons, Proc. Natl. Acad. Sci. USA, 77: 2465-2469
7. M. S. Meng, R. E. Gregg, E. J. Schaefer, J. M. Hoeg, and H. B. Brewer, Jr., 1983, Presence of two forms of apolipoprotein B in patients with dyslipoproteinema, J. Lipid Res. 24: 803-809
8. J. P. Kane, G. Chi Chen, R. L. Hamilton, D. A. Hardman, M. J. Malloy, and R. J. Havel, 1983, Remnants of lipoproteins of intestinal and hepatic origin in familial dysbetalipoproteinemia, Arteriosclerosis 3:47-56
9. C. E. Sparks, and J. B. Marsh, 1981, Analysis of lipoprotein apoproteins by SDS gel filtration colum chromatography, J. Lipid Res. 22:514-518
10. K. Weber, and M. Osborn, 1969, The reliability of molecular weight determinations by dodecyl sulfate-polyacrylamide gel electrophoresis, J. Biol. Chem. 244:4406-4412
11. A. C. Peacock, and C. W. Dingman, 1968, Molecular weight estimation and separation of ribunocleic acid by electrophoresis in agarose-acrylamide composite gels, Biochemistry 7:668-674
12. R. J. Havel, H. A. Eder, and J. H. Bragdon, 1955, The distribution and chemical composition of ultracentrifugally separated lipoproteins in human serum, J. Clin. Invest. 34:1345-1353
13. R. J. Folch, M. Lees, and G. H. Sloan-Stanley, 1957, A simple method for the isolation and purification of total lipids from animal tissue, J. Biol. Chem. 226:497-509
14. H. Towbin T. Staehlin, and J. Gordon, 1979, Electrophoretic transfer of proteins from polyacrylamide gels to nitrocellulose sheet, Proc. Natl. Acad. Sci USA, 76:4350-4354
15. C. Gabelli, D. G. Stark, R. E. Gregg and H. B. Brewer Jr., Separation of apolipoprotein B species by agarose-acrylamide gel electrophoresis, Submitted for publication.
16. A. L. Be Blas, H. M. Cherwinski, 1983, Detection of antigens on nitrocellulose paper immunoblots with monoclonal antibodies, Anal. Biochem. 133:214-219

APOLIPOPROTEIN C-II DEFICIENCY

A.L. Catapano and A. Capurso*

Institute of Pharmacology and Pharmacognosy Via A. Del
Sarto 21, Milano and* Istituto di Clinica Medica II
Università di Bari, Bari, Italy

Apolipoprotein C-II (Apo C-II) is a protein component of chylomicrons, very low density (VLDL) and high density lipoproteins (HDL) (1) which plays a key role in the activation of lipoprotein lipase (LPL), an enzyme located at the capillary endotelium of the muscle, heart and adipose tissue (2). Its primary structure consists of 79 aminoacids as determined by protein sequence and from the cDNA (3,4). It also consist of two functionally distinct regions. The HH_2 terminal, up to approx residue 45, which contains the lipid binding region (high probability of helix) and the COOH terminal region responsible for the activation of and binding to LPL (5,6). Studies performed using synthetic peptide (5) has allowed a detailed mapping of the Apo C-II region involved in the LPL activation (7,8). A clear cut demonstration of the pivotal role of Apo C-II in the catabolism of triglyceride rich lipoproteins in vivo is the Apo C-II deficiency syndrome (9).

Here we review the data available in literature on Apo C-II deficiency in terms of clinical as well biochemical hallmarks of the disease.

In TABLE 1 a list the cases of Apo C-II deficiency so far reported in literature is reported (9-15). These are listed as kindreds in agreement with the fact that Apo C-II deficiency is transmitted as an autosomal recessive trait (16).

187

TABLE I

KINDREDS AFFECTED BY APO C-II DEFICIENCY

Kindred	N.of homozygotes	Age at Detection	Location
1 (9,21)*	12	17-62	Canada
2 (10)	2	13-15	Japan
3 (11)	1	30	England
4 (12)	4	31-36	Holland
5 (13)	2	4-8	Italy
6 (14)	2	35-37	Italy
7 (15)	1	5	USA

* numbers in brackets represent the references cited in the text

7 families have been reported since the original discovery in 1978 of a Canadian kindred (9) for a total of 23 patients affected by the homozygous form of Apo C-II deficiency, whose condition was detected as early as at 5 years of Age (15).

CLINICALS FEATURES

Apo C-II deficiency appears to be related to episodies of abdominal pain and pancreatitis , in several patients also hepatosplenomegaly has been reported. Xantomata are also present in a few patients. None of the patient was diabetic but one, furthermore Apo C-II deficiency does not appear to be linked to coronary heart disease (9-15).

Interestingly plasma triglycerides levels are relatively lower than the values seen in LPL deficiency, therefore it appears that the latter syndrome results in more overt clinical symptoms that Apo C-II deficiency. This is in agreement with the notion that Apo C-II is not a true cofactor for the LPL, i.e. the lipoprotein lipase has a basal activity towards lipoprotein triglycerides which is increased several fold by the presence of Apo C-II.

PLASMA LIPOPROTEINS AND APOPROTEINS

Among the homozygous patient studied the lipoprotein distribution is largely modified (table 2). Chylomicrons are present and VLDL are often increased with respect to controls. Several patients have, in fact, high VLDL (9-11) while some others do not (13) ;the reason for this discrepancy is unclear. Different dietary menagement as well as a possible heterogeneity of the disease or association with other metabolic deficiencies (12) can explain these findings . In addition to this the distribution of VLDL particles is changed towards larger ones (S_f 100) (11) thus suggesting that chylomicron remnants might be in part accumulating the VLDL density range. This is in agreement with data by Catapano et al (13). Furthermore low density lipoproteins LDL and HDL cholesterol are dramatically decreased (9-15). The ratio cholesterol to triglycerides in the LDL and HDL fractions is also decreased (13) suggesting that part of the decrease of LDL and HDL cholesterol can be accounted for by the exchange of lipoprotein cholesterol with an enlarged circulating pool of triglycerides. Catapano et al (13) and Miller et al (11), however, detected a decrease of LDL and HDL mass by analytical ultracentrifugation in the plasma of two C-II deficient patients.

Apolipoprotein levels have been evaluated in several patients (table 3). Apo A-I, Apo A-II and Apo B, in agreement with the low levels of LDL and HDL. (9-11,13-15). Another consistent finding is the increase of Apo C-III, as well as Apo E. Since the pool of TG rich lipoproteins is largely increased this is not surprising. (9-11,13-15). Apo B 100 and 48 are present in the VLDL of the probands (13) as determined by SDS gel electrophoresis. Chylomicron remnants floating in the VLDL density range might have contributed to the Apo B eterogeneity of VLDL. Apo C-II, of course, is not detectable by isoelectric focusing or immunochemistry. However a recent report (17) suggests that abnormal iso forms of Apo C-II are present and can be detected by immunoblotting. These protein do not activate lipoprotein lipase altough some but probably not all antigenic sites are present. These data clearly show that as abnormal C-II is produced. Whether this is a product of an abnormal gene or of an abnormal post traslattional processing is not known. We have not been able to detect such a protein in our patient by immunoblotting (18). This finding points towards a heterogeneity of the disease which leads to a common

TABLE 2

PLASMA LIPOPROTEINS IN HOMOZYGOTES WITH APOLIPOPROTEIN CII
DEFICIENCY

KINDRED	N. OF PAT.	PLSMA TG.	PLASMA CHOL.	VLDL CHOL.	LDL CHOL.	HDL CHOL.
1	12	high	normal	high	low	low
2	2	high	normal	high	low	low
3	1	high	normal	normal	low	low
4	4	high	normal	high	low	low
5	2	high	normal	low	low	low
6	2	high	normal	high	low	low
7	1	high	normal	N.D.	low	low

TABLE 3

PLASMA APOLIPOPROTEINS IN HOMOZYGOTES WITH APOLIPOPROTEIN
C-II DEFICIENCY

KINDRED	APO A-I	APO A-II	APO B	APO C-III	APO D	APO E
1	low	low	low	high	normal	high
2	N.D.	N.D.	N.D.	high	N.D.	N.D.
3	low	low	low	high	N.D.	high
4	N.D.	N.D.	N.D.	N.D.	N.D.	N.D.
5	low	low	low	high	N.D.	high
6	low	N.D.	low	N.D.	N.D.	N.D.
7	low	low	normal	N.D.	N.D.	high

phenotype as it is the case of familial homozygous hypercholeste-
rolemia(19).

That the deficiency of Apo C-II is responsible for the
hypertriglyceridemia and for the derangements of lipoprotein
distribution in these patients has been shown by providing the
patients with exogenous Apo C-II as plasma. In several patients
while C-II was very low after plasma infusion and sometimes not
detectable ,plasma TG rapidly fell and after a lack of 10 to 40h
LDL and HDL cholesterol started to raise (11-13). Apo A-I and Apo
B also increased in one study (11) ,Apo A-I in another (13). The
discrepancy on the Apo B may be related to technical problems due
to the large pool of Apo B carried by chylomicrons and VLDL which
could be underestimated, depending upon the method used.

The problem then arises as to whether C-II deficiency can be
related to a defective synthesis of the protein. Studies carried
with FRPL analysis of the DNA from two patients suggest that no
major rearrangements take place in their gene (20) furthermore,
we have shown ,in studies to be published elsewhere, that also our
patient has an apparently normal organization of the DNA. We were
also able to show that Apo C-II could be determined in the
intestinal mucosa of the proband by immunolocalization (18). This
finding suggests that Apo C-II is synthetyzed by the intestinal
mucosa of the patient but is either not secreted in appreciable
amounts or rapidly removed from the circulation. Further studies
are required to address these possibilities.

Apo C-II deficiency has clearly demonstrated that this
apoprotein also _in vivo_ is a must for a correct catabolism of
triglyceride rich lipoprotein. However this syndrome has raised
several other questions, for istance obligate heterozygotes have
30-50% of normal Apo C-II in their VLDL but their lipoprotein
pattern is still normal (13,21).This suggests, together with the
experiments of plasma infusion, that a large excess of Apo C-II is
present in plasma. One could speculate that since C-II must
shuttle from mature plasma lipoproteins to nascent ones its excess
may represent a functional reservoir. Alternatively Apo C-II may
play some other, not yet elucidated, functions.

Apo C-II deficiency also proved useful for in vitro studies
where the natural substrate for the action of LPL can be used.
This is of course a great advantage in order to understand the

mechanism by which the enzyme acts on triglyceride rich lipoproteins and how Apo C-II activates the LPL. Studies performed along these lines are in fact present in the literature (22,23).

The lipoproteins from the C-II homozygotes are largely modified in their lipid content. It has been recently shown that LDL rich in triglycerides are very frequently found in hypertriglyceridemia, and these lipoproteins have a reduced affinity for the cellular LDL receptor (24,25). We have tested this possibility with Apo C-II deficient VLDL and LDL. LDL from the proband failed to effectively suppress cholesterol biosynthesis in these cells. This finding is not surprising since LDL from the proband are rich in triglycerides, it suggests however that more lipoproteins are required to interact with cellular receptors to obtain the same effect on cholesterol biosynthesis. It is possible therefore that LDL receptors in vivo will be up regulated in Apo C-II deficient patients owing the reduced efficiency of the lipoprotein receptors interaction. LDL kinetics in vivo as well studies on cholesterol metabolism may shade more light on this point and could, at least in part, explain the massive response of Apo C-II deficient subjects to the infusion of small amounts of plasma. An high level of LDL receptors expression may in fact represent a preferential pathway for the removal of VLDL and chylomicron remnants from the plasma.

CONCLUSIONS

The discovery of several patients affected by Apo C-II deficiency has clearly demonstrated in vivo the pivotal role of Apo C-II in the catabolism of triglyceride rich lipoproteins (9-15).

Furthermore lipoprotein isolated from these patients are useful tools is explore the mechanism of activation of LPL Apo C-II using a natural substrate. A final point, which clearly deserves further attention is the clear heterogeneity of the disease in therms of the defective protein (Apo C-II) which seems to be either fully absent or present as abnormal isoforms which do not activate the enzyme lipoprotein lipase.

This field of research is clearly the most promising for the understanding of the moleculare basis of thes deficiency as well as to have a "nature experiment" which will further help in the understanding of the functionally relevant areas of Apo C-II involved in the activation of LPL.

ACKNOWLEDGEMENTS

This work was supported in part by a CNR grant Progetto Finalizzato Malattie Degenerative ob.43 to ALC and to AC. Miss Silvana Magnani typed the manuscript.

REFERENCES

1. Jackson R.L.,Baker H.N.,Gilliam E.B. and Gotto A.M. Primary structure of very low density apolipoprotein C-II of human plasma.Proc.Natl.Acad.Sci.USA 74:1942(1977).
2. Nilsson-Ehle P.,Garfinkel A.S. and Schotz M.C. Lipolytic enzymes and plasma lipoprotein metabolism.Ann.Rev.Biochem.49:667 (1980).
3. Hospattankar A.V.,Fairwell T.,Ronan R. and Brewer H.B. Amino acid sequence of human plasma apolipoprotein C-II from normal and hyperlipoproteinemic subjects. J.Biol.Chem. 259:318 (1984).
4. Myklebost S.,Rogers J.,Woods D.E. and Humphries S.E. The isolation and characterization of cDNA clones for human plasma apolipoprotein C-II. J.Biol.Chem. 259:4401 (1984).
5. Smith L.C.,Voyta J.C.,Catapano A.L.,Kinnunen P.K.J.,Gotto A.M. and Sparrow J.T. Activation of lipoprotein lipase by synthetic fragments of apo C-II. Ann.N.Y.Acad.Sci. 348:213 (1980).
6. Kinnunen P.K.J.,Jackson R.L.,Smith L.C. and Gotto A.M. Activation of lipoprotein lipase by native and synthetic fragments of human plasma apo C-II. Proc.Natl.Acad.Sci.USA 74:4848 (1977).
7. Catapano A.L.,Kinnunen P.K.J.,Breckenridge W.C.,Gotto A.M.,Jackson R.L.,Little J.A.,Smith L.C. and Sparrow J.T. Lipolysis of apo C-II deficient very low density lipoproteins.Enhancement of lipoprotein lipase activity by synthetic fragments of apo C-II. Biochem.Biophys.Res.Commun. 89:951(1979).
8. Musliner T.A.,Herbert P.N. and Church E.C. Activation of lipoprotein lipase by native and acylated peptides of apolipoprotein C-II. Biochim.Biophys.Acta. 573:501 (1979).
9. Breckenridge W.C.,Little J.A.,Steiner G.,Chow A. and Poapst M. Hypertriglyceridemia associated with deficiency of apolipoprotein C-II. N.Engl.J.Med. 298:1265 (1978).

10. Yamamura T.,Sudo H.,Ishikawa K. and Yamamoto A. Familial type I hyperlipoproteinemia caused by apolipoprotein C-II deficiency. Atherosclerosis 34:53 (1979).

11. Miller N.E.,Rao S.N.,Alaupovic P.,Noble N.,Slack J.,Brunzell J.D. and Lewis B. Familial apolipoprotein C-II deficiency :plasma lipoproteins and apolipoproteins in heterozygous and homozygous subjects and the effects of plasma infusion. Eur.J.Clin.Invest. 11:69 (1981).

12. Stalenhoef A.F.H.,Caspaire A.F.,Demaker P.N.M.,Stouten J.T.J.-Luttermann J.A. and Van't Laar A. Combined deficiency of apolipoprotein C-II and lipoprotein lipase in familial hyperchylomicronemia. Metabolism 30:919 (1981)

13. Catapano A.L.,Mills G.L.,Roma P.,La Rosa M. and Capurso A. Plamsa lipids,lipoproteins and apolipoproteins in a case of apo C-II deficiency. Clin.Chim.Acta 130:317(1983).

14. Fellin R.,Baggio G.,Poli A.,Augustin J.,Baiocchi M.R.,Baldo G.,Sinigalia M.,Greten H.and Crepaldi G. Familial lipoprotein lipase and apolipoprotein C-II deficiency. Atherosclerosis 49:55 (1983).

15. Saku K.,Cedres C.,Mc Donald B.,Hynd B.,Liu B.W.,Srivastava L.S. and Kashyap M.L. C-II anapolipoproteinemia and severe hypertriglyceridemia. Am.J.Med. 77:457 (1984).

16. Wilson Cox D.,Breckenridge W.C. and Little J.A. Inheritance of apolipoprotein C-II deficiency with hypertriglyceridemia and pancreatitis. N.Engl.J.Med. 299:1421 (1978).

17. Maguire G.F.,Little J.A.,Kakis G.and Breckenridge W.C. Apolipoprotein C-II deficiency àssociated with nonfunctional mutant forms of apolipoprotein C-II. Can.J.Biochem.Cell.Biol. 62:847 (1984).

18. Capurso A.,Catapano A.L.,Mogavero F.,La Rosa M and Reata F. Apolipoprotein C-II deficiency: a new mutant form with intestinal synthesis of an abnormal protein. Submitted for publication.

19. Goldstein J. and Brown M.S. Progress in the understanding of the LDL receptor and HMG CoA reductase two membrane proteins that regulate the plasma cholesterol. J.Lipid Res. 25:1450 (1984)

20. Humphries S.E.,Williams L.,Myklebost O.,Stalenhoef A.F.H., Demaker P.N.M.,Baggio G.,Crepaldi G.,Galton D.J. and Williamson R. Familial apolipoprotein C-II deficiency:a preliminary analysis of the gene defect in two independent families. Human Genet. 67:151 (1984).

21. Breckenrige W.C.,Alaupovic P.,Cox D.W. and Little J.A. Apolipoprotein and lipoprotein concentrations in familial apolipo-

protein C-II deficiency.Atherosclerosis 44:223 (1982).

22. Capurso A. and Catapano A.L. Manuscript in preparation.

23. Fitzharris T.S.,Quinn D.M.,Goh E.H.,Johnsonn D.,Kashyap M.L.,- Srivastava L.S.,Jackson R.L. and Harmony J.A.K. Hydrolysis of guinea pig nascent VLDL catalyzed by lipoprotein lipase activation by human Apo C-II. J.Lipid Res. 22:921 (1981).

24. Kleinmann Y.,Eisemberg S.,Oschry Y.,Gavish D.,Stein O and Stein Y. Defective metabolism of hypertriglyceridemic low density lipoproteins in coltured skin fibroblasts.J.Clin Invest.75:1280 (1985).

25. Eisemberg S. Personal communication

FAMILIAL APOLIPOPROTEIN CII DEFICIENCY:

AN ANALYSIS OF THE GENE DEFECT IN A DUTCH FAMILY

S.E. Humphries, [1], A. Stalenhoef,[2] and S. Wallis[1,3]

[1] Department of Biochemistry, St. Mary's Hospital
Medical School, Norfolk Place, London W2 1PG
[2] Department of Medicine, University of Nijmegen
Holland. [3] Clinical Research Centre, Northwick Park
Harrow, Middlesex.

At the present time the defect that causes apo
CII deficiency is not known. One possibility is that
there is a mutation in an enzyme involved in the
correct processing or catabolism of the apoprotein.
However, since heterozygotes for the deficiency
produce decreased amounts of functionally normal apo
CII, it seems more likely that the deficiency is
caused by a mutation in the apo CII gene itself. In
order to investigate this problem at the molecular
level we have used our recently isolated cDNA clone
for apo CII (1), to study the structure of the gene in
the family of a patient with apo CII deficiency.
Clinical information and chemical studies on the
patients have been reported previously (2).

DNA from the apo CII deficient patients and other
members of the family was digested with several
restriction enzymes that are known to cut within or
close to the apo CII gene. DNA fragments were
separated by size using electrophoresis on an agarose
gel and the fragments transferred to a nitrocellulose
filter using the Southern blotting technique (3).
Filters were hybridised with nick-translated apo CII
cDNA probe (4), washed and exposed to X-ray film. With
the enzymes BglI, PvuII, EcoRI, PstI, SstI, BamHI and
BglII, apo CII gene fragments indistinguishable in
size from those found in normal samples were observed

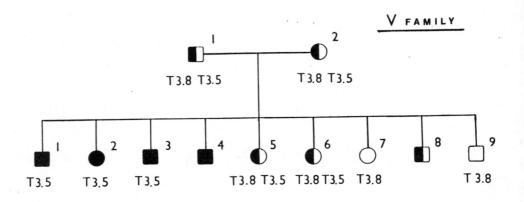

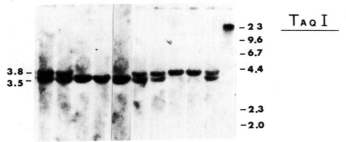

Figure 1 Inheritance of the apo CII gene. A Pedigree.
Individuals with: OO normal levels, OO half normal
levels, ● ■ no detectable apo CII. B Southern Blot
analysis. DNA samples from family and a normal
individual (N) digested with TaqI, and hybridised with
apo CII probe.

(data in 5). We estimate that deletions in the gene of
a little as 50 bp could have been detected in this
analysis and conclude that the defect in these
patients is not caused by any gross deletion or
sequence rearrangement.

This raises the possibility that the apo CII gene
is in fact normal in these individuals, and that apo
CII deficiency is due to a defect in some other gene,
involved for example in processing, glycosylating, or
degrading the protein. To investigate this we have
used a common TaqI restriction fragment length

TABLE I

STRATEGY TO ISOLATE APO CII DEFICIENT GENE

1. DNA FROM PATIENT DIGESTED WITH HIND III

2. FRACTIONATED ON SUCROSE GRADIENT - FRAGMENTS >10 KB

3. BACTERIOPHAGE λ L47 DIGESTED WITH HIND III (SUCROSE GRADIENT)

4. DNA PLUS ARMS LIGATED AND PACKAGED

5. PLATE ON SELECTIVE STRAIN OF BACTERIA (358/359)

6. SCREEN FOR APO CII GENE USING APO CII cDNA INSERT

7. PLAQUE PURIFY RECOMBINANTS

8. GROW DNA DICEST WITH BAM HI, PST I AND SST I

9. SUBCLONE BAM HI 4.7 KB FRAGMENT INTO PLASMID VECTOR (PUC8)

10. SUBCLONE PST I AND SST I FRAGMENTS INTO M13 FOR SEQUENCING

(FOR METHODS SEE 11)

polymorphism of the normal apo CII gene (4) to follow the inheritance of the apo CII genes in the families (Figure 1).

If the defect causing apo CII deficiency were a mutation in the apo CII gene, then in both the parents of the V family the defective apo CII gene could be inferred to be on the 3.5 kb TaqI fragment. The affected children are homozygous for this fragment, both normal children are homozygous for the 3.8 kb fragment, and both carrier children are heterozygous for the TaqI fragments. It is not possible using this polymorphism to distinguish whether the carrier children have inherited the deficient allele from the mother or father. The probability of obtaining this pattern of inheritance of the alleles of the apo CII gene by chance alone is about 1 in 1000 (lod score 3.01) and thus constitutes formal proof that the defect causing apo CII deficiency in this family is in, or very close to, the apo CII gene.

Encouraged by this we have started the isolation and sequencing of the apo CII gene from one of the patients. The strategy has been developed from the known restriction enzyme map of the normal apo CII gene. The steps involved are outlined in Figure 2 and the conditions used are as detailed in (6). Several points are worthy of mention. We have had difficulty

TABLE II
COMPARISON OF DIFFERENT APO CII PATIENTS

ORIGIN OF PATIENT	DETECTABLE APO CII PROTEIN	SIZE OF CII GENE TAQI FRAGMENT	REFERENCE
HOLLAND	?	3.5 KB	5
ITALY	YES[+]	3.8 KB	5
SICILY	YES[+]	3.8 KB	*
SICILY (VANCOUVER)	?	3.8 KB	9
CARRIBEAN	YES	?	10
BETHESDA	YES[+]	3.8 KB	^

* L. WILLIAMS, A. CAPURSO D. GALTON AND S. HUMPHRIES (UNPUBLISHED)
^ B. BREWER (PERSONAL COMMUNICATION)
+ THIS CONFERENCE

in purifying the Human DNA and the vector arms from agarose gels. Although the enrichment of specific DNA fragments is not so high, we have found using sucrose gradients gives ligatable DNA of acceptable purity. Packaging mix was purchased from Amersham. Although it is possible to screen the library with nick translated whole plasmid this usually gives high backgrounds. This can be avoided by purifying the plasmid DNA on two rounds of caseium chloride to remove all traces of contaminating bacterial DNA, or by simply excising the insert from the plasmid and isolating the fragment from an agarose gel. The DNA can then be labelled using a random oligonucleotide primer (7, 8). Hopefully progress on the sequencing of the isolated gene will enable us within the next few months to determine at the DNA level the defect causing apo CII deficiency in this patient.

How many different mutations are there causing apo CII deficiency? It is now clear that in all of the patients so far studied the apo CII gene is grossly normal, and that a re-examination of the apolipoproteins from many of these patients reveals the presence of low levels of apo CII protein with an altered size or isoelectric point (this conference). It seems likely that many of the independently ascertained families will represent independent and different mutations. Because apo CII deficiency is so rare, it is most likely that the individuals are homozygous for the same defect, caused by inbreeding from a distant ancestor. One way of examining this is to see if the defective alleles are on the same TaqI allele of the apo CII gene. It is interesting that all the patients so far examined are indeed homozygous for one or the other TaqI allele (Table I). However this may be purely by chance, and a detailed examination of this must await an elucidation of the defects at the DNA level in these patients. It is likely that this analysis of defects causing apo CII deficiency will also shed some light on the functions and mechanism of action of apo CII in the regulation of triglyceride levels in normal individuals and in patients.

References

1. O. Myklebost, R. Williamson, A.F. Markham, S. Myklebost, J. Rogers J, D.E. Woods and S.E. Humphries, The isolation and characterisation of cDNA clones for human apolipoprotein CII, J. Biol. Chem. 259:4401-4404 (1984).
2. A.F.H. Stalenhoef, A.F. Casparie, P.N.M. Demacker, J.T.J. Stouten, J.A. Lutterman and A. Van 't Laar, Combined deficiency of apolipoprotein CII and lipoprotein lipase in familial hyperchylomicronemia, Metabolism 30:919-926 (1981).
3. E. Southern, Detection of specific sequences among DNA fragments separated by gel electrophoresis, J. Mol. Biol. 98:503-517 (1975).
4   S.E. Humphries, N.I. Jowett, L. Williams, A. Rees, M. Vella, A. Kessling, O. Myklebost, A. Lydon, M. Seed, D.J. Galton and R. Williamson, A DNA polymorphism adjacent to the human apolipoprotein CII gene, Mol Biol Med. 1:463-471 (1984).
5. S.E. Humphries, L. Williams, O. Mykelbost, A.F.H. Stalenhoef, P.N.M. Demacker, G. Baggio, G. Crepaldi, D.J. Galton and R. Williamson, Familial apolipoprotein CII deficiency: A preliminary analysis of the gene defect in two independent families, Hum. Genet 67:155-156 (1984).

6.   S.C. Wallis, J.A. Donald, L.A. Forrest, R. Williamson and S.E. Humphries, The isolation of a genomic clone containing the apolipoprotein CII gene and the detection of linkage disequilibrium between two common DNA polymorphisms around the gene, Hum. Genet. 68:286-289 (1984).

7.   A.P. Feinberg and B. Vogelstein, A technique for radiolabelling DNA restriction endonuclease fragments to high specific activity, Anal. Biochem. 132:266-267 (1983).

8.   A.P. Feinberg and B. Vogelstein , Addendum "A technique for radiolabelling DNA restriction endonuclease fragments to high specific activity", Anal. Biochem. 137:266-267.

9.   M. Hayden, R. McLeod, J. Frohlich, S.E. Humphries, E.A. Jones, N. Jetha, L. Kirby and P. Munk, Apolipoprotein CII deficiency: A clinical pathological and biochemical investigation and preliminary study of its molecular pathology, Annals of Int. Med., submitted.

10. W.C. Breckenridge, J.A. Little, G. Stenier, A. Chow and M. Poapst, Hypertriglyceridemia associated with deficiency of apolipoprotein CII, N. Eng. J. Med. 298:1265-1272 (1978).

11. T. Maniatis, Molecular Cloning (A laboratory manual), Cold Spring Harbour Laboratory, (1982).

APO C-II$_{Padova}$: A NEW APOPROTEIN VARIANT IN TWO PATIENTS WITH APO

C-II DEFICIENCY SYNDROME

G.Baggio, C.Gabelli, E.Manzato, S.Martini, L.Previato,
F.Verlato, H.B.Brewer*, G.Crepaldi

Dept. of Internal Medicine, University of Padua, Via
Giustiniani, 2-35128 PADOVA, Italy- *Molecular Disease
Branch, National Heart, Lung, and Blood Institute, N.I.H.
Bethesda, Maryland 20205 U.S.A.

INTRODUCTION

Apoprotein C-II, present in chylomicrons, VLDL, and HDL is the
co-factor of lipoprotein lipase, the enzyme responsible for triglyceride-rich lipoproteins catabolism[1].

In 1978 a rare metabolic disorder, characterized by the absence
of this peptide had been described[2]. It was named apo C-II Deficiency
Syndrome. A deficiency or absence of either lipoprotein lipase or
apolipoprotein C-II results in severe plasma hypertriglyceridemia.
More than 90% of the plasma triglycerides of the affected subject
are in the d< 1.006 g/ml density fraction. The other major classes
of lipoprotein including LDL and HDL are reduced in concentration
and relatively enriched in their percent triglyceride content[3].

Seven kindreds have been found in the last seven years: in the
Carribean[2], Italy[4,5], Japan[6], England[7], Holland[8], U.S.A.[9].

The probands of these families had no apparent apo C-II, based
on immunodiffusion, electroimmunoassay, polyacrylamide gel electrophoresis, isoelectricfocusing and activation assays. Apo C-II is a
polypeptide chain of 79 aminoacids with a molecular weight of 8837[10]
Synthetic peptide fragments of apo C-II have been obtained[11]. An
isoform of apo C-II (apo C-II 2) was reported[12] with an isolectric
point different from that of the major isoform apo C-II 1, with the
same amino-acid composition and capacity to activate lipoprotein lipase.

Recently, the gene for apo C-II has been cloned, and the complete cDNA sequence of apo C-II determined[13-15].

Apo C-II is synthesized as a 101 amino-acid precursor protein, pre-apo C-II, containing a 24 amino-acid peptide which is co-translationally cleaved during synthesis.

Apo C-II gene have been localized to chromosome 19 [15,16] which also contains the genes for apo E [17] and for LDL receptor[18].

Recent analysis of the apo C-II gene in the patients presented here and an independent kindred by restriction enzyme analysis established that the apo C-II gene was present in members of these two affected kindreds, and there were no major insertions or deletions in the apo C-II gene [19].

In this paper apoprotein and lipoprotein levels in 2 patients with apo C-II deficiency syndrome are presented. Moreover an apoprotein C-II isoform, different from normal known isoforms, is described. This variant has been called apoprotein C-II$_{Padova}$.

MATERIAL AND METHODS

Plasma lipoproteins were isolated by preparative ultracentrifugation utilizing an L5-65 Beckman ultracentrifuge and a Ti-50 rotor at densities 1.006, 1.065, and 1.210 g/ml to obtain chylomicron plus VLDL, LDL, and HDL respectively[20].

Triglycerides[21], cholesterol[22], and phospholipids[23] were quantitated by standard procedures using buffers and enzymes obtained by Boehringer - Mannheim GmbH. Apolipoprotein A-I, was quantitated by radial immunodiffusion[24]. Apo C-II was measured by radioimmunoassay[25]. Apolipoprotein B was quantitated by rocket immunoelectrophoresis[26]. Two dimensional electrophoresis was performed as recently reported[27] and immunoblotting by the procedure of Towbin et al.[28].

RESULTS AND DISCUSSION

The family tree of the first degree relatives of the patients with apo C-II deficiency is illustrated in Fig. 1. No consanguineity was found in the family history of this kindred.

Apoprotein C-II, A-I and B, as well as cholesterol and triglyceride level in fasting plasma of the probands with apo C-II deficiency and of their first degree relatives are presented in Table 1.

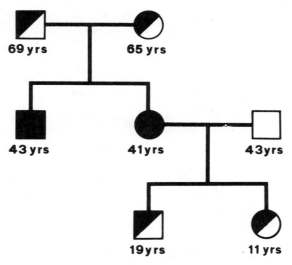

Fig. 1 Family tree of the first degree relatives of 2 patients
with apo C-II deficiency

Apo C-II was detected by radioimmunoassay in the 2 patients
and its concentration was about 2 percent of a normal level. While
the father, the son, and the daugther of female patient have apo
C-II levels in the low range of normal value, the mother has normal
level.

Table 1. Apoprotein C-II, A-I, B, Cholesterol (CT) and
Triglyceride (TG) levels (mg/dl) in whole serum
of 2 probands with apo C-II deficiency and of
their first degree relatives

	C-II	A-I	B	CT	TG
PROBAND 1	0.13	63	105	275	1610
PROBAND 2	0.12	56	157	183	1630
MOTHER	7.98	145	146	281	80
FATHER	3.18	143	142	238	108
SON of P.2	1.97	116	100	165	84
DAUGHTER of P.2	3.13	123	90	166	134

This is contrasting with the data of other authors, who found a 30-50% of the normal amount of apo C-II in obligate heterozygotes.

Apo A-I concentration in patients is low (less than 50% of normal). This is in agreement with the low level of HDL (Table 2).

Apo B and total cholesterol levels are within the normal range in spite of the low LDL concentration.

As described in previous report[4],[29] plasma triglycerides and cholesterol are mainly tranported by the d < 1.006 g/ml fraction. All these parameters are normal in the 4 obligate heterozygotes here presented.

Two dimensional gel electrophoresis followed by immunoblot with a monospecific antibody to apo C-II of plasma from both probands revealed a variant of apo C-II (Fig. 2) with lower apparent molecular weight and more acid pI.

Analysis of a mixture of normal plasma and plasma from one of the proband clearly demonstrated the difference in electrophoretic mobility of normal apo C-II in comparison to the apo C-II variant. The apo C-II variant identified in this kindred was designated apo C-II$_{Padova}$.

Table 2. VLDL, LDL, and HDL Cholesterol (CT) and Triglyceride (TG) levels (mg/dl) in 2 probands with apo C-II deficiency and in their first degree relatives

	VLDL*		LDL		HLD	
	CT	TG	CT	TG	CT	TG
PROBAND 1	196	1166	24	22	21	b.s.
PROBAND 2	106	1490	26	30	21	b.s.
MOTHER	5	32	164	28	81	10
FATHER	17	66	135	22	55	17
SON of P.2	9	49	102	20	48	8
DAUGHTER of P.2	14	87	99	15	52	19

* VLDL = d < 1.006 g/ml
  b.s. = below sensitivity of the method

Recently another apo C-II variant different from apo C-II$_{Padova}$ has been found in a patient affected by the apo C-II Deficiency Syndrome in Bethesda[30].

Both apo C-II$_{Padova}$ and apo C-II$_{Bethesda}$ do not correspond to any of the normal known apo C-II isoforms.

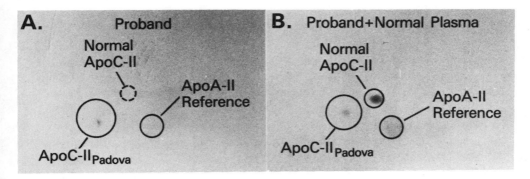

Fig. 2   Two dimensional gel electrophoretogram and immunoblot of plasma from proband 1 with apo C-II deficiency (A) and a mixture of plasma from a normal subject and patient with apo C-II deficiency (B)

The inheritance of these molecular defects are important to understand the genetics of this Syndrome.

Up to now we can conclude that in different kindreds there is an heterogeneity of molecular defects resulting in similar metabolic disorder and similar clinical features.

ACKNOWLEDGEMENTS

This work was supported by grants from Progetto Finalizzato C.N.R.: Ingegneria Genetica e Basi Molecolari delle Malattie Ereditarie: Sottoprogetto Basi Molecolari delle Malattie Ereditarie.

REFERENCES

1.   J. C. LaRosa, R. I. Levy, P. Herbert, S. E. Lux, and D. S. Fredrickson, 1970, A specific apoprotein activator for lipoprotein lipase. Biochem. Biophys. Commun. 41:45-62
2.   W. C. Breckenridge, J. A. Little, G. Steiner, A. Chow, and M. Poast, 1978, Hypertriglyceridemia associated with deficiency of apolipoprotein C-II, N. Eng. J. Med. 298:1265-1273

3. E. A. Nikkilä, 1983, Familial lipoprotein lipase deficiency and related disorders of chylomicron metabolism, In The Metabolic Basis of Inherited Disease, J. B. Stanbury, J. B. Wyngaarden, D. S. Fredrickson, J. L. Goldstein, and M. S. Brown, editors, McGraw-Hill, New York, 5th ed. 622-642

4. G. Crepaldi, R. Fellin, G. Baggio, J. Augustin, and H. Greten, 1980, Lipoprotein and apoprotein, adipose tissue and hepatic lipoprotein lipase levels in patients with hyperchylomicronemia and their immediate family members, In Atherosclerosis V, A. M. Gotto, Jr., L. C. Smith, and B. Allen, editors, Springer-Verlag, New York, Heidelberg, Berlin, 250-254

5. A. L. Catapano, G. L. Mills, P. Roma, M. LaRosa, and A. Capurso, 1983, Plasma lipids, lipoproteins and apoproteins in a case of apo C-II deficiency, Clin. Chim. Acta 130:317-327

6. T. Yamamura, H. Sudo, K. Ishikawa, and A. Yamamoto, 1979, Familial type I hyperlipoproteinemia caused by apolipoprotein C-II deficiency, Atherosclerosis 34:53-65

7. N. E. Miller, S. N. Rao, P. Alaupovic, N. Noble, J. Slack, J. D. Brunzell, and B. Lewis, 1981, Familial apolipoprotein C-II deficiency: plasma lipoproteins and apolipoproteins in heterozygous and homozygous subjects and the effects of plasma infusion. Eur. J. Clin. Invest. 11:69-76

8. A. F. H. Stalenhoef, A. F. Casparie, P. N. M. Demaker, F. T. Y. Stouten, F. A. Luttermann, and A. Van't Laar, 1981, Combined deficiency of apolipoprotein C-II and lipoprotein lipase in familial hyperchylomicronemia, Metabolism 30:919-926

9. K. Saku, C. Cedres, B. McDonald, B. A. Hynd, B.W. Liu, L. S. Srivasteva, and M. L. Kashyap, 1984, C-II anapolipoproteinemia and severe hypertriglyceridemia - Report of a rare case with absence of C-II apolipoprotein isoforms and review of the literature, Am. J. Med. 77:457-462

10. A. V. Hospattankar, T. Fairwell, R. Ronan, and H. B. Brewer, Jr., 1983, Amino acid sequences of human apolipoprotein C-II from normal and hyperlipoproteinemia subjects, J. Biol. Chem. 259:318-322

11. P. K. J. Kinnunen, R. L. Jackson, L.C. Smith, A. M. Gotto Jr., and J. T. Sparrow, 1977, Activation of lipoprotein lipase by native and synthetic fragment of human plasma apolipoprotein C-II, Proc. Natl. Acad. Sci. USA 74:4848-4851

12. R. J. Havel, L. Kotite, and J. P. Kane, 1979, Isoelectric heterogeneity of a co-factor protein for lipoprotein lipase in human blood plasma, Biochem. Med. 21:121-128

13. S. S. Fojo, S. W. Law, and H. B. Brewer, Jr., 1984, Human apo-lipoprotein C-II: Complete nucleic acid sequence of preapo-lipoprotein C-II, Proc. Natl. Acad. Sci. USA 81:6354-6357

14. C. R. Sharp, A. Sidoli, C. S. Shelley, M. A. Lucero, C. C. Shoulders, and F. E. Baralle, 1984, Human apolipoprotein A-I, A-II, C-II, and C-III, cDNA sequence and mRNA abundance, Nucl. Acid Res. 12:3917-3932

15. S. S. Fojo, S. W. Law, H. B. Brewer, Jr., A. Y. Sakaguchi, and S. L. Naylor, 1984, The localization of the gene for apolipo-protein C-II to chromosome 19, Biochem. Biophys. Res. Commun. 122:687-693

16. R. L. Jackson, G. A. P. Bruns, and J. L. Breslow, 1984, Isola-tion and sequence of a human apolipoprotein C-II cDNA clone and its use to isolate and map to human chromosome 19, the gene for apolipoprotein C-II, Proc. Natl. Acad. Sci. USA 81:2945-2949

17. B. Olaisen, P. Teisburg, and T. Gedle-Dahl, Jr., 1982, The locus for apolipoprotein E (apo E) is linked to the comple-ment component C3 (C3) locus on chromosome 19, In Manual of Human Genetics, 62:233-236

18. V. Francke, M. S. Brown, and J. L. Goldstein, 1984, Assignment of the human gene for the low density lipoprotein receptor to chromosome 19: synteny of a receptor, a ligand, and a genetic disease, Proc. Natl. Acad. Sci. USA 81:2826-2830

19. S. E. Humphries, L. Williams, O. Myklebost, A. F. H. Stalenhoef, P. N. M. Demaker, G. Baggio, G. Crepaldi, D. J. Galton, and R. Williamson, 1984, Familial apolipoprotein C-II deficiency: A preliminary analysis of the gene defect in two independent families, Hum Genet. 67:151-155

20. R. J. Havel, H. A. Eder, and J. H. Bragdon, 1955, The distri-bution and chemical composition of ultracentrifugally sepa-rated liproteins in human serum, J. Clin. Invest. 34:1345-1353

21. A. W. Wahlefeld, 1974, Triglycerides determining after enzymatic hydrolysis, In Methoden der Enzymatischen Analyse, H. U. Bergmeyer, editor, Verlag Chemie, Weinheim, 3rd edition, 2:1878-1882

22. J. Roschlau, P. E. Bernt, and W. Gruber, 1974, Enzymatische Bestimmung des Gesamt-Cholesterins in Serum, J. Clin. Chem. Clin. Biochem. 12: 403:407

23. D. B. Zilversmit, and A. K. Davis, 1950, Microdetermination of plasma phospholipids by trichloroacetic acid precipitation,

J. Lab. Clin. Med. 35:155-163

24. O. Ouchterlony, 1953, Antigen-antibody reactions in gels: IV types of reactions in coordinated system of diffusion, Acta Pathol. Microbiol. Scand. 32:231-236

25. M. L. Kashyap, L. S. Srivastava, C. Y. Chen, G. Perisutti, M. Campbell, R. F. Lutmer, and C. J. Glueck, 1977, Radioimmunoassay of human apolipoprotein C-II: A study in normal and hypertriglyceridemic subjects, J. Clin. Invest 69:171- 178

26. M. D. Curry, A. Gustafson, P. Alaupovic, and W. J. McConathy, 1978, Electroimmunoassay, radioimmunoassay and radial immunodiffusion assay evaluated for quantitation of human apolipoprotein B, Clin. Chem. 24:280-286

27. D. L. Sprecher, L. Taam, and H. B. Brewer, Jr., 1984, Two-dimensional electrophoresis of human plasma apolipoproteins, Clin. Chem. 30:2084-2092

28. H. Towbin, T. Staehlin, and J. Gordon, 1979, Electrophoretic transfer of proteins from polyacrylamide gels to nitrocellulose sheets - procedure and some applications, Proc. Natl. Acad. Sci.USA 76:4350-4354

29. E. Manzato, G. Baggio, S. Żambon, C. Gabelli, S. Martini, R. Marin, and G. Crepaldi, 1985, Plasma Lipoproteins in apo C-II deficiency, Elsevier Science Publishers, in press

30. D. L. Sprecher, L. Taam, R. E. Gregg, S. S. Fojo, D. M. Wilson, M. L. Kashyap, B. H. Brewer, Jr., 1985, Apolipoprotein C-II Deficiency: identification of an apo C-II variant (apo C-II$_{Bethesda}$) associated with hypertriglyceridemia, Submitted for publication

THE APOLIPOPROTEIN E GENE: CHROMOSOMAL LOCALIZATION

AND TISSUE EXPRESSION

Yen-Chiu Lin-Lee, Fa-Ten Kao, Peter Cheung, and Lawrence Chan

Baylor College of Medicine, Houston, Texas and University of Colorado Health Sciences Center Denver, Colorado

Apolipoprotein E (apoE)[1] is an apoprotein found in chylomicrons, chlyomicron remnants, very low density lipoproteins, and high density lipoproteins in man and in other mammalian species. The complete amino acid sequence of apoE was reported by Rall et al. (1982). It is a polypeptide of 299 amino acids. There are a series of amphipathic helices (Segrest et al., 1974) in the carboxyl-terminal third of the polypeptide chain that may represent the lipid binding site(s) for apoE (Rall et al., 1982). An important function of apoE appears to be the mediation of cellular uptake of lipoproteins through specific cell-surface receptors. ApoE binds to the low density lipoprotein receptor of various cells and tissues. It also binds to a specific apoE receptor in the liver and mediates the hepatic uptake of chylomicron remnants (Mahley & Innerarity, 1983; Hui et al., 1981; Sherill et al., 1980).

Our laboratory has been interested in apoE gene expression for a number of years (Lin-Lee et al., 1981a,b; Tanaka et al., 1982). To further understand the molecular basis for apoE expression, we have cloned the cDNA for human hepatic apoE mRNA. Using the cloned cDNA as a hybridization probe, we have localized the structural gene for apoE to human chromosome 19 by Southern blot analysis of DNAs from a panel of human-Chinese hamster somatic cell hybrids. We have also used the probe to study the tissue-specific expression of apoE in the primate.

Materials and Methods

Human ApoE cDNA Cloning. A full-length human apoE cDNA was isolated from a library of human liver cDNA clones by the technique of

211

oligonucleotide hybridization (Cheung & Chan, 1983). It was completely sequenced (Lin-Lee et al., 1985) and its sequence was found to match the "normal" sequence of McLean et al. (1984).

Localization of ApoE Structural Gene By Somatic Cell Hybrids. Mapping of the apoE structural gene on human chromosomes was performed by Southern blot analysis of DNAs isolated from a panel of human-Chinese hamster somatic cell hybrids. The conditions for culture of the parental cell lines (CHO-K1 and HT-1080), fusion between the auxotrophic mutants of CHO-K1 cells and human cells, and the characterization of the panel of somatic cell hybrids with respect to their chromosome content and isozyme complements have all been described previously (Kao et al., 1976, 1982; Cheung et al., 1984; Kao & Chan, 1985). For DNA preparation, cells were grown in 150 mm dishes to confluency and harvested by trypsinization. They were treated with proteinase K after washing, and DNA was isolated as described (Kao et al., 1982; Cheung et al., 1984).

Detection of Functional ApoE mRNA in Various Human and Baboon Tissues. The cloned human apoE cDNA clone was labeled with ^{32}P by nick-translation. It was used to detect apoE mRNA sequences by Northern blot hybridization (Thomas, 1980), and quantitative slot-blot hybridization (Lin-Lee et al., 1985). The biological activity of the apoE mRNA sequences was assayed by in vitro translation in a reticulocyte lysate system (Pelham & Jackson, 1976).

Results

Hybridization of pAE155 Probe with Somatic Cell Hybrid DNA. The somatic cell hybrid DNAs were digested with HincII, transferred to nitrocellulose paper, and hybridized to the ^{32}P-labeled human apoE cDNA probe, pAE155. In pilot experiments, the HincII-digested parental cell (HT-1080) DNA showed an ~ 10 kb band on Southern analysis. Chinese hamster DNA failed to show any hybridization signal under our conditions of hybridization. Table I summarizes the results of Southern blot analysis of a panel of 13 human-Chinese hamster somatic cell hybrid DNAs. Five of the 13 hybrid DNAs gave positive hybridization signals, and eight of them did not show any signal even on prolonged exposure of the X-ray film. In our synteny analysis, concordant hybrids are those that have the particular human chromosome and the apoE gene either present or absent together. Conversely, those hybrids having either the chromosome or the apoE gene present singly are discordant hybrids. Concordant segregation frequency is expressed by dividing the number of concordant hybrids by the total number of hybrids analyzed (13 hybrids in this study). By such analyses, the presence or absence of the ~ 10 kb human apoE band correlates exclusively with human chromosome 19 (Table I). Furthermore, the apoE gene co-segregates with human chromosome 19 isozyme marker glucose phosphate isomerase in all the hybrids examined (Table I). These

Table 1. Synteny Analysis of the Human ApoE Gene in 13 Human Cho-K1 Cell Hybrids By Molecular Hybridization Using a cDNA Probe

Hybrids	Human Chromosomes[*]																							GPI[+]	ApoE[@]
	1	2	3	4	5	6	7	8	9	10	11	12	13	14	15	16	17	18	19	20	21	22	X		
CP3-1	-	-	-	+	+	-	-	-	-	-	+	+	-	+	-	+	+	+	-	+	+	-	+	-	-
CP4-1	-	-	-	+	+	-	-	+	-	-	+	-	-	+	-	-	-	-	-	-	-	+	+	-	-
CP5-1	+	-	-	-	+	-	-	+	+	-	-	+	-	+	+	-	+	-	+	-	+	+	-	+	+
CP6-1	-	-	-	+	-	-	-	-	-	-	+	-	+	-	-	+	+	+	-	+	+	-	+	+	+
CP11-1	-	-	-	-	+	-	-	-	-	-	-	+	-	-	-	-	+	-	+	-	+	-	-	-	-
CP12-1	-	+	-	+	-	-	-	+	+	+	+	+	+	+	-	-	-	-	-	-	+	+	+	-	-
CP14-1	-	-	-	+	+	-	-	-	-	-	-	-	-	-	-	+	-	-	+	+	+	-	-	-	-
CP16-1	-	-	-	+	-	-	-	-	-	-	+	-	+	-	-	+	-	+	+	+	+	-	+	+	+
CP17-1	+	-	-	+	+	-	-	-	+	-	-	+	-	-	-	-	-	-	-	-	-	-	-	-	-
CP18-1	+	-	-	-	-	+	-	+	-	-	+	-	-	+	+	-	+	+	+	-	-	+	+	+	+
CP20-1	-	+	-	+	-	-	-	+	-	-	-	-	-	+	-	-	+	-	-	+	-	-	-	-	-
CP26-1	+	-	-	+	+	+	+	-	+	+	+	+	+	-	-	-	+	-	-	-	+	-	-	-	-
CP28-1	+	-	-	+	+	-	-	+	+	-	-	-	-	-	-	-	+	+	+	-	-	-	+	+	+
Number of Concordant Hybrids	9	6	8	4	4	7	7	9	7	6	5	6	6	9	10	7	7	9	13	9	5	7	4		

Percent of Concordance
```
    69.2       61.5       30.8       53.8       53.8       38.5       46.2       76.9       53.8      100.0       38.5       30.8
          46.2       30.8       53.8       69.2       46.2       46.2       69.2       53.8       69.2       69.2       53.8
```

[*]Identified by trypsin-banding and Giemsa-11 differential staining in sequential steps.

[+]Identified by isozyme analysis for detecting the human chromosome 19 isozyme marker glucose phosphate isomerase (GPI).

[@]Identified by Southern blot analysis using apoE cDNA probe.

results allow assignment of the structural gene for human apoE to chromosome 19 and to no other chromosomes.

Northern Blot Analysis of ApoE mRNA. Northern blot analysis of various polyA RNA preparations from human and baboon tissues using ^{32}P-labeled pAE155 as a probe indicates the presence of hybridizable apoE mRNA sequences of ~ 18 S in human liver and in baboon liver, intestine, kidney, spleen, brain, and adrenal gland, but not in baboon skeletal muscle.

Quantitation of ApoE mRNA Sequences by Slot-Blot Analysis. When increasing quantities of total RNA from the various organs and tissues were directly blotted on Zeta-Probe membrane, there was a linear relationship between the amount of RNA blotted and the radioactivity on the filter. From the slopes of the curves generated by the various RNA samples, the relative concentrations of apoE mRNAs were determined. Taking baboon liver RNA as 100%, the various organs contained hybridizable apoE mRNA sequences at the following relative concentrations: adrenal gland, 59.6%; spleen, 11.8%; brain, 5.6%; kidney, 3.2%; small intestine, 0.8%; skeletal muscle, 0.5% or less.

<u>Cell-Free Translation of ApoE mRNA From Various Tissues</u>.   To
assess the functional state of the hybridizable apoE RNA sequences
in some of the tissues, we have translated the polyA RNAs in a
reticulocyte lysate translation assay.   ApoE mRNA activity was
detected by specific immunoprecipitation using a monospecific
antiserum against human apoE.   There was good cross-immunoreacti-
vity between human and baboon apoE.   By this analysis, biologically active apoE mRNA activity was detected in RNAs isolated from
baboon liver, small intestine, kidney, spleen, and brain, but not
that from baboon skeletal muscle.

Discussion

In this report, we have used cloned human apoE cDNA as a
hybridization probe to map the apoE structural locus on human
chromosomes, and to detect the presence of apoE mRNA sequences in
various human and baboon tissues.   Southern blot analysis of
HincII-digested DNAs from 13 human-Chinese hamster somatic cell
hybrids has localized the apoE gene to human chromosome 19.   This
observation indicates that apoE is syntenic to at least two other
genes related to lipid metabolism, those for the low density lipoprotein receptor (Francke et al., 1984), and apoC-II (Jackson et
al., 1984).   Furthermore, our chromosomal mapping results are in
agreement with pedigree analysis, which shows linkage of the gene
for apoE with complement 3 on human chromsome 19 (Olaisen et al.,
1982, 1984).   To date, there are five apolipoprotein genes that
have been assigned to specific human chromosomes: apoA-I to the
long arm of chromosome 11 (Cheung et al., 1984); apoA-II to chromosome 1 (Moore et al., 1984); apoC-I and apoC-II to chromosome 19
(Knott et al., 1984; Jackson et al., 1984); and now, apoE also to
chromosome 19.   In the future, the determination of the exact
chromosomal localization of the various apolipoprotein genes at
the fine banding level will be useful in our understanding of the
structure, organization, and evolution of these genes.

In our studies on tissue-specific apoE gene expression, we
detected the presence of intact and biologically active apoE mRNA
in human liver and in baboon liver, adrenal gland, spleen, brain,
kidney, small intestine, but not in baboon skeletal muscle.   Our
observation on the presence of apoE gene transcript in non-lipo-
protein producing tissues such as brain raises interesting
questions on the role of this apolipoprotein in such tissues and
organs.

Acknowledgment

This work was supported by grants from the National Institutes of Health HL-27341 and HD-02080, and the March of Dimes
Birth Defects Foundation.

References

Cheung, P., & Chan, L. (1983) Nucleic Acids Res. 11, 3703-3715.

Cheung, P., Kao, F.-T., Law, M.L., Jones, C., Puck, T.T., & Chan, L. (1984) Proc. Natl. Acad. Sci. USA 81, 508-511.

Francke, U., Brown, M.S., & Goldstein, J.L. (1984) Proc. Natl. Acad. Sci. USA 81, 2826-2830.

Hui, D.Y., Innerarity, T.L., & Mahley, R.W. (1981) J. Biol. Chem. 256, 5646-5655.

Jackson, C.L., Bruns, G.A.P., & Breslow, J.L. (1984) Proc. Natl. Acad. Sci. USA 81, 2945-2949.

Kao, F.-T., Jones, C., & Puck, T.T. (1976) Proc. Natl. Acad. Sci. USA 73, 193-197.

Kao, F.-T., Hartz, J.A., Law, M.L., & Davidson, J.N. (1982) Proc. Natl. Acad. Sci. USA 79, 865-869.

Kao, F.-T., & Chan, L. (1985) Methods Enzymol. (in press).

Knott, T.J., Eddy, R.L., Robertson, M.E., Priestley, L.M., Scott, J., & Shows, T.B. (1984) Biochem. Biophys. Res. Commun. 125, 299-306.

Lin-Lee, Y.-C., Bradley, B.A., & Chan, L. (1981a) Biochem. Biophys. Res. Commun. 99, 654-661.

Lin-Lee, Y.-C., Tanaka, Y., Lin, C.T., & Chan, L. (1981b) Biochemistry 20, 6474-6480.

Lin-Lee, Y.C., Kao, F.T., Cheung, P., & Chan, L. (1985) Biochemistry 24, 3751-3756.

Mahley, R.W., & Innerarity, T.L. (1983) Biochem. Biophys. Acta 737, 197-222.

McLean, J.W., Elshourbagy, N.A., Chang, D.J., Mahley, R.W., & Taylor, J.M. (1984) J. Biol. Chem. 259, 6498-6504.

Olaisen, B., Teisberg, P., & Gedde-Dahl, T., Jr. (1982) Hum. Genet. 62, 233-236.

Olaisen, B., Teisberg, P., Gedde-Dahl, T., Jr., Wihelmy, M., Mevag, B., & Helland, R. (1984) Cytogenet. Cell Genet. 37, 559.

Pelham, H.R.B., & Jackson, R.J. (1976) Eur. J. Biochem. 67, 247-256.

Rall, S.C., Jr., Weisgraber, K.H., & Mahley, R.W. (1982) J. Biol. Chem. 257, 4171-4178.

Segrest, J.P., Jackson, R.L., Morrisett, J.D., & Gotto, A.M., Jr. (1974) FEBS Lett. 38, 247-253.

Sherrill, B.C., Innerarity, T.L., & Mahley, R.W. (1980) J. Biol. Chem. 255, 1804-1807.

Tanaka, Y., Lin-Lee, Y.-C., Lin-Su, M.H., & Chan, L. (1982) Metab. Clin Exp. 31, 861-865.

Thomas, P. (1980) Proc. Natl. Acad. Sci. USA 77, 5201-5205.

APOPROTEIN E3-LEIDEN: A VARIANT OF HUMAN APOLIPOPROTEIN E3 ASSOCIATED WITH FAMILIAL TYPE III HYPERLIPOPROTEINEMIA

L. Havekes*, E. Klasen**, and G. Utermann***

*TNO Gaubius Institute for Cardiovasculas Research
and **Dept. of Human Genetics, State University of
Leiden, Leiden, The Netherlands; *** Institute for
Medical Biology and Genetics, University of Innsbruck, Innsbruck, Austria

As determined with isoelectric focusing, human apo E can be saparated into three major isoforms, i.e. E2, E3 and E4 and a number of minor glycosylated isoforms (1,2). The heterogeneity of apo E is proposed to be the result of different apo E alleles, at one single genetic locus (1,2,3). At present a number of apo E variants have been described (for reference see 4). Most of these variants are the underlying metabolic defect in familial type III HLP due to a more or less pronounced defect of these variants in binding to the hepatic lipoprotein receptors (5,6). It is reported that the potential receptor binding region of the apo E molecule lies between residues 126 and 218 (7,8). Most of the type III HLP patients exhibit the apo E2 (Arg$_{158}$ $\rightarrow$ Cys) or E2 (Arg$_{145}$ $\rightarrow$ Cys) variant. Recently, we described a type III HLP patient (C.V.) with apolipoprotein phenotype E3/3 as evaluated by isoelectric focusing (9). We reported that apo E3 from patient C.V. was defective in binding to the LDL receptor on cultured fibroblasts at 4°C, as compared with apo E3 isolated from a type IV HLP patient. In this paper we describe the partial characterization and the mode of inheritance of this defective apo E3, denoted apo E3-Leiden.

Chemical cheracterization of apo E3-Leiden

Treatment of proteins with cysteamine results in a reversible mixed disulfide linkage with cysteinyl residues converting cysteine to a positively charged analogue of lysine. Therefore, this chemical modification adds one and two extra

217

positive charge units to apo E3 and E2 (Arg$_{158}$→Cys) or E2 (Arg$_{145}$→Cys) respectively. This implies that after cysteamine treatment both normal apo E3 and apo E2, that contain respectively one and two cysteine residues, will migrate at the position of apo E4 upon isoelectric focusing. In Fig. 1 it is shown that after treatment with cysteamine the apo E3–Leiden does not focus in the E4 position, thus indicating that either the apo E3–Leiden does not contain any cysteine residues, or that in apo E3–Leiden cysteine residues are not accessible for reaction with cysteamine. Amino acid analysis of apo E3–Leiden, isolated by preparative SDS polyacrylamide gel electrophoresis, revealed that apo E3–Leiden does not contain cysteine residues.

On SDS gel electrophoresis apo E2 (Arg$_{158}$→Cys) migrates as a distinctly separable band with a higher apparent molecular weight than the other variant forms of apo E tested, e.g., apo E3, E2 (Arg$_{145}$→Cys), E2 (Lys$_{146}$→Gln) and E4 (Cys$_{112}$→Arg) (10). Using the same technique of SDS polyacrylamide gel electrophoresis we found the apo E3–Leiden migrated as one single band between slow apo E2 (Arg$_{158}$→Cys) and fast normal apo E3 (Fig. 2). Furthermore, apo E3–Leiden does not represent a sialylated derivative of apo E4 (Cys$_{112}$→Arg), as evaluated by neuraminidase treatment. Consequently, we conclude that apo E3–Leiden differs from all other hitherto described apo E variants, that are defective in binding to the LDL receptor.

Study of the V kindred

The mother and all siblings of the propositus (II.6) were investigated (Table I). All members except two (II.1 and II.7) have elevated plasma triglyceride, cholesterol and apo E levels and show the presence of IDL as evaluated by density gradient ultracentrifugation (member II.4 has not been investigated). Some of the affected family members have xanthomatosis. Characterization of the apo E of the family members revealed that all members have the E3/3 phenotype. Further characterization of the apo E of the family members using cysteamine treatment (Fig. 1) and SDS polyacrylamide gel electrophoresis (Fig. 2) of VLDL showed that all members are apparently homozygous for the apo E3–Leiden phenotype except members II.1 and II.7, who had normal lipid levels and were apparently homozygous for normal apo E3. HLA typing did not indicate non-paternity in II.1 and II.7.

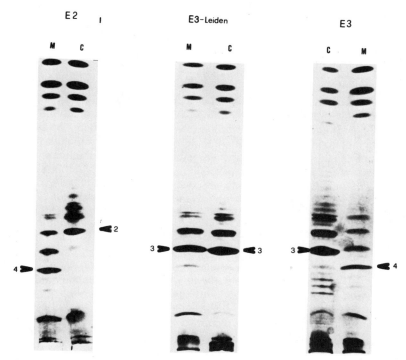

Fig. 1 - Effect of treatment of VLDL with cysteamine on isoelectric focusing patterns of apo E. (M = modified by cysteamine treatment; C = control). The pI of E3 from patient C.V. (apo E3-Leiden) was not increased by a single charge unit after cysteamine treatment.

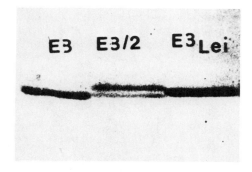

Fig. 2 - SDS polyacrylamide gel electrophoresis of apo VLDL. Only the apo E region of the slab gel is shown. Apo E3-Leiden shows an intermediate mobility between fast apo E3 and slow apo E2.

Table 1. Family V.

Position	Sex	Age y	TC (mmol/l)	TG	IDL	Apo E (mg/dl)	Phenotype	Binding to LDL receptor
I.1	F	76	9.0	2.3	yes	21.7	E3-Leiden	defective
II.1	M	54	6.0	2.1	no	4.5	E3	
II.2	M	52	12.6	3.9	yes	20.5	E3-Leiden	
II.3	F	49	11.3	3.1	yes	30.8	E3-Leiden	defective
II.4	F	46	7.2	nd	yes	nd	nd	
II.5	F	44	8.0	2.7	yes	23.7	E3-Leiden	
II.6	M	41	6.6	2.4	yes	18.4	E3-Leiden	defective
II.7	F	40	5.3	0.6	no	4.2	E3	
II.8	M	38	8.1	2.5	yes	13.7	E3-Leiden	

Discussion

Our data indicate that the LDL receptor binding deficient apo E3-Leiden variant does not contain cysteine residues and differs therefore from all other hitherto described apo E variants. It is noteworthy that within the family studied the apo E3-Leiden phenotype is 100% linked with type III hyperlipoproteinemia. This is in sharp contrast with, for example, E2/E2 nomozygotes, of which only about 4% display hyperlipidemia.

We observed that the mother and all siblings of the propositus (II.6), except II.1 and II.7, are apparently homozygous for apo E3-Leiden, whereas numbers II.1 and II.7 are apparently homozygous for wild type apo E3. This mode of inheritance is difficult to explain. The presence of a silent allele in both the father and mother is hardly to be expected. It is possible that the mutation has not occurred in the apo E gene itself but rather in a "modifier" gene coding for an enzyme that in the mutant form modifies the cysteine residue in position 112 of apo E3 (for example by methylation). The mother then had to be heterozygous for this "modifier" gene. Another possibility is that the apo E3-Leiden variant is derived from a mutation of apo E4, which has no cysteine residues. In that case the family members with the apo E3-Leiden variant are obligate E3/E3-Leiden heterozygotes. However, we were not able to detect normal apo E3 in these subjects. Additional experiments will be performed in order to further elucidate the mode of inheritance of apo E3-Leiden.

REFERENCES

1. G. Utermann, M. Hees and A. Steinmetz, Polymorphism of apolipoprotein E and occurrence of dysbetalipoproteinemia in man, Nature, 269:604 (1977)..
2. V.T. Zannis, and J.L. Breslow, Human very low density lipoprotein apoprotein E isoprotein polymorphism is explained by genetic variation and posttranslational modification, Biochemistry, 20:1033 (1981).
3. V.T. Zannis, J.L. Breslow, G. Utermann, R.W. Mahley, K.H. Weisgraber, R.J. Havel, J.L. Goldstein, M.S. Brown, G. Schonfeld, W.R. Hazzard, and C. Blum, Proposed nomenclature of apo E isoproteins apo E genotypes and phenotypes, J. Lipid Res., 23:911 (1982).
4. T.L. Innerarity, K.H. Weisgraber, K.S. Arnold, S.C. Rall, and R.W. Mahley, Normalization of receptor binding of apolipoprotein E. Evidence for modulation of the binding site conformation, J; Biol. Chem., 259:7261 (1984).
5. S.C. Rall, K.H. Weisgraber, T.L. Innerarity, and R.W. Mahley, Structural basis for receptor binding heterogeneity of apolipoprotein E from type III hyperlipoproteinemic subjects, Proc. Natl. Acad. Sci., USA, 79:4696 (1982).
6. W.J. Schneider, P.T. Kovanen, M.S. Brown, J.L. Goldstein, G. Utermann, W. Weber, R.J. Havel, L. Kotite, and J.P. Kane, Familial dysbetalipoproteinemia: Abnormal binding of mutant apolipoprotein E to low density lipoprotein receptors of human fibroblasts and membranes from liver and adrenal of rats, rabbits and cows, J. Clin. Invest., 68:1075 (1981).
7. T.L. Innerarity, E.J. Friedlander, S.C. Rall, K.H. Weisgraber, and R.W. Mahley, The receptor-binding domain of human apolipoprotein E. Binding of apolipoprotein E fragments, J. Biol. Chem., 285:12341 (1983).
8. K.H. Weisgraber, T.L. Innerarity, K.J. Harder, R.W. Mahley, R.W. Milne, Y.L. Marcel, and J.T. Sparrow, The receptor binding domain of human apolipoprotein E. Monoclonal antibody inhibition of binding, J. Biol. Chem. 258:12348 (1983).
9. L.M. Havekes, J.A. Gevers Leuven, E. Van Corven, E. De

Wit, and J.J. Emeis, Serum lipids, lipoproteins and apolipoprotein E phenotypes in relatives of patients with type III hyperlipoproteinemia, Eur. J. Clin. Invest., 14:7 (1984).

10. G. Utermann, K.H. Weisgraber, W. Weber, and R.W. Mahley, Genetic polymorphism of apolipoprotein E: a variant form of apolipoprotein distinguished by sodium dodecyl sulfate-polyacrylamide gel electrophoresis, J. Lipid Res., 25:378 (1984).

RECENT STUDIES ON THE MOLECULAR DEFECT IN

APOLIPOPROTEIN E DEFICIENCY

H.B. Brewer, Jr., M. Anchors, R.E. Gregg, and S.W. Law

Molecular Disease Branch, National Heart, Lung, and
Blood Institute, National Institutes of Health
Bethesda, MD.   20892

INTRODUCTION

Apolipoprotein (apo)E, a 34,000 molecular weight
protein, functions in lipoprotein metabolism by modulating
the hepatic catabolism of remnants of triglyceride rich
lipoproteins (1,2). ApoE has been proposed to bind to a
specific hepatic apoE receptor (3,4), and to the LDL receptor
on peripheral cells and on the liver (3-6).

ApoE deficiency is a rare genetic disease characterized
by a virtual absence of plasma apoE (7). Subjects with apoE
deficiency have hyperlipidemia, type III hyperlipoproteinemia, tuberoeruptive xanthomas, and premature
cardiovascular disease. This report summarizes the current
information available on the clinical, biochemical, and
molecular defect in the proband with apoE deficiency .

MATERIAL AND METHODS

Plasma Lipoproteins   and Apolipoproteins

Plasma lipoproteins were isolated by ultracentrifugation, and apolipoproteins quantitated as previously
reported (8). Two dimensional gel electrophoresis and
immunoblotting were performed by the methods of Sprecher et
al (9).

Cell Culture

Blood-macrophages were cultured in RPMI 1640 in 5% human

serum. ApoE was quantitated in the media by radioimmunoassay as previously described (10).

Isolation of RNA and Preparation of the ApoE cDNA Probe

Total RNA was isolated from monocyte - macrophages from normal subjects and the patient with apoE deficiency in quanidinium thiocyanate and sodium N-lauroyl sarcosinate, and fractionated in CsCl in vanadyl ribonucleoside as detailed previously (11).

The apoE cDNA probe was 1.1 kb, and was isolated from a human liver cDNA library (12). This probe contained the complete sequence of apoE.

Northern and Southern Blotting Procedures

Northern blot analysis was performed on total monocyte-macrophage RNA following separation by 1% agarose electrophoresis (13).

Leukocyte DNA was analyzed following restriction enzyme digestion by Southern blot as previously reported (14). Restriction enzymes were purchased from Bethesda Research Laboratories and used as specified by the manufacture.

RESULTS

The plasma lipoproteins from the apoE deficient patient are charcteristic of type III hyperlipoproteinemia (15). No significant quantity of apoE (<1% of normal) was present in plasma, and no apoE in plasma or very low density lipoproteins was detected by two-dimensional gel electrophoresis followed by immunoblot analysis in the apoE deficient subject. All other apolipoproteins were present, however, there was a marked elevation of plasma apoB-48, a marker of intestinal lipoproteins, present primarily in low and intermediate density lipoproteins (7). These results indicated that the only abnormality in the plasma apolipoproteins was a deficiency of apoE.

In order to elucidate the molecular defect in the patient with apoE deficiency , the gene and mRNA for apoE were evaluated. High molecular weight DNA from blood leukocytes was isolated from normal and apoE deficient subjects. The DNA was digested with six different restriction enzymes, and the fragments analyzed by agarose gel electrophoresis followed by Southern blot analysis. The apoE gene was present and there were no major insertions or deletions in the apoE gene in the apoE deficient subject.

Monocyte-macrophages have been previously shown to secrete apoE (16). The media from cultured monocyte-macrophages from normal subjects but not the apoE deficient patient contained apoE.

The mRNA from normal and apoE deficient subjects was isolated, and analyzed by Northern blot analysis following agarose gel electrophoresis. The apoE mRNA present in the apoE deficient macrophages was similar in size to normal apoE mRNA, but was reduced to 1-3% that of the apoE present in monocyte-macrophages isolated from normal subjects.

DISCUSSION

An elucidation of the role of apoE in lipoprotein metabolism has been markedly facilitated by the characterization of the lipoproteins from the apoE deficient patient. The plasma lipoproteins were elevated, and characteristic of type III hyperlipoproteinemia. There was a marked elevation of plasma apoB-48 reflecting a decreased clearance of intestinal lipoproteins. These results are consistent with the proposed role of apoE in mediating the clearance of remnants of triglyceride rich lipoproteins.

No detectable defects in the immunological or neurological systems have been detected in the apoE deficient patients. The deficiency of apoE therefore may not play a pivotal role in these systems.

The molecular defect in the apoE deficient patient was evaluate by a detailed analysis of the apoE gene. In these studies no major insertions or deletions could be detected by Southern blot analysis of restriction enzyme digests of leukocyte DNA isolated from the patient with apoE deficiency.

The cellular mRNA in monocyte-macrophages isolated from the apoE deficient patient was similar in size to normal apoE mRNA, but reduced to 1-3% the level of apoE mRNA in normal monocyte-macrophages. The combined results from these studies indicate that the deficiency of apoE in the apoE deficient kindred is due to a marked reduction in cellular apoE mRNA. The decrease in apoE mRNA may be due to a defect in transcription and processing of the apoE mRNA or the biosynthesis of an unstable mRNA.

REFERENCES

1. Blum, C.B., Aron, L., and Sciacca, R. (1980) Radio-immunoassay studies of human apolipoprotein E. J. Clin. Invest. 66, 1240-1250.

2. Havel, R.J., Kotite, L., Vigne, J.L., Kane, J.P., Tun, P., Phillip, N., and Chen, G.C. (1980) Radioimmunoassay of human arginine-rich apolipoprotein, apoprotein E. J. Clin. Invest. <u>66</u>, 1351-1362.

3. Hui, D.Y., Innerarity, T.L., and Mahley, R.W. (1981) Lipoprotein binding to canine hepatic membranes. Metabolically distinct apoE and apoB,E receptors. J. Biol. Chem. <u>256</u>, 5646-5655.

4. Hoeg, J.M., Demosky, S.J., Jr., Gregg, R.E., Schaefer, E.J., and Brewer, H.B., Jr. (1984) Distinct hepatic receptors for low density lipoprotein and apoE in humans. Science <u>227</u>, 759-761.

5. Quarfordt, S.H., Shelburne, F.A., Meywers, W., Jakoi, L., and Hanks, J. (1981) Effect of apolipoproteins on the induction of hepatic steatosis in rats. Gastroenterology <u>80</u>, 149-153.

6. Innerarity, T.L., and Mahley, R.W. (1978) Enhanced binding by cultured human fibroblasts of apoE containing lipoproteins as compared with low density lipoproteins. Biochem. <u>17</u>, 1440-1447.

7. Ghiselli, G., Schaefer, E.J., Gascon, P., and Brewer, H.B., Jr. (1981) Type III hyperlipoproteinemia associated with apoE deficiency. Science <u>214</u>, 1239-1241.

8. Gregg, R.E., Zech, L.A., Schaefer, E.J., and Brewer, H.B., Jr. (1984) Apolipoprotein E metabolism in normalipoproteinemic human subjects. J. Lipid Res. <u>25</u>, 1167-1176.

9. Sprecher, D.L., Taam, L., and Brewer, H.B., Jr. (1984) Two-dimensional electrophoresis of human plasma apolipoproteins. Clin. Chem. <u>30</u>, 2084-2092.

10. Gregg, R.E., Wilson, D., Rubacaba, E., Ronan, R., and Brewer, H.B., Jr. (1982) Proceedings of the Workshop on Apolipoprotein Quantification (Lippel, K. ed.) NIH Publication No. 83-1266, p. 383-401.

11. Chirgivin, J.M., Przybyla, A.E., MacDonald, R.J., and Rutter, W.J. (1979) Isolation of biologically active ribonucleic acid from sources enriched in ribonuclease. Biochem. <u>18</u>, 5294-5299.

12. Law, S.W., Gray, G., and Brewer, H.B., Jr. (1983) cDNA cloning of human apoA-I: Amino acid sequence of preproapoA-I. Biochem. Biophys. Res. Comm. <u>112</u>, 257-264.

13. Alwine, J.C., Kemp, D.J., and Stark, G.R. (1977) Method for detection of specific RNAs in agarose gels by transfer to diazobenzyloxymethyl-paper and hybridization with DNA probes. Proc. Natl. Acad. Sci. U.S.A. <u>74</u>, 5350-5354.

14. Southern, E.M. (1975) Detection of specific sequences among DNA fragments separated by gel electrophoresis. J. Mol. Biol. 98, 503-517.

15. Brewer, H.B., Jr., Zech, L.A., Gregg, R.E., Schwartz, D., and Schaefer, E.J. (1983) Type III hyperlipoproteinemia: Diagnosis, molecular defects, pathology, and treatment. Ann. Intern. Med. 98, 623-640.

16. Basu, S.K., Brown, M.S., Ho, Y.K., Havel, R.J., and Goldstein, J.L. (1981) Mouse macrophages synthesize and secrete a protein resembling apolipoprotein E. Proc. Natl. Acad. Sci. U.S.A. 78, 7545-7549.

INDEX

229

Mutagenesis, 153
Mutants, 51–54, 55–59
Mutations, 55

Plasmid, 153–156, 200
Polymorphism, 18, 21
  genetic, 139
  restriction-fragment length
  (RFLP), 17, 20–21, 40, 101,
      175, 191

Recombinant vectors, 153–154
Restriction enzymes, 40, 100,
      139, 175, 197, 204
Risk factors, 51, 67

Tangier disease, 3, 5–7, 69,
      129–132

  clinical symptoms, 5, 129
  heterozygotes, 6–7
  metabolic defect, 129–132
  molecular defect, 6
  monocytes, 6–7

Very low density lipoproteins
(VLDL), 8–9, 52, 161, 163, 179,
      182–184, 187, 189–192,
      203–204, 211, 219, 224
ß–, 12–15